WEST of the ROCKIES

RECIPES FROM CAMPFIRE TO CANDLELIGHT

Junior Service League
of
Grand Junction, Colorado

WEST OF THE ROCKIES

The Grand Junction Junior Service League is an organization founded in 1983 and dedicated to promoting volunteerism within our community. Proceeds from the sale of this cookbook will be used to benefit and enhance western Colorado projects.

Past volunteer placement of volunteer time and monies:

KPRN Public Radio
Mesa County Public Library Adult Literacy Program
Dinosaur Valley Museum
Mesa County School District #51 — Art Heritage Program
Riverfront Project (Trail System and Parks)
Museum of Western Colorado
Mesa Young Parents
Hilltop Rehabilitation Hospital
Make a Difference Days (Spring and Fall Clean-up for Senior Citizens)

Additional copies may be obtained by addressing:
West of the Rockies
Junior Service League of Grand Junction
PO Box 3221
Grand Junction, Colorado 81502
For your convenience, order blanks are included in the back of the book.

First Edition — October, 1994
Second Printing — December, 1994
ISBN: 0-9641314-0-4

Printed in the USA by

WIMMER
The Wimmer Companies, Inc.
Memphis • Dallas

TABLE OF CONTENTS

LIFE WEST OF THE ROCKIES

	Committee	4
	Introduction	5
	Menus	8

IN THE BEGINNING   Appetizers and Beverages   17

SOUP'S ON   Soups, Stews, and Chowders   41

THE GARDEN PATCH   Salads and Dressings   61

WAVES OF GRAIN   Breads, Muffins, and Coffee Cakes   77

EGGSTRORDINARY   Egg Dishes   99

FROM STREAMS AND BEYOND   Fish and Seafood   109

THE GRAND EVENT   Meats and Poultry   127

ON THE WILD SIDE   Game and Wild Fowl   161

FARMER'S MARKET   Vegetables   175

ANYTHING'S PASTABLE   Pasta   191

CLEAN LIVIN'   Light and Healthy   205

RIO GRANDE   Southwestern Fare   221

CAMPFIRE CAFÈ   Western Outdoor Specialties   245

THE COOKIE JAR   Cookies and Candy   263

GRAND FINALE   Pies, Cakes, and Desserts   281

FROM THE PANTRY   Canning, Sauces, Miscellaneous   323

SPECIAL GUIDES   Wine Guide, Measurements, Substitutions   335

Contributors and Testers   345
Index   348
Order Forms   359

COOKBOOK COMMITTEE

Chairman	Patti Milius
Editor	Patti Milius
Editorial Associate	Marilyn Jones
Steering	Janice Copeland, Marilyn Jones, Linda LaCroix, Patti Milius, Elisabeth Moore, Diana Osborne
Recipe Collection and Coding	Linda LaCroix, Marilyn Jones
Section Coordinators	
Appetizers	Lori Howard
Soups and Salads	Karen Roberts
Meats	Judi Kugeler
Poultry and Campfire Cafè	Janice Copeland
Game	Chris Gilmor
Fish and From the Pantry	Stephanie Martin
Vegetables	Nancy Petersburg
Breads	Gayle Gerson
Pasta and Egg Dishes	Ruth Leever
Southwestern and Light and Healthy	Marilyn Jones
Desserts	Cydne Simons, Carol Tompkins
Marketing	Diana Osborne
Public Relations	Barbara Bowman, Caryn Penn
Proofreading	Elisabeth Moore
Computer Inputting	Gayle Gerson
Graphics and Layout	Amy Nuernberg
Watercolor Cover	Shirley Dickinson
Pen and Ink Illustrations	Gail Collins

Special thanks to William Milius for the use of office, supplies, and lots of encouragement to the committee; Nancy Mohler for nutritional information and analysis; Pyramid Printing for all their assistance in this project; and to all the members of the Junior Service League for their help and confidence in this project.

LIFE WEST OF THE ROCKIES

Our Grand Valley is the home of the communities of Grand Junction, Palisade and Fruita and is the heart of Western Colorado. Grand Valley residents live amidst a bold and angular landscape including cliffs, plateaus, canyons and mesas. Vertical-walled canyons of the Colorado National Monument (cover) overlook the broad Grand Valley of the Colorado River moving westward in a flat, fertile sweep of irrigated green. The Grand Mesa, Mt. Garfield and the red rock canyons of the Colorado National Monument are the dominant topographic features surrounding the Grand Valley, which was carved by the Colorado and Gunnison Rivers.

Exposed rock layers bear evidence of the ancestral Rocky Mountains, numerous advances and retreats of seas, deserts and dunes, rivers with broad flood plains, lush forests, ancient lakes and lava flows. Dinosaurs once roamed through the ancient forests and today the Grand Valley is known worldwide as a paleontological treasure trove of dinosaur remains. Our unique geological features have also yielded rich sources of coal, oil shale, uranium and precious metals which continue to be mined to the present day.

The first prehistoric people are thought to have appeared in the area during the Pleistocene Epoch, followed by a series of early Indian peoples. The "old ones", as many Native Americans call them, were believed to have appeared around A.D. 700. They abandoned their fields about A.D. 1200 and, as a cultural group, disappeared into the mists of history. Their legacy to us is the mysterious petroglyphs they painted on the canyon walls. Several of their designs are used in this cookbook as symbols, the most famous being Kokopelli, the flute-player.

In 1776, the Dominquez-Escalante Expedition explored the area after setting out from Santa Fe to seek a more northern route to California. The Ute Indians, members of the Shoshone family, were in the region when the Spanish explorers entered the area. The Grand Valley was a favorite hunting and wintering place. The Utes, armed with bows and arrows and the horse (after the sixteenth century), were able hunters and feared warriors.

The Grand Valley became part of the Ute Reservation set aside by an 1868 treaty, but continuous pressure was applied to remove the Indians so the land could be settled. In a treaty signed in 1880, the Utes gave up all land in Colorado with the exception of a narrow strip in the southwest corner of the state. In 1881, the Utes were escorted from the Grand Valley at gunpoint, forced to leave their mountain homeland to relocate on a desolate reservation near Vernal, Utah. Local legend tells us that as they left their home, the Utes cast a spell on the valley so that if anyone moved here, they could never move away again for very long. Many people claim they are victims of the "Ute Curse" when, as often happens, they move to another part of the country and soon return because they miss our friendly lifestyle.

In September of 1881, the first settlers arrived in the area. They camped at a site near the junction of the Grand (now the Colorado) and Gunnison Rivers. Grand Junction became the name for the settlement at the fork of those two rivers in November 1881. Within the next few years, other small towns cropped up throughout the Grand Valley. By 1890, settlement of this part of Colorado was well-advertised and rapid, due in part to the advancing Denver and Rio Grande and Colorado Midland Railroads. By the 1890's, large groups of immigrants from the Midwest, particularly, Kansas, Iowa and Arkansas found homes here.

The Denver and Rio Grande Western Railroad played a vital role in the economic development of the area. The railroad has been one of the largest and longest-lived employers, shipping fruit crops, produce, livestock and manufactured goods to markets all over the country, but has also served as an inward conduit for settlers, supplies and communications. Other smaller railroads also operated in the area, the Interurban, dedicated in 1910, hauled passengers and freight from Grand Junction to Fruita.

When early settlers entered the Grand Valley, they saw sage, grease-wood and a few trees. Irrigation canals built during the late 1800's and early 1900's turned dry desert portions of the Grand Valley into lush green fields and orchards.

Because of the success of fruit produced in neighboring Utah, where soil and growing conditions were similar to those of the Grand Valley, settlers were encouraged to grow fruit. The first fruits grown in the area included strawberries, raspberries, blackberries, sweet and sour cherries, almonds, currants, plums, pears, peaches, apples and apricots. One orchard reputedly contained 84 varieties of apples!

Peak years for fruit profits were in the first decades of the century. In 1911, the year of the greatest yield, shipment of apples alone amounted to over 1,800 railroad cars. Apples, pears and peaches became central to the local economy. Grapes were grown as a cash crop to supplement income from peach and apple production.

Fruit production continues to be a vital part of the economy of Western Colorado. Palisade peaches are famous for their wonderful flavor and size. Recently, grape production has again increased and several local vineyards and wineries have been established. The Junior Service League's most successful fundraiser, Viva El Vino, celebrates Western Colorado's best wines each spring.

Tourism has become one of the most important industries in Western Colorado. The beautiful canyons of the Colorado National Monument and the scenery and multitude of hunting and fishing opportunities on the

Grand Mesa and surrounding areas attract hundreds of thousands of visitors annually. The explosion in popularity of mountain biking, river rafting and the current fascination with dinosaurs have all combined to make the Grand Valley a favorite vacation destination.

The local economy has recently recovered from the most recent "boom and bust" cycle caused by the pullout of several major oil companies from development of oil shale holdings in adjacent Garfield County in the early 1980's. Agriculture, tourism and high quality regional health care facilities have combined to make the Grand Valley a healthy growing community of approximately 100,000 people.

LOGO INFORMATION — *From Anasazi Petroglyphs*

Signifies Do Ahead Recipe

Fast and Easy Recipes

Historic Notes
   Kokopelli, the flute player

Ladies' "Let's Get Together" Luncheon

Mimosa

Spinach and Strawberry Salad

Leaf-Wrapped Stuffed Salmon

Baby Steamed Vegetables

Almost Brioche Bread

Bessie's Chocolate Cake

Tea   Coffee

Appropriate Wines

Grande River Viognier

Carlson Prairie Dog Red

Plum Creek Grand Valley Chardonnay

Carlson Cherry Wine

Candlelight Dinner for Two

Grapefruit and Spinach Salad
or
Mixed Greens with Raspberry Vinaigrette

Apple-Stuffed Veal Rolls

Wild Rice with Piñon Nuts and Brandied Raisins

Grandma B's Dinner Rolls

Lemon Napoleans with Raspberry Sauce
or
Apple Pie with Warm Cinnamon Cider Sauce

Coffee   Amaretto

Appropriate Wines

Carlson Gewurzasaurus

Grande River Barrel Select Chardonnay

St. Patrick's Day "I Want to Be Irish" Dinner

Pesto Artichoke Dip

Frozen Pea Salad

Potato and Leek Soup

Steak Rolls with Mushrooms

Colcannon   Roasted Green Beans, Onion and Garlic

Irish Soda Bread

Chocolate Angel Pie
or
Enstrom's Oatmeal Chocolate Toffee Cake

Coffee   Irish Cream Liqueur

Appropriate Wines

Plum Creek Grand Mesa Red

Carlson Tyrannosaurus Red

Grande River Merlot

Skiing In

Twice Dressed Salad   Mixed Greens with Choice of Dressing

Veal and Barley Stew

Toasted Grape Nut Bread

Milk Chocolate Pound Cake with Dark Chocolate Fudge Sauce

Powderhorn Warm-Up   Coffee

Appropriate Wines

Grande River Syrah

Plum Creek Cabernet Franc

Carlson Tyrannosaurus Red

Carlson Cherry Wine

Palisade Peach Festival Picnic or "How Many Ways Can I Eat Fresh Peaches?"

Peach Smash   Apricot Iced Tea

Seafood Stars   Nutty Crabmeat Spread

Baked Ham with Spicy Mustard Sauce

Silver Dollar Slaw

Ditch Bank Asparagus and Scallion Toss

Bread and Butter Pickles

Edith's Cracked Wheat Bread   Palisade Peach Bread

Palisade Peach Pie   Chocolate Chip Meringue Bars

Appropriate Wines

Grande River Meritage White

Grande River Sauvignon Blanc

Grande River Semillon

Plum Creek Merlot

Carlson Peach Wine

Mountain Morning Breakfast

Cowboy Coffee

Eggs in a Tortilla

Iron Man Mix

Fresh Fruit or Crested Butte Banana in Foil

Beer Can Biscuits

Appropriate Wines

Grande River Meritage White

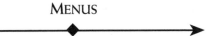

Brunch for Any Reason

Fresh Squeezed Orange Juice

Fresh Fruit served with Sour Cream and Brown Sugar

Steamed Shrimp with Cocktail Sauce

Smoked Salmon Cheesecake

Asparagus or Broccoli Quiche

Cinnamon Rolls   Bran Muffins

Double-Decker High Altitude Cheese Biscuits

Coffee   Tea

Appropriate Wines

Grande River Viognier

Plum Creek Sauvignon Blanc

Carlson Dry White

I Won't Tell It's Healthy

Creamy Caesar Salad

Pork Chops Normandy

Vegetable Rice Toss

Bran Muffins

Pumpkin Apple Bundt Cake

Coffee   Tea

Appropriate Wines

Grande River Barrel Select Chardonnay

Carlson Apple Wine or Pearadactyl (Pear Apple)

11

Tailgate Party

Smoked Salmon Cheesecake

Crudités with Lemon Cream

Perfect Grilled Chicken

Plum-Marinated Pork Ribs

Orange Bowl   Light Rye with Anise Seed and Black Pepper Bread

Spiced Apple Muffins

Chocolate Sheet Cake   Crisp Oat Cookies

Appropriate Wines

Carlson Riesling or Gewurzasaurus

Plum Creek Dry Riesling

Grande River Meritage White

Grande River Merlot

Plum Creek Merlot

Grande River Meritage Red

Saddle Bag Lunch

Carrot and Celery Sticks

Health Bread with Versatile Cheese Spread

Health Bread with Paul's Ham Salad

Lemon Loaf Pound Cake

Wild West Oatmeal Cookies

Appropriate Wines

Grande River Barrel Select Chardonnay

Carlson Pearadactyl

Alpine Meadow Trail Ride

Silver Dollar Slaw

Timberline Steak Sandwich with Corn Salsa

Fruit Leather   Mocha Chip Cookies

Appropriate Wines

Grande River Merlot

Grande River Cabernet Franc

Gourmet Camp Dinner by Candlelight

Fresh Fruit in Gingered White Wine

Mountain Trout in Foil
or
Crab Fettuccine

Baked Potatoes in Foil

Beaver Creek Blueberry Binge   Turtle Cookies

Cowboy Coffee

Appropriate Wines

Carlson Colorado Dry White

Grande River Meritage White

Are You Game?

Glazed Brie   Lime Garlic Shrimp with Mango Mint

Orange, Avocado, and Onion Salad

Braised Stuffed Duck Pullman Style

Ruby Carrots   Herbed Green Beans

Quick Butter Dips

White Chocolate Mousse with Raspberry Sauce

Coffee   Tea

Appropriate Wines

Grande River Meritage White

Carlson Plum Wine

Grande River Merlot or Syrah

Hunter's Bountiful Dinner

Smoky Mountain Trout Pâtè   Hot Gouda Cheese

Onion Soup Fondue or Wild Rice Soup

Grilled Venison with Apricot and Green Peppercorn Glaze

Sautéed Mushrooms and Spinach with Shallots

Mashed Potatoes

High Country Carrot Muffins

Diana Torte
or
Lemon Meringue Pie

Appropriate Wines

Grande River Barrel Select Chardonnay

Carlson Prairie Dog Red

San Juan Fiesta

Elam BLT Peach Margarita   Skip and Go

Salsa de Leonardo with Tortilla Chips

Creamy Salsa Dip

Mexican Corn Soup

Marinated Enchilada with Green Chili and Melon Salsa

Jalapeño Corn Bread

Individual Orange Flan   Silverton Indian Fry Bread with Cinnamon and Honey

Appropriate Wines

Grande River Meritage White

Sleigh Bell Holiday Buffet

Cranberry Punch   Lands End Nog

Warmed Cranberry Brie   Rumaki Pâté

Spanakopita   Cheese and Artichoke Appetizer

Waldorf Salad   Tossed Greens

Seafood and Wild Rice Salad   Buffet Ham

Weekend Chicken

Orange-Cranberry Bread   North African Coriander Bread

Lemon Glazed Cheesecake   Pecan Pie Squares

Molasses Sugar Cookies   Fantastic Frosted Fattening Brownies

Appropriate Wines

Plum Creek Merlot

Carlson Merlot or Gewurtzasaurus

This Can't Be a Healthy Dinner!

Molded Gazpacho Salad

Black Canyon Bean Salad

Parmesan Chicken

Low-Fat Broccoli, Bacon and Cheddar Toss

Toasted Health Bread

Chocolate Angel Food Cake with Low-Fat Crème Anglaise

Tea   Coffee

Appropriate Wines

Plum Creek Colorado Chardonnay

Grande River Meritage White

Carlson White Riesling

Very Important Person Coming to Dinner

Onion Pissaladiere   Baked French Bread Dip

Vegetable Melange

Fresh Pear Ice

Leg of Lamb Swedish Style

Grilled Garlic Squash

Fascinating Fast Bread   Rolls

Smooth as Silk Cheesecake or Wild Berry Cobbler

Appropriate Wines

Plum Creek Redstone Chardonnay

Grande River Syrah

In the Beginning

SUGAR AND NUT GLAZED BRIE

Yield: 10 appetizers

¼ cup brown sugar, packed
¼ cup broken almonds, walnuts, or pecans
1 tablespoon whiskey or brandy
1 (14 ounce) wheel of Brie cheese
Assorted crackers, apple slices, pears, seedless grapes

◆ Prepare glaze: mix sugar, nuts, and whiskey or brandy (may be made ahead, covered and placed in refrigerator).

◆ Place Brie in 9-inch pie plate or like container.

◆ Put sugar mixture into 2-cup glass measuring cup. Microwave uncovered on high for 1 minute.

◆ Pour sugar mixture over cheese. Microwave uncovered on 50% power about 2 minutes until cheese is heated but not melted.

Variation: Can also be done in oven. Bake cheese at 500° for 4 to 5 minutes. Sprinkle sugar mixture over top, bake 2 to 3 minutes more.

STUFFED MUSHROOMS

Yield: 24 appetizers

2 pounds fresh mushrooms, rinsed and patted dry
½ cup Parmesan cheese, grated
¾ cup dry breadcrumbs
½ cup onion, grated
2 cloves garlic, pressed
3 tablespoons parsley, minced
1 teaspoon salt
½ teaspoon pepper
½ teaspoon oregano
¾ cup olive oil

◆ Cut stems from mushroom caps. Chop stems and mix with the remaining ingredients.

◆ Loosely stuff mushroom caps. Grease pan with olive oil. Place stuffed mushrooms in pan and bake 25 minutes at 350°.

CRAB PUFFS WITH SWEET AND SOUR SAUCE *Yield: 16 appetizers*

CRAB PUFFS:
- 3 ounces cream cheese
- 4 ounces crabmeat
- 1 green onion, minced
- ½ teaspoon garlic salt
- ⅓ pound wonton skins

CRAB PUFFS:
- ◆ Mix cream cheese, crabmeat, onion, and garlic salt.
- ◆ Place one teaspoon crab mixture in the middle of wonton skin. Dab water around edges, and fold into a triangle. Press to seal edges.
- ◆ Deep fry in hot oil until light brown. Serve with sweet and sour sauce.

SWEET AND SOUR SAUCE:
- ⅓ cup water
- ⅓ cup rice vinegar
- 1½ tablespoons cornstarch
- ⅔ cup sugar
- 1 tablespoon soy sauce

SWEET AND SOUR SAUCE: *Yield: 1 cup*
- ◆ Mix water, rice vinegar, and cornstarch until cornstarch is dissolved.
- ◆ Add sugar and soy sauce.
- ◆ Heat on medium heat until thick and serve warm.

WARMED CRANBERRY BRIE *Yield: 5 to 6 appetizers*

- ⅓ cup crushed cranberry sauce
- 2 tablespoons brown sugar (packed)
- ¼ teaspoon rum extract
- ⅛ teaspoon ground nutmeg
- 8 ounces Brie cheese
- 2 tablespoons chopped pecans or almonds (if desired)

- ◆ Combine all ingredients except Brie cheese. (Can be made ahead of time.)
- ◆ Spread cranberry mixture over Brie. Sprinkle nuts over top, if desired.
- ◆ Bake in preheated 500° oven for about 5 minutes.
- ◆ Serve with assorted crackers and Granny Smith apple slices.

Oriental Chicken Wontons

Yield: Makes about 25 appetizers

8 ounces ground raw chicken or pork
½ cup shredded carrots
¼ cup finely chopped celery or water chestnuts
1 tablespoon soy sauce
1 tablespoon dry sherry
2 teaspoons cornstarch
2 teaspoons grated ginger root
½ (16 ounce) package of wonton wrappers
2 tablespoons margarine or butter, melted
Plum or sweet and sour sauce (optional)

◆ For filling, in a medium skillet cook and stir ground chicken (or pork) until no pink remains; drain.

◆ Stir in carrot, celery or water chestnuts, soy sauce, sherry, cornstarch, and ginger root; mix well.

◆ Spoon one rounded teaspoon of the filling on to a wonton wrapper. Lightly brush edges with water.

◆ To shape each wonton, carefully bring two opposite points of the square wrapper up over the filling and pinch together in the center. Carefully bring the two remaining opposite points to the center and pinch together. Pinch together edges to seal.

◆ Place wontons on greased baking sheet. Repeat with remaining filling and wonton wrappers.

◆ Brush the wontons with melted margarine or butter. Bake in a 375° oven for 8 to 10 minutes or until light brown and crisp. If desired, serve with plum or sweet and sour sauce.

HOT GOUDA CHEESE

Yield: 6 to 8 appetizers

½ package refrigerator
crescent rolls
2 tablespoons Dijon mustard
7 ounce round of Gouda
cheese, peeled
Egg white
Sesame seeds or poppy
seeds

◆ Do not separate crescent rolls
into triangles, but press seams
together making a square.

◆ Spread with Dijon mustard and
place the cheese in the center.

◆ Pull the edges of the dough to
the top of the cheese and press
together.

◆ Place the cheese in an oven-proof
dish, seam side down. Brush with
lightly beaten egg white. Sprinkle
the top with sesame seeds or
poppy seeds.

◆ Bake at **350°** for approximately
20 minutes or until nicely
browned. Let cool for 10 minutes.

◆ Serve with plain crackers, apple,
or pear wedges.

*This is a simple, very tasty and
impressive dish.*

◎ CHICKEN ALMOND SPREAD

Yield: 12 to 15 appetizers

2 tablespoons water
⅓ cup almonds, sliced
1 tablespoon curry powder
1 cup mayonnaise
1 cup cooked chicken, diced
Salt to taste

◆ Place water and almonds in
blender. Cover and blend at high
speed until smooth.

◆ Add remaining ingredients and
blend until smooth.

◆ Chill until serving time.

◆ Serve with crackers.

◎ MUSHROOM SPREAD

Yield: Makes about 2½ cups.

4   slices bacon
8   ounces fresh mushrooms, chopped
1   medium onion, finely chopped
1   clove garlic, minced
2   tablespoons flour
¼   teaspoon salt
⅛   teaspoon pepper
1   (8 ounce) package cream cheese, cubed
2   teaspoons Worcestershire sauce
1   teaspoon soy sauce
½   cup sour cream

◆ Cook bacon until crisp. Drain, reserving 2 tablespoons drippings. Crumble the bacon and set aside.

◆ Cook the mushrooms, onion, and garlic in the drippings until they are tender and most of the liquid has evaporated.

◆ Stir in the flour, salt and pepper. Add the cream cheese, Worcestershire sauce, and soy sauce.

◆ Heat slowly and stir until the cheese is melted. Stir in the sour cream and bacon and heat through. Do not boil.

This may be made ahead and refrigerated. Prior to serving, pour into an oven-proof dish and reheat.

CREAMY SALSA DIP

Yield: 30 to 35 appetizers

1   large onion, chopped
2   large tomatoes, chopped
1   (7 ounce) can green chiles, diced
1   (8 ounce) package cream cheese
¼   cup picante sauce (medium hot)
    Salt and pepper to taste

◆ Stir onion and tomato together in large skillet. Sauté until onion is clear on medium heat.

◆ Add green chiles and cream cheese, stir until smooth.

◆ Add picante sauce, salt and pepper.

◆ Do not overcook.

◆ Serve with tortilla chips.

Rumaki Pâté

Yield: Makes about 1½ cups

½ pound chicken livers, cooked
3 tablespoons soy sauce
½ cup butter or margarine, softened
½ teaspoon onion salt
½ teaspoon dry mustard
¼ teaspoon nutmeg
Dash hot pepper sauce
1 (8 ounce) can water chestnuts, drained and coarsely chopped
6 slices bacon, cooked and crumbled
2 tablespoons green onion, chopped
Melba toast or crackers

◆ In blender container or food processor bowl, finely chop chicken livers, a few at a time.

◆ When all are chopped, return to blender container and add soy sauce, butter, onion, salt, mustard, nutmeg, and hot pepper sauce. Blend until smooth and well mixed, scraping down sides frequently. Add water chestnuts and bacon. Mix in thoroughly by hand.

◆ Spoon into 1 large or 5 small molds, pressing firmly so all air pockets are removed.

◆ Chill. Unmold by dipping quickly into hot water up to rim and allow to soften to room temperature before serving.

◆ Garnish with green onion. Serve with Melba toast.

Hot Cheese Balls

Yield: 36 appetizers

½ pound Parmesan cheese, grated
½ pound cream cheese, softened
2 eggs
½ teaspoon salt
Dash of cayenne
1 cup fresh white breadcrumbs
Peanut or salad oil for frying

◆ In medium bowl combine both kinds of cheese, eggs, salt, and cayenne. Beat with wooden spoon until smooth. Form into 1-inch balls.

◆ Roll each ball lightly in breadcrumbs, place on waxed paper. Refrigerate.

◆ In a deep skillet or fryer, slowly heat oil (about 2 inches) to 350°.

◆ Fry cheese balls until golden brown. Drain on paper towels.

◆ Serve hot with sweet and sour or hot mustard sauce.

SEAFOOD STARS

Yield: 24 appetizers

1	package egg roll wrappers
½	pound of imitation crabmeat
½	cup frozen peas
4 - 5	green onions, chopped
8	ounce package bean sprouts
¼	cup carrots, grated
½	cup celery, cut into small pieces
3 - 4	broccoli heads, chopped to make ¼ to ½ cup
	Salad dressing of your choice

◆ Cut egg roll wrappers in half, press one egg roll wrapper in each muffin tin to form star. Bake at **350°** until brown.

◆ Combine crab, vegetables, and dressing, fill 24 stars.

SESAME SHRIMP TOAST

Yield: 24 appetizers

½	pound cooked shrimp, shelled and deveined
6	water chestnuts
2	tablespoons scallions, chopped
½	teaspoon ginger root, chopped
1	egg
1	teaspoon salt
½	teaspoon sugar
1	teaspoon sherry
3	tablespoons cornstarch
6	slices firm white bread
	Sesame seeds
	Oil for frying

◆ Chop shrimp, water chestnuts, scallions, and ginger until well chopped (use food processor).

◆ Add egg, salt, sugar, sherry, and cornstarch and continue chopping until well combined.

◆ Remove crusts from bread (which should be at least 2 days old) and spread with shrimp mixture.

◆ Cut each slice into 4 triangles, and dip into sesame seeds.

◆ Fry in hot oil, placing shrimp side down first, turning once.

These may be cooked, frozen, and reheated when needed.

CRABBY CHEESE CRESCENTS

Yield: 16 appetizers

1 (8 ounce) package cream cheese
1 can crabmeat
1 stalk celery, minced fine
2 teaspoons Worcestershire sauce
2 cloves garlic, minced
1 - 2 tablespoons fresh basil (according to taste) or 1-2 teaspoons dried basil
2 - 3 scallions, minced
Salt and pepper to taste
2 cans crescent rolls

◆ Mix all ingredients except crescent rolls.

◆ Unwrap rolls according to directions, spread with crabby cheese mixture and roll up as directed.

◆ Bake at 350° for 10 to 15 minutes until browned.

Can also be served as a light entrée with a salad.

SAUSALITO CRAB DIP

Yield: 26 appetizers

1 (2.4 ounce) package leek soup mix
1½ cups sour cream
1 tablespoon lemon juice
⅛ teaspoon red pepper sauce
6 ounces frozen crabmeat, thawed
1 (14 ounce) can water packed artichoke hearts
1 cup shredded Swiss cheese
1 teaspoon dillweed

◆ Combine soup mix, sour cream, lemon juice, and hot sauce together. Spread on platter.

◆ Chop crabmeat and artichoke hearts and layer on sour cream mixture. Top with shredded Swiss cheese and dillweed.

◆ Serve with assorted crackers.

◎ SHRIMP NEW ORLEANS

Yield: 4 appetizers

1 pound medium sized shrimp
¼ cup vegetable oil
1 tablespoon prepared mustard
2 tablespoons lemon juice or vinegar
2 green onions, thinly sliced
¼ cup celery, chopped fine
½ teaspoon salt
¼ teaspoon pepper

◆ Remove shells down to tail and clean shrimp.

◆ Steam or poach for about 3 minutes, until the shrimp turns pink, stirring occasionally.

◆ Mix together ingredients and marinate shrimp in mixture overnight.

◆ Serve on a bed of chopped greens for a luncheon or as an appetizer.

 SHRIMP MOLD

Yield: 20 appetizers

1 (3 ounce) package lemon jello
1 cup boiling water
½ cup chili sauce
1 tablespoon vinegar
2 drops hot pepper sauce
1 teaspoon Worcestershire sauce
2 tablespoons prepared horseradish
2 cups bay, or chopped shrimp

♦ Dissolve lemon jello in boiling water, set aside.
♦ Mix chili sauce, vinegar, pepper sauce, Worcestershire sauce, and horseradish. Add water to make 1 cup.
♦ Combine with jello mixture.
♦ When slightly thickened, add shrimp.
♦ Pour into buttered mold. Refrigerate until set.
♦ Unmold, garnish with shrimp and serve with crackers.

◎ LIME GARLIC SHRIMP WITH MANGO MINT SALSA

LIME GARLIC SHRIMP:

Yield: 12 appetizers

1 lime, juiced
2 cloves garlic, crushed
1 teaspoon Chinese hot oil
½ teaspoon salt
¼ teaspoon pepper
12 large shrimp, shelled and deveined

MANGO MINT SALSA:
2 cups mango, diced
¾ cup red onion, finely minced
1 red bell pepper, seeded and diced
2 jalapeño peppers, seeds removed and diced
1 bunch fresh mint (about 4 teaspoons), chopped
1 lime, juiced

♦ In a medium bowl, combine the lime juice, garlic, Chinese hot oil, salt, and pepper.
♦ Add the shrimp and marinate in refrigerator for 45 minutes.

♦ Combine Mango Mint Salsa ingredients and place in a serving bowl.
♦ Grill the shrimp for about 2 minutes on each side, or until they are pink. Serve with Mango Mint Salsa.

COCKTAIL MEATBALLS

Yield: 30 to 36 appetizers

MEATBALLS:

1	pound ground beef
2	eggs, slightly beaten
1	cup dried breadcrumbs
2	tablespoons onions, minced
2	tablespoons sweet pepper flakes
9	drops red pepper sauce
¼	teaspoon garlic powder

SAUCE:

¾	cup ketchup
½	cup water
¼	cup vinegar
⅓	cup packed brown sugar
1½	tablespoons minced onion
1	teaspoon prepared mustard
1¼	teaspoons salt
4	teaspoons Worcestershire sauce
6	drops red pepper sauce

◆ Combine all ingredients except sauce. Shape into bite size meatballs.

◆ Place single layer of meatballs in 13 x 9–inch baking pan. Bake at 350° for 30 minutes.

◆ Place meatballs in casserole. Combine sauce ingredients and pour over meatballs. Bake 1 hour longer.

◆ Serve warm with toothpicks.

Meatballs can be made ahead and frozen.

JOSEFINAS

Yield: 20 to 24 appetizers

1	cup butter
1	cup chopped pickled jalapeños or 6 to 8 ounces chopped mild green chiles for a milder version
1	clove garlic, crushed
1	cup mayonnaise
8	ounces Monterey Jack cheese, grated
1	baguette French bread (thin loaf)

◆ Mix butter, chopped peppers, and garlic. Set aside.

◆ Mix mayonnaise and Jack cheese. Set aside.

◆ Cut baguette into ½–inch pieces and toast in broiler on one side.

◆ Spread the pepper mixture on the untoasted sides of the bread slices. Top with layer of mayonnaise and Jack cheese mixture.

◆ Broil until cheese mixture is brown and puffy. Serve warm.

People will say these are really warm, but watch them disappear. If you do not use all of the butter/chile mixture, keep it for future use. The same for the mayonnaise/Jack cheese mixture. These are also good left over or served cold with soup.

SAUSAGE STRUDEL

Yield: 10 servings

1 pound smoked sausage (beef or turkey)
¾ cup cheese (Swiss, Jack, or Cheddar), grated
⅓ cup breadcrumbs
1 egg
4 - 5 sheets phyllo dough (or puff pastry sheets)
3 tablespoons melted margarine

◆ To prepare the stuffing: Peel sausage and grind. Combine sausage, cheese, breadcrumbs, and egg.

◆ To prepare the strudel: Thaw strudel dough if necessary. Working quickly and keeping dough moist is essential.

◆ Place a large, slightly dampened napkin or tea towel on the counter (not terry cloth). A spray bottle works well to dampen the cloth.

◆ Lay down one sheet of phyllo, spray lightly with cooking spray, lay down another sheet and spread with margarine. Layer 2 or 3 more sheets as above, ending with brushed margarine (or continue to use cooking spray).

◆ Place stuffing along the short side of the phyllo sheet and roll with the aid of a towel if needed.

◆ Place strudel on a buttered cookie sheet and bake at **400°** for 30 minutes.

See Special Guide Section for phyllo hints.

ARTICHOKE HEART DIP

Yield: 26 appetizers

1 (14 ounce) can water packed artichokes, drained
1 cup mayonnaise
1 cup Parmesan cheese
1 cup mozzarella cheese, shredded
1 teaspoon garlic salt
Paprika

◆ Smash artichoke hearts. Mix with mayonnaise, cheeses, and garlic salt.

◆ Spread in 9 x 12–inch baking dish. Sprinkle top with paprika.

◆ Bake at **350°** for about 30 minutes.

◆ Serve hot with crackers.

SHEEP DIP
(Artichoke Cheese Dip)

Yield: 1 gallon of dip

8 ounces water-packed artichoke hearts
6 ounces Asiago cheese or Parmesan cheese
3 ounces fresh spinach, washed and patted dry
1 pint half and half
20 ounces sour cream
24 ounces cream cheese
8 ounces whipping cream
4 bags of pita bread with each pita cut into 2–inch wedges

◆ Blend together all ingredients in food processor or blender until smooth (you will still have chunks of artichoke).

◆ Serve warm with side of toasted pita wedges.

This recipe is the product of a number of people. My mother came up with the idea and coached the chef who added together the right ingredients. I came up with the name as a joke since my father had been a sheep rancher for 50 years. We forgot to change the name in the final printing of the menu, but it sure draws attention to our best selling item.

This recipe is from Georgann Jouflas, owner of River City Cafe and Bar.

◎ TROUT PÂTÉ

Yield: 18 appetizers

12 ounces smoked trout
8 ounces cream cheese
2 tablespoons lemon juice
2 teaspoons onion, grated
1 teaspoon Worcestershire sauce
½ teaspoon (or less) salt
1 clove garlic, minced
Dillweed
Dash red pepper sauce

◆ Place ingredients in food processor and blend until creamy.

◆ Put in a bowl lined with plastic wrap (or spray mold with non-stick spray). Refrigerate until well chilled.

◆ Unmold and serve with crackers.

ARTICHOKE DIP WITH PESTO

Yield: 21 to 25 appetizers

8 ounces cream cheese, softened
½ cup pesto sauce (see recipe below)
¼ cup sour cream
1 (14 ounce) can water packed artichoke hearts, drained and coarsely chopped
½ cup grated Parmesan cheese

◆ Combine cream cheese and pesto sauce in a large bowl on medium speed until blended. Add sour cream, artichoke hearts, and Parmesan cheese and blend together.

◆ Bake uncovered at 350° in a shallow glass casserole dish for 30 minutes or until bubbly and golden color on top.

◆ Serve hot with assorted crackers.

⦿ PESTO SAUCE

Yield: Makes about 1¾ cups

2 cups fresh basil leaves, washed and lightly packed
4 garlic cloves, peeled and coarsely chopped
1 cup shelled pine nuts
¾ cup olive oil
1 cup grated Parmesan cheese
¼ cup grated Romano cheese
½ teaspoon salt
½ teaspoon pepper

◆ Combine basil, pine nuts, and garlic in the bowl of food processor or blender.

◆ With the blender running, add the olive oil slowly. Stop the motor and add the cheeses, salt, and pepper. Process to combine.

◆ Place in bowl with cover, and chill until ready to use.

ROASTED PEPPERS AND ARTICHOKES

Yield: 42 appetizers

2 tablespoons unsalted butter
1 bunch scallions, trimmed and minced
2 cloves garlic, minced
1 (13¾ ounce) can artichoke bottoms, drained and cut in quarters
3 ounces thinly sliced prosciutto, minced
3 tablespoons finely shredded fresh basil leaves
½ cup grated Parmesan cheese
½ cup Jarlsberg or Gruyère cheese, grated
1 tablespoon fresh lemon juice
Freshly ground black pepper to taste
½ cup mayonnaise
3 red bell peppers
3 yellow bell peppers
Salt to taste

◆ Melt butter in small skillet over medium-high heat. Add scallions and garlic and cook, stirring frequently, until softened (2 to 3 minutes). Transfer to medium size mixing bowl.

◆ Add artichoke bottoms, prosciutto, basil, Parmesan, and Jarlsberg to the scallions and toss. Sprinkle with lemon juice and pepper. Blend with mayonnaise and refrigerate 1 hour.

◆ Meanwhile, prepare peppers: preheat oven to 400°. Stem and seed peppers. Cut into chunks about 2 x 1½ inches.

◆ Place peppers in single layer in large shallow baking dish. Sprinkle with salt and pepper. Roast peppers 15 minutes, stirring once halfway through. Remove and cool.

◆ When ready to serve, preheat broiler. Mound about 2 teaspoons of artichoke mixture onto each pepper wedge. Arrange in rows on baking sheet (sprayed lightly with no-stick cooking spray).

◆ Broil 3 to 4 inches from heat until puffed and bubbly (about 2 to 3 minutes). Remove from broiler and cool for a few minutes. Place on serving tray. Enjoy!

Onion Pissaladière

Yield: 12 appetizers

TOPPING:

- ¼ cup (½ stick) unsalted butter
- 5 tablespoons olive oil
- 4 medium onions, thinly sliced
- 4 bay leaves
- 1 tablespoon sugar
- ½ teaspoon salt
- 2 tablespoons white wine

DOUGH:

- 1 teaspoon dry yeast
- ½ teaspoon sugar
- ¾ cup warm water
- ½ teaspoon salt
- 1¾ cups unbleached flour
- 2 tablespoons Parmesan cheese, grated

◆ For topping: Melt butter with oil in large heavy skillet over low heat. Add half of onions and 2 bay leaves.

◆ Sprinkle with half of sugar and half of salt. Top with remaining onions, bay leaves, sugar, and salt. Cover and cook 20 minutes. Increase heat to medium and cook uncovered 15 minutes, stirring occasionally. Increase heat to medium-high and cook until onions are deep golden, stirring often, about 15 minutes.

◆ Add wine and bring to a boil, scraping up any browned bits.

◆ Chill (can be made one day ahead).

◆ Bring to room temperature before using.

◆ To prepare dough: Sprinkle yeast and sugar over ¾ cup warm water in small bowl or food processor, stir to dissolve. Let stand until foamy, about 5 minutes.

◆ Add salt and flour. Process until well blended and dough forms ball. Continue processing one minute more. (Dough will be slightly sticky.)

◆ Lightly oil large bowl. Add dough, turning to coat. Cover and let stand in warm place until doubled (about 1 hour).

◆ Preheat oven to 500°. Punch down dough. Roll out dough on lightly floured surface to form large circle.

◆ Transfer to large, oiled pizza pan. Drizzle 1 tablespoon olive oil over dough. Spread onion

Continued on next page

Onion Pissaladière (continued)

mixture over dough. Sprinkle Parmesan cheese on top.

◆ Bake until golden, about 15 minutes.

◎ SPANAKOPITA

Yield: 15 appetizers

1	medium onion, minced
2	tablespoons butter
1	pound fresh spinach, chopped (or 1 package frozen chopped spinach)
¼	pound feta cheese, crumbled
6	ounces dry cottage cheese
¼	cup fresh breadcrumbs
½	cup scallions, chopped
2	eggs
	Salt and freshly ground pepper, to taste
	Nutmeg, to taste
¼	cup parsley, chopped
1	tablespoon dillweed
	Fresh breadcrumbs
½	pound phyllo leaves
½	pound sweet butter, melted

◆ Remove phyllo leaves from the refrigerator 4 hours before using.

◆ If using fresh spinach, wash and cook briefly. If using frozen spinach, defrost and drain.

◆ Sauté onions in butter until soft. Add the spinach and cook until the moisture has evaporated. Remove from heat and add the next 9 ingredients. Mix well. Set aside.

◆ Stack 4 phyllo leaves atop one another, brushing each leaf with melted butter.

◆ Place a ¾–inch strip of filling along the end of the phyllo leaves, sprinkle with breadcrumbs and roll jelly roll fashion, tucking the ends underneath.

◆ Place on a lightly greased cookie sheet and make small slits across the top diagonally.

◆ Brush with butter and bake at 375° for 35 to 40 minutes.

◆ Slice diagonally into 1–inch pieces. Serve on a bed of fresh parsley.

Baked Spanakopitas freeze well. Recrisp in 350° oven before serving.

See Special Guide Section for phyllo hints.

CHEESE AND ARTICHOKE APPETIZER

Yield: 4 servings

4 baked patty shells, fresh or frozen
2 (3 ounce) packages cream cheese, softened
2 tablespoons butter, softened
1 egg
4 drops hot pepper sauce
6 drops Worcestershire sauce
1 tablespoon fresh chives, chopped
4 artichoke hearts, drained

◆ Preheat oven to **425°**.

◆ Place the patty shells on an oven-proof serving dish. Beat the cream cheese with the butter, egg and seasonings.

◆ Just before baking, place a spoonful of cheese mixture in each shell, set an artichoke heart in the center and cover with remaining cheese mixture.

◆ Bake for 20 to 25 minutes in the upper third of the oven, until the cheese filling has puffed slightly and browned on top.

◆ Serve on a small plate with a fork.

This must be assembled at the last minute, but your guests will love it!

BAKED FRENCH BREAD DIP

Yield: 16 to 20 appetizers

1 large round loaf French bread (slice off top and set aside. Scoop out most of bread, not to be used in this recipe)
1½ pounds Monterey Jack cheese, grated
1 small can diced chiles
1 bunch green onions, chopped
2 packages (about 8 to 10 ounces) chipped beef, paper thin and chopped small
1 whole tomato, chopped small
Garlic powder and onion powder, to taste
Hot red pepper sauce
Salt and pepper

◆ Combine all ingredients together, except bread.

◆ Place filling in bread, replace top of bread.

◆ Wrap in foil and bake at **350°** for 45 minutes. Uncover, and continue baking 30 minutes more.

◆ Serve with large corn chips for dippers. When nearly all of the filling is eaten, slice bread in pie wedges to finish every last drop!

THE "BEST EVER" DEVILED EGGS

Yield: 12 deviled eggs

6 hard boiled eggs
¼ cup real mayonnaise
1 teaspoon prepared mustard
1 teaspoon vinegar
½ teaspoon salt
Paprika

◆ Boil eggs 20 minutes, cool.

◆ Cut eggs in half lengthwise and remove yolks.

◆ Place yolks in bowl, mash well with fork. Add mayonnaise, mustard, vinegar, and salt. Mix well.

◆ Stuff egg white halves with mixture. Garnish with paprika.

Add 1 teaspoon prepared horseradish for additional "zip".

VERSATILE CHEESE SPREAD

Yield: 2 cups

1 (8 ounce) package cream cheese (nonfat is okay)
2 tablespoons green onions, minced
3 tablespoons sweet pickles, finely chopped
2 hard boiled eggs, chopped
2 tablespoons mayonnaise (lowfat is okay)

◆ Bring cream cheese to room temperature.

◆ Add green onions, pickles, eggs, and mayonnaise to cream cheese. Mix well.

Variations: Can be spread on toasted bagel for a quick breakfast. Use on crackers for an appetizer. Stuff in celery.

LEMON CREAM (A DIP FOR CRUDITÉS)

Yield: Makes 4 cups

2 cups mayonnaise
2 cups sour cream
¼ cup fresh lemon juice
2½ teaspoons lemon peel, finely grated
2 teaspoons white horseradish
2 teaspoons Dijon mustard
1 teaspoon salt

◆ Combine all ingredients in a large bowl and blend.

◆ Cover and refrigerate.

◆ Adjust seasonings to taste before serving.

May be used for crudités, artichokes, or asparagus. Its refreshing lemon flavor complements them all!

CRANBERRY JUICE PUNCH

Yield: 30 to 35 servings

3 pints cranberry juice
½ cup lime juice, chilled, (bottled)
2 cups pineapple juice
¼ cup sugar
½ teaspoon almond extract
1 quart ginger ale, chilled
1 bottle champagne, chilled

◆ Combine all the ingredients, except the ginger ale and champagne ahead of time to allow flavors to mingle; refrigerate.

◆ When you are ready to serve, add in the chilled ginger ale and champagne.

Variation: If a non–alcoholic punch is desired, substitute an additional bottle of ginger ale for the champagne.

LANDS END NOG

Yield: 17 cups

6 eggs
¼ cup sugar
¼ teaspoon cinnamon
¼ teaspoon cardamom
¼ teaspoon cloves
1 quart vanilla ice cream, softened
6 cups orange juice
¼ cup lemon juice
1 quart ginger ale, chilled
Ice mold, optional
Ground nutmeg, optional
Stick cinnamon, optional

◆ Beat eggs on low speed until blended. Add sugar and spices, beat at medium speed until sugar dissolves.

◆ On low speed, beat in soft ice cream, add juices, cover and chill.

◆ To serve, pour mixture in punch bowl and slowly pour in ginger ale stirring with an up and down motion. Add ice ring.

◆ For each serving sprinkle with nutmeg and insert cinnamon stick if desired.

Can substitute 1 cup orange liqueur for 1 cup of orange juice.

◎ HOT BUTTERED RUM MIX

Yield: 30 servings

1 quart vanilla ice cream, softened
1 pound butter, softened
1 pound brown sugar
1 pound powdered sugar
1-2 teaspoons nutmeg
2 teaspoons cinnamon

◆ Mix all ingredients together well and freeze. Keep frozen.

◆ To serve: mix 3 tablespoons of mix with 6 ounces of boiling water and 1 jigger of rum.

Pumpkin Punch Bowl with Hot Mulled Cider

Yield: 15 servings

1	gallon apple cider
½	cup light brown sugar, packed (optional)
4-5	3–inch cinnamon sticks, broken into pieces
10-15	whole allspice
20-25	whole cloves
1	medium pumpkin (about 12 inches in diameter)

◆ In a 6–quart kettle bring cider, brown sugar, cinnamon, allspice and cloves to boiling; simmer uncovered for 30 minutes.

◆ Wash and dry pumpkin. Remove a 2–inch slice from top, scoop out seeds, discard pulp.

◆ Using a 2–cup glass measuring cup or a small saucepan, transfer cider into pumpkin punch bowl and serve.

When cider has been used, prepare pumpkin shell for use in another recipe; its flavor will be enhanced by the spicy cider. You may also want to save the seeds for toasting.

⟨ Vail Hot Spiced Wine

Yield: 2 quarts

1	quart Burgundy wine
1	quart cranberry juice
½	cup sugar
½	cup brown sugar
6	cloves
6	whole allspice
½	stick cinnamon

◆ Combine all ingredients in a large pan, mix thoroughly. Heat on medium until the sugar dissolves. Do not boil. Serve hot.

⟨ Amaretto

Yield: 6½ cups

2	cups brandy
2	cups vodka
2	teaspoons almond extract
2	cups sugar
2	cups water

◆ Bring sugar and water to boil, then simmer for 10 minutes, cool.

◆ Add brandy, vodka, and almond extract to sugar and water mixture.

◆ Store in corked bottle in cool, dark place.

Irish Creme Liqueur

Yield: 12 to 15 servings

1	pint half and half
1	can sweetened condensed milk
3	eggs
2 - 3	tablespoons chocolate syrup
2	teaspoons vanilla extract
8	ounces blended whiskey

♦ Blend all ingredients except whiskey, in blender. Stir in whiskey. Keep refrigerated.

Powderhorn Warm–Up

Yield: 2 cups dry mix

½	cup instant coffee
½	cup sugar
1	cup dry creamer
2	tablespoons cocoa powder

♦ Combine all ingredients and mix together thoroughly. Store in air tight container.

♦ To prepare, add 2 rounded teaspoons of mix to 6 to 8 ounces of hot water.

Variation: Add peppermint schnapps.

Gold Diggers' Painkillers

Yield: 1 serving

1	ounce cream of coconut milk
1	ounce orange juice, pulp–free
4	ounce pineapple juice
1	ounce dark rum
⅛	teaspoon nutmeg, freshly grated

♦ Ingredients need to be at room temperature.

♦ Blend all ingredients together until frothy.

♦ Pour over crushed ice. Top with fresh grated nutmeg.

Rum may be increased to 2 or 3 ounces depending on the amount of pain you are in or the amount of pain you will have the following day.

🐏 PEACH SMASH

Yield: 4 to 6 servings

1 (6 ounce) can orange juice, frozen
½ cup rum, vodka or gin
1 large peach, fresh, peeled and pitted, or 5 ounces of frozen sliced peaches
1 tablespoon orange liqueur
4 - 5 ice cubes
   Mint sprigs dipped in powdered sugar

◆ Place orange juice, rum, peaches, orange liqueur and ice into blender and blend until smooth and slushy.

◆ Pour immediately into glasses, garnish with mint sprigs and serve.

Good for summer or for after dinner drink.

🐏 SKIP AND GO

Yield: 4 to 6 servings

1 (6 ounce) can limeade, frozen
6 ounces tequila
6 ounces beer
   Ice

◆ Pour limeade into blender. Fill limeade can with beer and pour into blender. Fill limeade can with tequila and pour into blender. Fill blender with ice, blend.

🐏 ELAM BLT PEACH MARGARITA

Yield: 1 serving, multiply as desired

1 peach half, fresh (peeled)
1 ounce tequila
½ ounce Triple Sec
½ ounce fresh lemon juice
   Peach slice or lemon wedge (garnish)
   Ice as needed

◆ Place all ingredients except garnish in blender with ice and whirl until smooth and slushy.

◆ Garnish with peach slice or lemon wedge

Note: Can make a pitcher ahead, add ice and blend just before serving.

Ladies playing in this golf tournament enjoy this drink at the 19th hole.

MESA MARGARITAS

Yield: 4 to 6 servings

1   (6 ounce) can limeade
    concentrate (frozen)
¾   can tequila
½   can Triple Sec
¼   can lemon juice
2   egg whites, or egg white
    substitute
    Crushed ice

♦ Pour limeade in blender.

♦ Fill the limeade can with tequila and add to blender (if you want lighter ones add only ¾ of a can of tequila). Use the can to measure the Triple Sec and lemon juice.

♦ Add 2 egg whites (makes it frothy).

♦ Fill the blender with crushed ice to within 2 inches of top. Blend on high speed until combined; has frozen, frothy appearance.

Note: A favorite high desert drink.

Soup's On

• CRYSTAL MILL– ASPEN •

PEACH SOUP

Yield: 5 (⅔ cup) servings

2 cups peaches, coarsely
   chopped
⅓ cup sugar
¼ cup lemon juice
⅛ teaspoon ground cinnamon
1 cup water
¾ cup dairy sour cream

◆ Place peaches, sugar, lemon juice
  and cinnamon in blender or food
  processor and process until
  smooth.

◆ Add water and sour cream and
  blend until smooth.

CANTALOUPE SPLASH SOUP

Yield: 6 to 8 servings

2 ripe cantaloupes
¼ cup dry white wine
½ cup canned, unsweetened
   coconut milk
½ cup whipping cream
4 tablespoons fresh lime juice
½ teaspoon white pepper
¼ teaspoon nutmeg
2 tablespoons orange juice
4 thin slices ham, julienned
4 tablespoons coconut,
   shredded
   Grated zest of 1 lime
   Salt to taste

◆ Halve, seed and peel cantaloupes.
  Cut flesh into small pieces. Purée
  in food processor or blender.

◆ Place purée in bowl, add wine,
  coconut milk, cream, lime zest
  and juice, salt, pepper, nutmeg
  and orange juice. Blend well.

◆ Taste and correct seasonings, if
  needed. Chill at least 1 hour.

◆ When ready to serve, sprinkle
  with ham & shredded coconut.

*Note: Serve in chilled small tulip
bowls. Excellent for brunch!*

Chilled Summer Squash Soup with Curry

Yield: 4 servings

2 tablespoons (¼ stick) unsalted butter
2 large shallots, minced
1 large clove garlic, minced
1½ teaspoons curry powder (adjust to taste)
1½ pounds yellow crookneck squash, peeled and diced
2 cups (or more) chicken stock or canned broth
   Plain yogurt
   Mint leaves, minced

◆ Melt butter in heavy large saucepan over medium-low heat.

◆ Add shallots, garlic and curry and sauté 3 minutes.

◆ Add squash. Cover and cook until squash is tender, stirring occasionally (approximately 10 minutes).

◆ Purée in batches in blender or food processor. Transfer to bowl, whisk in broth.

◆ Cover and chill.

◆ May be thinned by adding additional stock, or by adding a little milk or cream.

◆ Season with salt, ladle into bowls and top with dollop of yogurt. Garnish with minced mint leaves.

This soup is delicious served hot, as well. Butternut squash may be substituted for the yellow crookneck. It may be prepared the day before.

Cold Pimiento Soup

Yield: 4 to 6 servings

2¼   pounds ripe tomatoes
2   large sweet red peppers
1   tablespoon unsalted butter
½   pound onions, coarsely chopped
¼   celery rib, coarsely chopped
1   small carrot, coarsely grated
4   cups rich chicken stock
      Sour cream

◆ Put tomatoes on a low-sided baking sheet and set under the broiler. Roast them as you would peppers, turning with tongs until the skin blackens, about 10 minutes. Put them on a plate and set aside. They will give up quite a bit of liquid by the time you are ready to use them; drain it off and discard.

◆ Roast the red peppers as you did the tomatoes. When they are blackened, put them in a paper bag and fold the top shut. Set aside.

◆ Put butter, onions, celery, and carrot in a saucepan with a tablespoon or two of the stock. Simmer, covered, over low heat for 10 minutes. Shake or stir to prevent sticking. Do not allow to brown. When vegetables are soft, set aside.

◆ Peel the tomatoes and cut out the stem ends.

◆ Add tomato pulp to wilted onion mixture and simmer, covered, for 15 minutes. Stir occasionally to prevent scorching.

◆ Dump this all into a strainer and mash the solids thoroughly to get rid of the seeds. (Putting the strained pulp through a food processor or food mill first makes this a bit easier.)

◆ Return strained vegetables to saucepan and add chicken stock.

◆ Simmer 30 minutes, uncovered. Skim as necessary.

◆ Peel and then purée the peppers.

Continued on next page

COLD PIMIENTO SOUP (Continued)

Add to the tomato mixture and let simmer for just a few minutes.

◆ Let cool and then correct seasonings.

◆ Serve slightly chilled with a large spoonful of sour cream.

Variation: Try spicing it up with a little hot pepper sauce to taste.

Truly a different kind of soup - try it!

GAZPACHO

Yield: 8 to 10 servings

1 cup tomatoes, peeled and minced
½ cup green pepper, minced
½ cup celery, minced
½ cup cucumber, minced
¼ cup onion, minced
1 small clove garlic, minced
2 teaspoons parsley
1 teaspoon chives
2-3 tablespoons tarragon wine vinegar
2 tablespoons olive oil
1 teaspoon salt
¼ teaspoon pepper
½ teaspoon Worcestershire sauce
3 cups tomato juice
Croutons and cilantro garnish

◆ Combine all ingredients, except croutons and cilantro, in a glass or stainless steel bowl. Cover and chill more than 4 hours.

◆ Serve in chilled soup bowls, garnished with croutons and fresh cilantro.

Note: This is really easy to make and delicious.

 SALMON BISQUE

Yield: 6 to 8 servings

1 tablespoon saffron threads, or 1 teaspoon powdered saffron (optional)

¾ cup heavy (whipping) cream, or low-fat evaporated milk

4 tablespoons (½ stick) unsalted butter

6 tablespoons minced shallots or green onions, white portions only

6 tablespoons unbleached all-purpose flour

1 tablespoon tomato paste

4½ cups homemade fish or chicken stock, or canned chicken broth (preferably low-sodium)

1 pound salmon fillet, skinned, rinsed, dried, and coarsely chopped

3 egg yolks
Salt
Ground cayenne pepper

1 teaspoon freshly squeezed lemon juice, or to taste
Fresh whole chives or parsley leaflets, preferably flat-leaf Italian type, for garnish

◆ In a small bowl, stir the saffron into the cream and set aside.

◆ Melt the butter in a large saucepan over medium heat. Add the shallots or green onions and sauté until soft but not browned, about 3 minutes.

◆ Using a wire whisk or wooden spoon, blend in the flour and cook, stirring, until bubbly, about 2 minutes.

◆ Quickly stir in the tomato paste.

◆ Gradually pour in the stock, whisking it into the flour until the mixture is thick and smooth, about 10 minutes.

◆ Add the salmon, reduce the heat to low, partially cover, and simmer until the salmon falls apart, about 15 minutes.

◆ Transfer the soup to a food processor or blender and purée until smooth.

◆ Then pour it through a fine wire sieve into a large bowl, pressing the salmon with the back of a wooden spoon to force as much through as possible. Discard whatever remains in the sieve.

◆ Pour the strained soup into a clean saucepan.

◆ Whisk together the egg yolks and saffron-flavored cream and then whisk in about ½ cup of the soup.

◆ Whisk the yolk mixture into the remaining soup and place the pan over medium heat. Cook, whisking constantly, until the soup almost comes to a boil.

Continued on next page

SALMON BISQUE (CONTINUED)

◆ Season to taste with salt, cayenne pepper, and lemon juice. Strain again through a fine sieve.

◆ Reheat, if necessary. Ladle into individual bowls, garnish, and serve immediately.

Hint: Can be transferred to a covered container and refrigerated as long as overnight. Reheat gently just before serving, stirring to prevent the bisque from boiling.

Note: Serve small portions of this rich soup to begin a special meal.

◎ ONION SOUP FONDUE

Yield: 12 servings

¾ cup unsalted butter
4 to 6 large onions, thinly sliced
8 cups beef broth
1 teaspoon chicken stock base
White pepper
12 ounces Monterey Jack cheese
French or sourdough bread, sliced 1-inch thick
Garlic Toast
¼ cup sherry (optional)

◆ Melt butter in large kettle, add onions, and sauté until transparent but not browned.

◆ Add beef broth and chicken stock base. Cover and simmer 2 to 3 hours.

◆ Remove from heat and refrigerate overnight or several hours. Discard chilled surface fat.

◆ Reheat and season to taste with white pepper. Add sherry.

◆ Slice cheese into 12 slices.

◆ Lightly toast 12 bread slices and top each with 1 slice Jack cheese.

◆ Pour soup into individual ovenproof serving bowls and top with slice of bread and cheese. Run bowls under broiler just until cheese bubbles and is soft but not browned.

Hint: Serve with Garlic Toast on the side.

Note: Fantastic as a first course; or make a meal of it on a cold blustery night.

BEATRICE FARNHAM OTTO'S TOMATO BISQUE

1 can tomatoes
1 can condensed milk

♦ Dilute can of milk with water until about quality of "real" milk.

♦ Bring to boiling point and thicken with corn starch or flour.

♦ Season well and let boil slowly (keeping out lumps) while tomatoes are put in another saucepan brought to boiling point and seasoned (salt, chile, or pepper), tablespoon full of sugar.

♦ Have equal parts tomato and milk—let both cook slowly until ready to serve. Then add pinch of soda to tomatoes and combine with milk.

♦ Do not let it cook or boil as it will "go bad" (curdle) after put together.

♦ This is camp style of course—at home it's usually strained through a colander to remove all lumps. Enjoy!

Note: Taken from a letter to Whipple Chester from Beatrice on Hotel Park Avenue stationery, September 1911.

This was served at Beatrice Farnham's wedding to John Otto, trailblazer and promoter of the Colorado National Monument. The ceremony was performed at the base of Independence Rock in the Colorado National Monument (see cover).

TODAY'S RECIPE: TOMATO SOUP

Yield: 6 or more servings

4   large, ripe tomatoes (about 1¾ pounds)
2   Bermuda onions (about 1¾ pounds)
2   tablespoons olive oil
4   cups beef broth
    Salt and pepper, to taste
¼   teaspoon dried hot pepper flakes
½   cup fresh basil leaves
¼   cup parsley, finely chopped
1   tablespoon fresh pesto (optional)

◆ Don't peel tomatoes, but cut away their cores and dice into small cubes, making about 4 cups. Set aside.

◆ Peel onions and cut in cubes no larger than ½ inch in diameter, about 5 cups.

◆ Heat olive oil in large pan and add onions cooking them until they look translucent (do not brown). Add tomatoes and cook 10 minutes, stirring often from the bottom of pan, until the mixture is sauce-like.

◆ Put in food processor and process until almost smooth.

◆ Add beef broth, salt, pepper, pepper flakes, basil, and parsley.

◆ Cook, stirring occasionally, about 20 minutes or longer. Add about 1 tablespoon fresh pesto if available. Serve with fresh toast on the side.

A very different taste!

OURAY SWISS CHEESE SOUP

Yield: 6 to 8 servings

1	tablespoon butter
¼	cup flour
2½	cups milk
1¼	cups chicken stock
8	ounces Cheddar cheese, shredded
8	ounces Swiss cheese, shredded
	Salt and white pepper to taste
1¼	cups white wine

Croutons:

3	cups bread crumbs made from dense-style bread
3	tablespoons olive oil
½	stick of butter

♦ Melt butter in saucepan and slowly add flour to make a roux.

♦ Add milk and chicken stock, stirring constantly. Bring to a boil and let simmer for 15 minutes.

♦ Stir in cheeses, stirring constantly. Simmer for an additional 5 minutes.

♦ Add salt and pepper.

♦ Just before serving, add wine and let simmer for an additional minute.

♦ Cube bread about ½-inch square (approximately). Melt butter in heavy skillet, add olive oil. Sauté bread cubes until brown on all sides. Salt lightly after removing from pan. Cool before serving.

GOURMET SPINACH SOUP

Yield: 4 to 6 servings

5	tablespoons unsalted butter
¼	pound fresh mushrooms, washed, dried, trimmed, and diced
1	scallion, chopped
5	tablespoons flour
2	cups chicken broth
2	cups milk
½	teaspoon salt (optional)
	Black pepper (preferably freshly ground)
	Ground nutmeg (optional)
¼	pound cream cheese, softened and cut into cubes
1	cup grated Swiss cheese (recommended: Jarlsberg)
¾	pound fresh spinach, washed, trimmed, cooked, and chopped

♦ Melt the butter in a large saucepan. Slowly sauté the mushrooms and scallion until tender.

♦ Add flour and stir just until flour is cooked, a couple of minutes.

♦ Whisk in chicken broth first, then milk, stirring until thickened.

♦ Add salt, pepper, nutmeg, cream cheese, and Swiss cheese; stir until melted.

♦ Stir in spinach.

♦ Heat and stir very gently. Season to taste. Serve hot.

Fresh and lovely taste.

CREAM OF MUSHROOM SOUP

Yield: 6 to 8 servings

1 pound fresh mushrooms, chopped
½ cup butter (1 stick)
6 tablespoons flour
¼ teaspoon dry mustard
¼ cup chives, finely chopped
Salt and white pepper to taste
2 cups chicken broth
2 cups half and half (1 pint)
¼ cup whipping cream
¼ cup sherry

◆ Melt butter in 2- to 3-quart saucepan.

◆ Add mushrooms and cook until mushrooms reduce in size, approximately 3 to 5 minutes.

◆ Add flour, dry mustard, chives, salt and white pepper. Mix well. Flour mixture should stick to mushrooms.

◆ Add chicken broth and cook on medium heat until hot, approximately 5 minutes.

◆ Add half and half and cook another 5 minutes on medium.

◆ Add whipping cream and sherry and cook until warm, another 3 minutes.

◆ Turn heat to low and cook to desired heat and thickness.

Note: This recipe was originally found on a coffee cup in the Delta, Colorado Post Office. It is very rich in taste and has a wonderful flavor. Serve it as the first course to a meal. It also makes a great soup and half sandwich dinner.

CREAMY POTATO SOUP

Yield: 4 servings

1 pound potatoes, peeled and thinly sliced
1½ cups chicken broth, low sodium with fat removed
1 cup skim milk
2 teaspoons margarine
⅓ cup green onion, thinly sliced
2 tablespoons parsley, chopped
½ teaspoon celery seed
¼ teaspoon tarragon
⅛ teaspoon pepper
Salt to taste

◆ Combine potatoes and broth in 2-quart saucepan. Bring to a boil, cover and cook until potatoes are tender. Cool slightly.

◆ Pour into blender and blend until smooth. Return to saucepan.

◆ Stir in milk, margarine, onion, parsley, celery seed, tarragon and pepper. Bring to boil, stir in salt.

◆ Serve warm or cold.

This soup is an all around winner— low cost, low-fat, yet rich and flavorful.

POTATO LEEK SOUP

Yield: 4 to 6 servings

2 tablespoons butter
1 cup onion, chopped (1 medium)
1 leek, white part chopped
4-5 baked potatoes (or pre-cook in another manner)
4 cups chicken broth
1 cup milk
Salt and pepper to taste

◆ Melt butter in a 2-quart saucepan.

◆ Sauté onion and leek until limp but not browned.

◆ Peel and dice 4 to 5 baked potatoes.

◆ Add potatoes and chicken broth to onion/leek mixture. Cook on medium heat about 15 minutes.

◆ Salt and pepper to taste. Add milk and heat through.

Variation: Serve cold with dollop of yogurt and fresh dill. Add cheese for another twist.

Hint: Soup can be refrigerated for later use before adding milk. If refrigerated, heat, add milk and heat through.

Serve with warm crusty French bread and green salad.

CORN CHOWDER WITH SHRIMP AND PEPPERS

Yield: 4 (1½ cup) servings

2	(10 ounce) packages of frozen whole kernel corn, thawed and divided in half
½	cup onion, finely chopped
¼	cup (2 ounces) butter or margarine, divided
1½	teaspoons fresh garlic, minced
1½	tablespoons cornstarch
¼	cup cold water
2	cups milk
1	cup heavy cream
1	Poblano chile pepper, roasted, seeded and diced
1	red pepper, roasted, seeded and diced
1½	teaspoons salt (optional)
1	pound medium-size shrimp, shelled and deveined
3	tablespoons chopped fresh cilantro
½	cup (2 ounces) crumbled goat or farmer cheese

◆ Place 3 cups of the corn in processor or blender; set aside remaining corn.

◆ In small skillet, sauté onion in 2 tablespoons of the butter until soft but not browned (about 6 to 8 minutes). Add garlic and sauté 1 minute longer.

◆ Add to corn in processor with cornstarch and water, process until fairly smooth.

◆ In a 3-quart saucepan, melt remaining butter over medium heat. Add puréed corn mixture. Cook, stirring constantly until quite thick (about 5 to 6 minutes).

◆ Whisk in milk. Partially cover and simmer 15 minutes, stirring often.

◆ Strain mixture through wire mesh sieve into large bowl.

◆ Rinse out saucepan.

◆ Pour strained soup back into saucepan. Stir in cream, diced peppers, the reserved corn and salt. Bring just to boiling.

◆ Reduce heat and simmer 10 minutes, stirring often.

◆ Add shrimp. Cook just until shrimp turn pink in color (about 3 minutes). Stir in cilantro and serve immediately garnished with crumbled cheese.

Note: Wonderful flavor. Makes a great meal served with corn bread and a salad.

WILD RICE CLAM CHOWDER

Yield: 8 to 10 servings

½ cup uncooked wild rice
(1½ cups cooked rice)
1 medium onion, chopped
¼ green pepper, diced
1 stalk celery, diced
½ cup fresh mushrooms,
diced
¼ cup butter (2 ounces)
½ cup all-purpose flour
2½ cups chicken stock or
chicken broth
1 pint half and half
¼ cup white wine
2 (6½ ounce) cans minced
clams
Salt and pepper to taste

◆ Partially cook wild rice (about 20 minutes) following one of the basic methods on wild rice package.

◆ Sauté onion, green pepper, mushrooms and celery in butter until vegetables are soft.

◆ Blend in flour, stirring until mixture is bubbly.

◆ Gradually stir in chicken stock. Heat to boiling, stirring constantly.

◆ Boil and stir one minute.

◆ Stir in half and half and wine. Simmer about 10 minutes.

◆ Stir in clams with juice and wild rice.

◆ Season with salt and pepper. Simmer about 20 minutes.

Note: Excellent, hearty chowder—a meal in itself. Serve with corn bread.

WILD RICE SOUP

Yield: 8 to 10 servings

1 ½	cups wild rice
4	cups chicken broth
1	teaspoon salt
1	large onion, chopped fine
1	cup celery, thinly sliced
½	cup carrot, chopped
2	cups sliced mushrooms
½	cup butter or margarine
½	cup flour
8	cups chicken broth, preferably homemade
1	teaspoon thyme, dried
3	bay leaves
1	teaspoon black pepper
½	cup dry sherry
2	cups heavy cream
1	teaspoon fine quality curry powder
2	cups cooked chicken, optional

◆ Rinse wild rice until water is clear. Cook rice in chicken broth with salt over medium heat until rice is tender (approximately 35 minutes).

◆ In heavy soup pot, sauté onion, celery, carrot and mushrooms in butter (about 5 minutes). Mix in flour and cook over medium heat about 5 more minutes.

◆ Add chicken broth, seasonings and sherry and bring to a boil stirring constantly until slightly thickened (about 10 minutes).

◆ Add reserved wild rice and any remaining cooking liquid and cream and cook over low heat about 1 hour.

◆ Adjust seasoning and add curry powder and optional cooked chicken and simmer 30 minutes.

Hint: Best made 1 day ahead; may be frozen.

A wonderful, rich soup from the Crystal Cafe.

◎VEGGIE SOUTHWEST SOUP

Yield: 8 to 12 servings

2 (28 ounce) cans stewed tomatoes
1 large green pepper, chopped
1 large onion, chopped
2 cups celery, chopped
1 jalapeño pepper, chopped and seeded
1 (17 ounce) can corn
1 (29 ounce) can black beans
2 cups water
1 package vegetable soup mix
1 teaspoon cilantro leaves
1 teaspoon garlic powder
1 teaspoon pepper, coarsely ground
½ teaspoon basil
½ teaspoon chili powder
 Salt to taste

◆ Purée the tomatoes or leave as they are if you like chunkier texture.

◆ Combine all ingredients in a large pot. Bring to boil, reduce heat and simmer for 2 to 3 hours (or all day if possible).

◆ Freezes well and tastes better the second day.

Hint: Chicken bouillon or any broth can be substituted for the water and vegetable mix.

Note: This soup adds a wonderful aroma to your kitchen while cooking. Serve it with a chile corn bread.

Black Bean Soup

Yield: 6 to 8 servings

2 tablespoons olive oil
3 slices bacon
3 ham hocks
2 medium onions, diced
2 cloves garlic, minced
2 stalks celery, chopped
1½ cups dried black beans, washed, soaked overnight and drained
3 teaspoons chili powder
4 cups water
1 tablespoon beef base
½ teaspoon black pepper
¼ cup dry vermouth or sherry
⅛ cup white vinegar
1 tablespoon fresh or 1 teaspoon dry cilantro, minced or crumbled

◆ In a large soup pot, over medium heat, place the olive oil, bacon, ham hocks, onions, garlic, and celery. Sauté them until vegetables are tender.

◆ Add remaining ingredients. Bring to boil and simmer it for 2½ to 3 hours, or until beans are tender. Add more water if necessary. Occasionally skim excess fat from top.

◆ Remove ham hocks and allow to cool. Remove meat from ham hocks and return to soup, discarding any fat and bones. Place the soup in a food processor or blender and purée until smooth.

◆ When ready to serve, garnish with fresh cilantro.

Hint: Soup can be made ahead, placed in a tightly covered bowl in the refrigerator and reheated as desired. Freezes well.

Note: State Representative Dan Prinster prefers his black bean soup chunky. He feels that "life has chunks, soup should too".

VEGETARIAN WINTER SQUASH STEW

Yield: 4 servings

1 (29 ounce) can hominy (or fresh equivalent)
¾ pound or 1½ cups banana squash (or any winter squash)
2-3 tablespoons safflower or canola oil
1 medium onion, diced into ½-inch squares
1 teaspoon dried oregano
Salt to taste
1-2 large cloves garlic, minced
2 tablespoons New Mexico ground red chile
1 tablespoon flour
3½ cups water
1 green bell pepper, diced into ½-inch squares
½ cup sour cream or plain yogurt
Chopped cilantro for garnish

♦ Drain hominy and rinse.

♦ Peel squash; cut into ½-inch strips, then cut into ½-inch pieces.

♦ Warm oil in large skillet or pot and add onion, squash, oregano. Season with salt. Cook over medium-high heat for about 4 minutes.

♦ Add garlic, ground chile and flour and stir well to mix in flour.

♦ Add hominy and water.

♦ Lower heat and simmer for 30 to 40 minutes.

♦ Add green pepper and cook until all is tender (about 15 minutes).

♦ Taste and adjust salt if necessary.

♦ Just before serving, stir in sour cream or yogurt. Garnish with cilantro.

Note: Want a change? Try this stew—it's a vegetarian delight!

Freezes well!

VEAL AND BARLEY STEW

Yield: 4 to 6 servings

3 tablespoons butter
1 leek (white part only), chopped
2 stalks celery, chopped
1 onion, chopped
1 pound veal, cubed
4 cups chicken broth
⅓ cup barley
¼ cup fresh parsley, chopped
1 bay leaf
½ teaspoon thyme
Salt and pepper to taste
1 potato, diced
1 cup light cream

◆ Melt butter in a large stew pot. Sauté leek, celery, onion and meat over low heat for about 20 minutes, stirring occasionally.

◆ Add broth and barley. Bring to boil.

◆ Add parsley, bay leaf, thyme, salt and pepper.

◆ Cover and simmer for about 2 hours.

◆ Add potato. Cover and simmer for about 30 to 40 minutes.

◆ Remove bay leaf and stir in cream.

◆ Heat until warm, about 5 minutes.

Hint: Can be doubled and made ahead and even frozen up to adding the cream.

Note: This is a fabulous dinner stew. Serve with a warm crusty bread and a Merlot wine.

SOUTH OF THE BORDER STEW

Yield: 6 servings

2 tablespoons shortening
1½ pounds lean chuck, cut in 1-inch cubes
1½ pounds smoked pork, cut in 1-inch cubes
2 medium onions, chopped
2 cloves garlic, minced
2 green chiles, seeded and chopped (hot or mild)
2 sweet red peppers (or green peppers)
2 bay leaves
1 teaspoon oregano
1 teaspoon salt
½-1 teaspoon pepper
½ teaspoon cumin
1 (1 pound) can tomatoes
¼ cup lemon juice
1 cup dry red wine
1 cup beef broth
1 cup raisins
1 cup whole almonds

♦ OVEN METHOD:

♦ Brown beef in shortening in Dutch oven. Remove beef. Brown pork, onions and garlic; stir often, about 5 minutes.

♦ Return beef to Dutch oven and add chile peppers, red pepper, bay leaves, oregano, salt, pepper, cumin and tomatoes.

♦ Bring to boil, then lower heat.

♦ Simmer uncovered 5 minutes.

♦ Add remaining ingredients and cover.

♦ Bake at **300°** for 2 hours. Skim fat.

♦ SLOW COOKER METHOD:

♦ Brown meats, garlic and onions in skillet.

♦ Place in slow cooker. Add chile peppers, red pepper, bay leaves, oregano, salt, pepper, cumin, tomatoes, lemon juice, raisins, almonds, ½ cup wine, ½ cup beef broth. Cover.

♦ Cook 8 to 10 hours.

Note: Serve with warm flour tortillas or over rice.

The Garden Patch

HAIL CAESAR SALAD

Yield: 6 to 8 servings

¾ cup vegetable oil
⅓ cup Parmesan cheese, freshly grated
3 tablespoons lemon juice
2 tablespoons green onion, finely minced
½ teaspoon salt
1 teaspoon dry mustard
½ teaspoon Worcestershire sauce
½ teaspoon garlic salt
¼ teaspoon pepper, freshly ground
1 large head Romaine lettuce, torn into pieces
1 avocado
½ cup croutons
1 (2 ounce) can anchovies, chopped

◆ Combine first 9 ingredients in a jar. Cover tightly and shake well.
◆ Refrigerate overnight.
◆ Combine remaining ingredients in large bowl.
◆ Shake dressing well and pour over salad.
◆ Toss gently and serve immediately.

Variation: Place sliced grilled chicken breast on top of salad for a delicious main dish.

WALDORF SALAD

Yield: 6 servings

6 cups red apples, cored and cubed
½ cup walnuts or pecans, chopped
½ cup pineapple chunks
8-10 Maraschino cherries
1 cup small marshmallows
2 cups sour cream
2-3 tablespoons strawberry jam

◆ Mix the fruit together in a large bowl.
◆ Mix the sour cream and strawberry jam together until it is a light pink color and is not too sweet.
◆ Combine sour cream mixture with fruit and refrigerate.
◆ Serve garnished with sliced fresh strawberries and nuts.

Note: Ingredient amounts can be varied according to the amount of servings you wish. Flavors will continue to blend.

COBB SALAD

Yield: 6 servings

½ head iceberg lettuce
½ bunch watercress
1 small bunch curly endive
½ head Romaine
2 tablespoons chives, minced
2 medium tomatoes, peeled, seeded and diced
1 chicken breast, cooked, boned, skinned and diced
6 strips bacon, cooked and diced
1 avocado, peeled and diced
3 hard-cooked eggs, diced
½ cup Roquefort cheese, crumbled
   Special French Dressing

SPECIAL FRENCH DRESSING:

¼ cup water
¼ cup red wine vinegar
¼ teaspoon sugar
1½ teaspoons lemon juice
½ teaspoon salt
½ teaspoon black pepper
½ teaspoon Worcestershire sauce
¾ teaspoon dry mustard
½ clove garlic, minced
¼ cup olive oil
¾ cup vegetable oil

◆ Chop lettuce, watercress, endive and Romaine in very fine pieces.

◆ Mix together in one large wide bowl or individual wide shallow bowls. Add chives.

◆ Arrange tomatoes, chicken, bacon, avocado and eggs in narrow strips or wedges across top of greens. Sprinkle with cheese and chill.

◆ Meanwhile, combine water, vinegar, sugar, lemon juice, salt, pepper, Worcestershire, mustard, garlic and oils in a jar. Chill. Shake well before using. (Makes about 1½ cups).

◆ At serving time, toss with ½ cup Special French Dressing. Pass remaining dressing.

Add some hot French bread or rolls and you have an excellent lunch salad!

SZECHWAN CONFETTI SALAD

Yield: 15 to 20 servings

4 pounds fried chicken meat, julienne
1 pound jícama, julienne and cut 2 inches long
1 pound carrots, julienne and cut 2 inches long
1 pound china peas, julienne
2 red and/or yellow peppers, julienne
1 bunch green onions, julienne and cut 2 inches long
4 stalks celery, julienne and cut 2 inches long
2 cups slivered almonds, toasted

DRESSING:

1 tablespoon garlic, minced
3 tablespoons whole grain mustard
½ cup soy sauce
½ cup rice wine vinegar
¼ teaspoon cayenne pepper
Pinch salt
1 cup soy or sesame oil

◆ Mix chicken, vegetables and slivered almonds together in a large salad bowl.

◆ Mix all dressing ingredients together in a jar and shake well.
◆ Toss together and chill until ready to serve.

This is a wonderful salad! Can be cut in half for a smaller group.

⦿SZECHWAN NOODLE SALAD

Yield: 10 servings

8 ounces egg noodles
1 (8 ounce) can sliced water chestnuts, drained
1 cup mushrooms, sliced
½ cup green onions, sliced
6 cloves garlic, minced
4 teaspoons fresh ginger root, grated
½ cup soy sauce
2 tablespoons sesame oil
2 tablespoons chili paste or chili oil
2 tablespoons honey
1 cup unsalted cashews or peanuts

◆ Cook noodles according to directions on package. Rinse, drain and set aside.
◆ In a large bowl, mix next 9 ingredients.
◆ Add noodles and toss lightly to combine.
◆ Cover and refrigerate 2 to 24 hours, stirring occasionally.
◆ Add nuts just before serving.

Note: This salad is even better served the next day.

◎ CURRIED CHICKEN ARTICHOKE SALAD   *Yield: 10 to 12 servings*

1	chicken, boiled and boned
1	package chicken, beef or other flavored rice vermicelli mix
½	bell pepper, chopped
½	cup pimiento-stuffed olives, sliced
2	(6 ounce) jars marinated artichoke hearts, reserving liquid
¼	teaspoon curry powder
⅓	cup good quality mayonnaise
½	cup green onion, chopped

◆ Cook chicken, beef or other flavored rice vermicelli mix as directed, omitting butter. Cool to room temperature.

◆ Add green onions, pepper, olives and artichokes.

◆ Add chicken.

◆ Mix curry, mayonnaise and the artichoke liquid from 1 jar of artichoke hearts together.

◆ Pour over salad and chill 24 hours.

◎ TOMATOES STUFFED WITH ARTICHOKE HEARTS   *Yield: 4 servings*

4	medium-large ripe, whole tomatoes, cored, peeled and seeded
1	cup water-packed artichoke hearts, drained and halved

MARINADE:

¼	cup olive oil
¼	cup vinegar
1	teaspoon salt
1	teaspoon black pepper
1	tablespoon relish, (optional)
1	tablespoon pimiento, chopped
1	tablespoon parsley, chopped
1	tablespoon green onion, chopped
1	teaspoon capers

◆ Day before or early in the day, make marinade and add artichoke hearts. Refrigerate.

◆ 4 hours before serving, peel and core whole tomatoes by placing whole tomatoes in 2 quarts of boiling water. Blanch for approximately 1 to 2 minutes. Place tomatoes in cold water. When cool, peel skin from tomatoes and core.

◆ Stuff tomatoes with artichoke hearts and pour remaining marinade on top. Chill up to 4 hours.

◆ Serve on bed of lettuce and garnish with fresh parsley.

Very attractive and appealing.

Carol's
Oriental Food & Gifts

JAPANESE CHICKEN SALAD

Yield: 4 to 6 servings

8 ounces chicken meat, cooked and shredded
2 ounces sai fun (bean thread) noodles, deep fried
1 head lettuce, shredded
4 green onions, sliced thin
2 tablespoons toasted almonds
2 tablespoons toasted sesame seeds

DRESSING:
4 tablespoons sugar
2 teaspoons salt
1 teaspoon pepper
2 tablespoons salad oil
6 tablespoons rice vinegar

◆ Cook chicken and shred into thin strips by hand.

◆ Fry noodles in hot oil (3 to 4 cups) until they expand. Remove from oil immediately.

◆ Shred lettuce and slice onions.

◆ Toast almonds and sesame seeds.

◆ Prepare dressing and mix all together.

Note: Delicious on any occasion.

From the kitchen of Carol's Oriental Food

ORIENTAL CABBAGE SALAD

Yield: 8 to 10 servings

2 packages chicken flavored ramen noodles (spice packets removed)
1 cup slivered almonds
½ teaspoon margarine or sesame oil
1 medium head of cabbage, finely chopped
1 red bell pepper, cut into julienne strips
2 tablespoons sesame seeds

DRESSING:
½ cup vegetable oil or canola oil
3 tablespoons sugar
¾ cup cider vinegar
½ teaspoon salt
Fresh ground pepper to taste
Spice packets from noodles

◆ Boil noodles according to directions on package. Do not add spice packets. Drain and rinse noodles in cold water and set aside.

◆ Toast almonds in margarine or oil until golden brown, stirring constantly, being careful not to burn.

◆ Combine toasted almonds, cooked noodles, shredded cabbage, red pepper and sesame seeds in large bowl.

◆ Prepare dressing by mixing together oil, sugar, vinegar, spice packets from noodles, salt and pepper. Pour over salad, toss and cover.

◆ Chill 2 to 3 hours before serving.

Note: This is a great salad to serve when cooking outdoors.

BROCCOLI SALAD

Yield: 10 to 12 servings

1   large bunch broccoli (4 to
    5 cups)
1   cup sunflower seeds
1   cup raisins
12 slices bacon, fried, drained
    and crumbled
1   medium red onion,
    chopped

DRESSING:
½   cup sugar
1   cup mayonnaise
2   tablespoons vinegar

◆ Clean and chop broccoli.
◆ Toss broccoli with remaining
  ingredients in a large salad bowl.

◆ Mix dressing together and pour
  over salad. Toss and refrigerate
  for 2 to 4 hours before serving.

This salad is a hit at any gathering.

DITCH BANK ASPARAGUS TOSS

Yield: 8 servings

2   pounds fresh asparagus
8   green onions, diagonally
    sliced
8   radishes, sliced

DRESSING:
¼   cup white vinegar
¼   cup olive oil
½   teaspoon thyme, dried
    (1½ teaspoons fresh)
½   teaspoon basil, dried
    (1½ teaspoons fresh)
¼   teaspoon salt
¼   teaspoon white pepper

◆ Snap off tough ends of asparagus.
  Remove scales from stalks with a
  knife or vegetable peeler, if
  desired. Cut spears diagonally
  into 1½-inch pieces.
◆ Cook asparagus, covered, in a
  small amount of boiling water 6
  minutes or steam until crisp-
  tender; drain.
◆ Place asparagus in a large bowl,
  cover and chill thoroughly.
◆ Add green onions and radishes to
  asparagus; set aside.
◆ Combine vinegar and remaining
  ingredients in a small jar. Cover
  tightly and shake until combined.
◆ Pour dressing over vegetables.
  Toss gently before serving.

*Note: An elegant dish served on a
plate with stuffed salmon.*

*Asparagus grows wild in the spring
time along the irrigation ditch banks
in Western Colorado.*

MARINATED MUSHROOM SALAD

Yield: 4 servings

1 pound large white
mushrooms, sliced
½ lemon, juice only
2 tablespoons parsley,
chopped
2 tablespoons chives,
chopped
Vinaigrette dressing
2 tomatoes, sliced
VINAIGRETTE DRESSING:
3 tablespoons vinegar
2 tablespoons Dijon-style
mustard
1 cup oil
Dash white wine
Salt and pepper to taste

♦ Whisk together vinegar and
mustard.

♦ Gradually add oil, pouring in a
thin stream and beating until
mixture thickens slightly.

♦ Add wine and season to taste
with salt and pepper.

♦ Slice mushrooms and toss with
lemon juice.

♦ Add parsley, chives and Vinaigrette Dressing. Toss, chill, then
toss again before serving.

♦ Garnish with a few tomato slices

A mushroom lover's delight!

MIXED GREENS WITH RASPBERRY VINAIGRETTE

Yield: 6 servings

6-8 cups Bibb, Romaine and
Red Leaf lettuce, well
washed and torn
1 cup pecan halves, roasted
and salted
⅓ cup mild blue cheese,
crumbled
4 small red onions, thinly
sliced
RASPBERRY VINAIGRETTE:
1 cup vegetable oil
⅓ cup red wine vinegar
2 tablespoons seedless
raspberry jam
½ teaspoon dill
¼ teaspoon dry mustard
⅛ teaspoon white pepper
¼ teaspoon salt
1 tablespoon granulated
sugar

♦ Combine together in large salad
bowl the lettuce, nuts, cheese and
onions.

♦ Mix together the oil, vinegar,
jam, dill, mustard, pepper, salt
and sugar. Blend well.

♦ Pour dressing on salad and toss
gently. Serve immediately.

Note: Can do dressing ahead.

*A delicious and colorful salad that
can stand alone. The pecans add
crunch to this zesty salad.*

MANDARIN SALAD

Yield: 4 to 6 servings

½ cup sliced almonds
3 tablespoons sugar
½ head iceberg lettuce
½ head Romaine lettuce
1 cup celery, chopped
2 whole green onions, chopped
1 (11 ounce) can mandarin oranges, drained

DRESSING:
½ teaspoon salt
Dash of pepper
¼ cup vegetable oil
1 tablespoon parsley, chopped
2 tablespoons sugar
2 tablespoons vinegar
Dash of hot pepper sauce

◆ In a small pan over medium heat, cook almonds and sugar, stirring constantly until almonds are coated and sugar dissolved. Watch carefully as they will burn easily. Cool and store in air-tight container.

◆ Mix all dressing ingredients and chill.

◆ Mix lettuces, celery and onions.

◆ Just before serving, add almonds and oranges. Toss with the dressing.

Compliments of "Colorado Cache" from The Junior League of Denver

ORANGE-AVOCADO-ONION SALAD

Yield: 6 servings

½ head iceberg lettuce, torn into bite-size pieces
½ head Romaine lettuce, torn into bite-size pieces
1 orange, sectioned and cut into bite-size pieces
½ avocado, sliced and drenched in lemon juice
½ red onion, sliced

 DRESSING:

¼ cup sesame seed
¼ cup sugar
½ teaspoon paprika
¼ teaspoon dry mustard
½ teaspoon salt
½ teaspoon Worcestershire sauce
3 tablespoons onion, grated
6 tablespoons oil
3 tablespoons cider vinegar

♦ Toast sesame seeds in 200° oven, stirring frequently.
♦ Combine sugar, paprika, mustard, salt, Worcestershire sauce and grated onion in large salad bowl.
♦ Add oil and vinegar gradually, stirring constantly with whisk.
♦ Transfer to large jar. Add sesame seeds and refrigerate.
♦ When ready to serve, toss dressing with salad.

Note: Great salad to serve with chicken, pork or ham.

SPINACH AND STRAWBERRY SALAD

Yield: 8 to 10 servings

1 pound fresh spinach, torn, stems removed
1 pint fresh strawberries

DRESSING:

½ cup sugar
2 tablespoons sesame seed
1 tablespoon poppy seed
1½ teaspoons onion, minced
1¼ teaspoons Worcestershire sauce
¼ teaspoon paprika
½ cup salad oil
¼ cup vinegar

♦ Mix dressing well in shaker.
♦ When ready to serve, mix spinach and strawberries in large bowl, add dressing and toss gently.
♦ Serve on chilled salad plates.

Variation: Substitute raspberries for strawberries.

A very nice summer-time salad. Would be delicious served with grilled fresh fish.

BREAD SALAD WITH TOMATOES

Yield: 6 servings

½ small sourdough or French baguette (about 12 inches)
1 large clove garlic, mashed
4 tablespoons olive oil
6 medium to large ripe summer tomatoes, cut into large chunks
½ cup green onions, chopped
3 tablespoons fresh basil, coarsely chopped
¼ cup balsamic vinegar
½ cup olive oil
   Salt and pepper to taste
   Bibb lettuce

◆ Heat oven to **300°**. Split the baguette in half lengthwise.
◆ Rub one half very well with the mashed garlic on the cut side and brush liberally with olive oil.
◆ Cut the bread into croutons about ¾ inch square.
◆ Place croutons on a cookie sheet, crust side down. Bake at 300° until dark golden (about 30 minutes).
◆ Place tomatoes in a large mixing bowl a bit before you intend to mix the salad. Drain away any juice that may have accumulated in the bowl.
◆ When ready to serve, add the croutons, onion and basil to the tomatoes.
◆ Whisk together the vinegar and oil. Season to taste.
◆ Pour over salad and toss.
◆ Serve on leaves of Bibb lettuce.

A great beginning to an Italian dinner.

STEAK SALAD

Yield: 4 servings

1 pound grilled flank steak, thinly sliced
2 ripe tomatoes, seeded and diced
1 small red onion, sliced thin
2 hard-boiled eggs, chopped or grated
DRESSING:
½ cup Italian-type dressing
1½ tablespoons capers, drained
2 teaspoons Dijon-style mustard

◆ Grill flank steak to desired doneness. Cool and slice into thin strips.
◆ Toss ingredients 1 through 4 in a large salad bowl.
◆ Add dressing and mix to coat.
◆ Chill about 2 hours and serve on a bed of mixed greens.

Men love this recipe!

ELAINE'S GREEK SALAD

Yield: 4 to 6 servings

3 firm red tomatoes, cut into wedges
2 cucumbers, peeled and sliced
3 green peppers, cut into strips
12 imported Greek black olives
8 ounces feta cheese, cut into ¾-inch cubes
1 medium onion, chopped

DRESSING:

½ cup olive oil
⅓ cup white or red wine vinegar
1 garlic clove, crushed
2 tablespoons fresh dill or basil, finely chopped
1 teaspoon oregano, dried (or 1 tablespoon fresh)
½ teaspoon salt
  Pepper to taste

◆ Combine dressing ingredients in a jar and shake vigorously.

◆ Combine salad in a large bowl. Pour dressing over salad and toss.

Variation: Serve alone or on a bed of mixed greens.

Wonderful with marinated flank steak.

FROZEN PEA SALAD

Yield: 8 to 10 servings

1 (16 ounce) package frozen peas
5 tablespoons bacon bits
½ cup celery, chopped
½ cup green onions, chopped
2 tablespoons mayonnaise
½ cup sour cream
1 cup cashew pieces

◆ Mix frozen peas together with remaining ingredients, except cashews, and let stand over night.

◆ Just before serving, mix in the cashews.

Note: Serve on a bed of mixed greens or Bibb lettuce leaf.

Great salad to take on a picnic or to a friend's barbecue.

SEAFOOD AND WILD RICE SALAD

Yield: 12 servings

1 cup wild rice
3-4 cups chicken stock
1½ cups frozen peas
¾ cup celery, diced with some leaves
½ cup whole green onions, sliced
1 (10 ounces) frozen sea legs, shredded
3 cups cooked baby shrimp

CURRY DRESSING:
1 large garlic clove, minced
3 tablespoons oil
1½ teaspoons curry
1 cup mayonnaise
1 cup sour cream
1 tablespoon sugar
2 tablespoons orange juice
2 tablespoons lemon juice
2 tablespoons chutney, chopped
2 tablespoons Dijon-style mustard

♦ Cook wild rice in chicken stock about 45 minutes. Drain. Refrigerate until cold.

♦ In the meantime, sauté garlic in oil for 3 minutes. Add curry and sauté 2 minutes more. Remove from heat.

♦ Add remaining dressing ingredients and stir until mixed thoroughly.

♦ Add peas, celery, onions, sea legs and shrimp to rice.

♦ Toss with Curry Dressing.

A very appealing dish. Your dinner guests will love this one.

TWICE-DRESSED SALAD

Yield: 6 to 8 servings

6 cups lettuce, washed and torn
½ small red onion, thinly sliced
Italian Vinaigrette of your choice
2 tomatoes, peeled, cut into wedges, for garnish

AVOCADO DRESSING:
6 hard-boiled eggs
¼-½ cup ranch-type dressing
½ teaspoon seasoned salt
¼ teaspoon white pepper
2 small avocados
Garlic powder to taste

♦ Toss lettuce and onions with Italian vinaigrette dressing and place on chilled salad plates.

♦ Process Avocado Dressing in food processor until blended (leave chunky). Adjust seasonings to taste.

♦ Top lettuce with Avocado Dressing and garnish with tomato wedges.

Variation: Use 3 green onions, sliced in place of red onion.

Hint: Use several different kinds of lettuce for an appealing look.

◎ TABBOULEH

Yield: 12 servings

2 cups bulgur wheat
2 bunches parsley, finely chopped
3 tomatoes, seeded, finely chopped
1 cucumber, seeded, finely chopped
1 bunch green onions, finely chopped
Juice of 3 lemons
1 tablespoon paprika
1 tablespoon cayenne pepper
1 cup olive oil
Salt and pepper to taste
Belgian Endive leaves

◆ Place the bulgur in a large-size bowl with cold water to cover and leave undisturbed for 45 minutes.

◆ Strain bulgur through a fine strainer or cheesecloth for 30 minutes, occasionally squeezing out excess water. Stir your hand through the bulgur several times to loosen and expose to air.

◆ Drain any excess liquid from tomatoes and cucumbers.

◆ In a large bowl, combine the bulgur, tomatoes, cucumbers, green onions and parsley.

◆ Add lemon juice, paprika, cayenne pepper and olive oil. Mix well.

◆ Add salt and pepper to taste.

◆ Allow tabbouleh to sit at room temperature for 30 minutes, then refrigerate.

Note: Tabbouleh is traditionally served spooned or scooped on to the Belgian Endive leaf and eaten with the hands.

Recipe by Becky Brehmer, Blue Moon Bar & Grille, Grand Junction, Colorado

SWEETWATER'S TARRAGON CHICKEN SALAD   *Yield: 4 servings*

1 pound cooked chicken, cut into chunks
1 good sized red onion, julienne
1 bunch of celery, diced large (about 4 cups)
½ cup almond slivers
1 green pepper, diced very small
2 cups cooked pasta (spirals, shells, etc.)
1 cup mayonnaise
¼ cup sour cream
2 tablespoons white vinegar
1 tablespoon tarragon, dried

◆ Mix all ingredients in no specific order.

◆ Salad should be refrigerated for 1 hour before serving.

Note: A crunchy, refreshing salad. A popular choice for a luncheon.

This recipe hails from Sweetwaters, Grand Junction, Colorado

FRENCH DRESSING   *Yield: About 2¾ cups*

1 cup oil
¾ cup ketchup
½ cup vinegar
½ cup sugar
1 teaspoon paprika
Grated onion to taste
Salt to taste

◆ Place all ingredients in jar and shake well.

◆ Refrigerate until ready to use.

ROMANO CHEESE DRESSING   *Yield: About 1 cup*

¼ cup egg substitute
1 clove garlic, minced
½ cup vegetable oil
½ cup Romano cheese, grated
⅓ teaspoon red pepper
½ teaspoon salt
5 teaspoons white vinegar

◆ Combine all ingredients in food processor and blend until smooth.

◆ Refrigerate until ready to use.

Wonderful on a mixed green salad.

BETTY'S DRESSING

Yield: 2½ cups

1   clove garlic
1   rib celery
½   medium onion
1   (2 ounce) can flat
     anchovies (optional)
2   tablespoons salad mustard
1   tablespoon lemon juice
1   teaspoon ground black
     pepper
¾   cup egg substitute
½   teaspoon sugar
2   cups salad oil

- Peel and slice garlic.
- Scrape and slice celery.
- Peel and slice onion.
- Combine garlic, celery and onion with anchovies, mustard, lemon juice, and pepper and process in food processor or blender until minced.
- Add eggs and blend to combine.
- Add salad oil in a stream with processor or blender on. Stop when combined.
- Refrigerate in a covered container until ready to use.

THOUSAND ISLAND DRESSING

Yield: 2 cups

1   cup mayonnaise
½   cup ketchup
½   cup green pepper, finely
     chopped
2-3 sweet pickles, finely
     chopped
1   tablespoon pimiento,
     chopped
2-3 tablespoons onion, finely
     chopped
½   teaspoon salt
½   teaspoon lemon juice

- Mix well and store in covered container in refrigerator until ready to use.

DOG TEAM DRESSING

Yield: 2½ cups

1⅓   cups sugar
⅓   cup dry mustard
¼   cup salt or to taste
1   tablespoon fresh basil,
     minced
1   tablespoon fresh marjoram,
     minced
4   cloves garlic, crushed
1½   cup light salad oil
1½   cup vinegar

- Mix all ingredients together.
- Chill before serving.

Hint: For best results mix garlic and salt together thoroughly before adding to mixture.

Makes a delicious light dressing that stores for weeks in the refrigerator.

Waves of Grain

LIGHT RYE BREAD WITH ANISE SEED AND BLACK PEPPER

Yield: Makes 4 long loaves or 2 larger round loaves

2 tablespoons dry yeast
2½ cups very warm water
2 tablespoons sugar
1 cup rye flour
5½ cups unbleached flour
1 tablespoon salt
4 tablespoons olive oil
3 tablespoons anise seed
2 tablespoons fresh black pepper, coarsely ground
Egg wash (1 egg white and ¼ cup water beaten together)
Non-stick spray shortening and cornmeal to prepare pans

◆ Dissolve yeast and sugar in very warm water in 8-cup container. Add 1 cup rye flour and allow to stand about one hour.

◆ Mix up to 5½ cups flour, salt and oil, stirring until smooth, elastic and doesn't stick to your hands (about 10 minutes). Can use food processor or dough hook on mixer.

◆ Sprinkle anise seed and pepper over dough and knead until seeds are spread throughout dough. Place in lightly oiled bowl, cover, and allow to rise until at least double. This takes perhaps 1 hour depending on yeast, temperature of room, etc.

◆ Form dough into 4 long loaves or two large round loaves and place on cookie sheets which have been sprayed with shortening and sprinkled with cornmeal. Allow to rise until at least double. Preheat oven to **400°**.

◆ Slash loaves decoratively, brush with egg wash and put in oven. Bake for 15 minutes. Brush again with egg wash. Reduce oven temperature to **350°** and bake 15 to 20 minutes longer or until loaves sound hollow when tapped on bottom. Cool on racks. Enjoy!

This is one of Caryl's hearty, homey breads from the Crystal Cafe

ALMOST BRIOCHE BREAD

Yield: 2 large braided loaves

1½ cups warm water
½ cup honey
2 packages dry yeast
   (2 tablespoons)
1 tablespoon salt
⅓ cup canola oil
2 eggs
4 egg yolks (reserve whites)
6 cups bread flour
   Sesame seeds or poppy
   seeds
   Non-stick spray shortening
   and cornmeal to prepare
   pans

◆ Combine first 4 ingredients in a bowl or food processor. Stir until yeast dissolves. Mix in oil, eggs and egg yolks.

◆ Gradually add enough flour (up to 6 cups) to form a soft dough. Knead on a lightly floured surface until smooth and elastic. Grease a large bowl. Place dough in bowl, turning dough ball over to coat with oil. Cover with a towel and let rise for about 1 hour.

◆ Spray a large cookie sheet with shortening and sprinkle with cornmeal. Punch down dough and divide in half. Cut each half into equal thirds (you will have 6 pieces of dough). Roll out each piece between hands on lightly floured surface to make a 9-inch rope. When you have 3 ropes, braid them together to make 1 loaf. Repeat rolling and braiding operation with remaining 3 pieces of dough to make another loaf. Be sure to pinch ends under on each loaf so that the braid won't unravel.

◆ Place loaves on cookie sheet and let rise 1 hour. Preheat oven to 400°.

◆ Brush each loaf with some of reserved egg whites and sprinkle with sesame seeds.

◆ Bake loaves at 400° for 15 minutes. Reduce oven temperature to 350°. Continue baking until loaves are golden brown, about 20 minutes.

Note: A food processor makes this recipe easy. Use a perforated pizza pan for even baking.

EDITH'S CRACKED WHEAT BREAD

Yield: 3 loaves

1½ cups dry milk
3½ cups water
1 stick margarine or butter
⅔ cup sugar (more if desired)
1 teaspoon salt
⅔ cup cracked wheat
⅓ cup bulghur wheat
8 cups flour, divided
1 package dry yeast
   (1 tablespoon)

◆ Warm first 5 ingredients in a pan on the stove long enough to melt butter. Place cracked wheat and bulghur wheat (see note below) in hot milk mixture and let stand 15 to 20 minutes.

◆ Pour above mixture into a large bowl or mixer. Stir in 4 cups of white flour, stir vigorously. Add yeast and beat well.

◆ Keep adding 2 cups of flour at a time until it is no longer sticky (total of 8 cups altogether).

◆ Turn dough onto counter and knead only until the dough holds a good shape.

◆ Let rise in greased bowl until well above rim.

◆ Shape into 3 loaves and place into bread pans, let rise for 20 more minutes.

◆ Bake at **350°** for 50 minutes. Butter tops of loaves when removed from pans.

This recipe makes up into good rolls.

Note: Buy cracked wheat and bulghur in health food store. Mix 2 bags (24 ounces) of cracked wheat with 1 bag (26 ounces) of bulghur.

FASCINATING FAST BREAD

Yield: 2 loaves or 30 rolls

RISER:

- 2 packages dry yeast (2 tablespoons)
- 1 cup warm water
- 2 tablespoons sugar
- ½ teaspoon salt
- ½ cup flour

REMAINDER OF RECIPE:

- 1¼ cups milk
- 2 tablespoons sugar
- 2 teaspoons salt
- 3 tablespoons shortening
- 5 cups flour, divided

◆ Combine ingredients for riser in a large mixing bowl. Cover and let stand in a warm place for 15 minutes or until bubbly.

◆ While riser is setting, scald the milk, and cool to lukewarm. Add the sugar, salt and shortening. When cool, add 2 cups of flour. Beat 2 minutes and add mixture to riser.

◆ Gradually stir in 3 cups flour. Form into a ball and put on well-floured surface, cover with a bowl and let rest for 10 minutes.

◆ Roll out dough to ½-inch thickness, fold in half, roll and fold 4 more times. Divide in half for 2 loaves or make 30 balls for rolls.

◆ Place loaves in well-greased bread pans or place rolls on well-greased cookie sheets. Cover and let rise in a warm place for 45 to 60 minutes or until doubled.

◆ Bake at **375°** for 35 minutes. Remove from pans immediately.

Hint: A microwave oven makes a great, draft-free place to put rising bread dough.

This is an old farm recipe.

GRANDMA B'S DINNER ROLLS

Yield: 16 rolls

1 ½ cups warm water
2 packages dry yeast
 (2 tablespoons)
2 eggs
1 stick margarine or butter,
 softened
1 teaspoon salt
4 tablespoons sugar
5 cups flour
2 tablespoons margarine or
 butter, melted

◆ In blender or food processor, mix all ingredients except the flour.

◆ Pour into a large bowl and add flour. Stir well.

◆ Let dough rise for about 30 minutes.

◆ Punch dough down and make into sixteen round balls. Place in lightly greased 9 x 13-inch baking pan (4 rows of 4 rolls each).

◆ Let rise in pan until doubled.

◆ Lightly spread melted butter or margarine on top of each roll. Bake at **375°** for 30 minutes.

Variation: These can be sprinkled with poppy seeds or sesame seeds after topping with the melted butter.

SWEET WALNUT CRESCENTS

Yield: 16 to 18 cookie-like rolls

½ pint cream-style cottage
 cheese
1 cup butter or margarine
2 cups flour
4 tablespoons butter or
 margarine, melted
¾ cup brown sugar
¾ cup walnuts, finely
 chopped

◆ In a large mixing bowl, blend cottage cheese and butter or margarine with a fork.

◆ Sift flour into butter mixture and blend until dough holds together.

◆ Roll out on floured board to ⅛-inch thickness.

◆ Spread dough with melted butter. Sprinkle with nuts and brown sugar.

◆ Cut into triangles, 3 inches wide at base. Roll each triangle from the wide end to point.

◆ Place on a lightly greased baking sheet and curve dough into a half-moon shape.

◆ Bake for 16 minutes or until golden brown at **400°**.

QUICK BUTTER DIPS

Yield: 18 bread sticks

¼ cup butter or margarine
1½ cups flour
2 teaspoons sugar
2 teaspoons baking powder
1 teaspoon salt
⅔ cup milk

◆ Heat oven to **450°**. Melt butter in 9 x 9-inch pan in oven. Remove as soon as butter melts.

◆ Stir dry ingredients together in bowl. Add milk. Stir 30 strokes with a fork until dough clings together. Turn out onto floured board.

◆ Knead lightly about 10 times. Roll out into an 8-inch square ½-inch thick. With floured knife, cut into strips 4 inches wide and then crosswise to make 18 pieces.

◆ Dip sticks in butter; place in 2 rows in pan.

◆ Bake for 15 to 20 minutes. Serve hot.

Variation: Sprinkle top with sesame seeds or poppy seeds before baking. Can also use wheat or oat flour or a combination.

This is a grandma's favorite recipe, the best kind!

ORANGE ROLLS

Yield: 20 rolls

2 cups milk
¼ cup butter
¼ cup sugar
2 teaspoons salt
2 packages dry yeast
(2 tablespoons)
¼ cup lukewarm water
5½-6½ cups flour, sifted
Melted butter or 1 egg
beaten with 1 teaspoon
water
Orange sauce

◆ Place milk in saucepan and bring to boil. Add butter, sugar and salt. Set aside to cool to luke-warm.

◆ Dissolve yeast in warm water. Add to cooled mixture. Add half of flour and mix well. Add enough remaining flour to make soft dough.

◆ Turn out onto floured board and let stand 10 minutes. Knead, working in flour until dough no longer sticks to board and is smooth and elastic, about 10 minutes.

◆ Place in greased bowl, cover and let rise in warm place until doubled.

◆ Turn dough out onto floured board and knead lightly until surface is smooth. Shape into rolls 1½ to 2 inches in diameter.

◆ Place close together in a 9 x 13-inch baking pan. Cover with towel and let rise until doubled.

◆ Brush with melted butter or egg-water mixture.

◆ Bake at **375°** for 20 to 25 min-utes, until browned. Turn out onto rack to cool.

◆ To serve, place generous table-spoon orange sauce on plate. Set warm roll on top. Drizzle with additional tablespoon orange sauce.

ORANGE SAUCE:
4 oranges
Water
1 cup sugar
4 teaspoons arrowroot

ORANGE SAUCE:
◆ Peel oranges with potato peeler. Remove any white pith from peel. Cut peel in fine strips.

Continued on next page

Orange Rolls (Continued)

◆ Place peel slices in saucepan and add water just to cover. Bring to boil, then drain under running water. Cover with water again and bring to boil. Drain and discard peel, reserving liquid.

◆ Blend sugar with arrowroot.

◆ Squeeze juice from oranges. Add orange juice and reserved liquid to sugar mixture.

◆ Bring to boil and cook and stir until thickened and clear, about 5 minutes.

◆ Makes 3 cups

DOUBLE-DECKER HIGH ALTITUDE CHEESE BISCUITS

Yield: 1 dozen

2 cups self-rising flour
½ teaspoon dry mustard
⅛ teaspoon cayenne pepper
2 tablespoons margarine or butter
¾ cup Swiss cheese, shredded
¾ cup buttermilk
1 large egg
1 egg yolk
1 tablespoon water
Parmesan cheese

◆ Mix flour, mustard, and cayenne. Cut in margarine with a pastry blender until mixture resembles fine crumbs.

◆ Stir in Swiss cheese, buttermilk, and egg until dough forms. Turn dough onto well-floured surface.

◆ With hands coated with flour, knead dough lightly 10 times. Roll dough ¼-inch thick. Cut with 2½-inch diameter cutter (a glass often works well). Make 24 rounds.

◆ Place 12 rounds on lightly greased baking sheet. Top each round with another and lightly press edges down to seal.

◆ Mix egg yolk and water. Brush over biscuits. Sprinkle with Parmesan cheese.

◆ Bake in preheated 475° oven about 10 minutes or until golden brown.

CINNAMON ROLLS

Yield: 36 rolls

1 cup milk
½ cup sugar
1 teaspoon salt
6 tablespoons shortening
2 packages yeast
  (2 tablespoons)
1 tablespoon sugar
1 cup lukewarm water
2 cups flour
3 eggs, beaten
4½-5 cups flour
6 tablespoons margarine or
  butter, melted
1½ cups white or brown sugar
1 tablespoon cinnamon
  Nuts and raisins to taste

◆ Scald the milk and add the next 3 ingredients.

◆ Put yeast and sugar in the lukewarm water. Add 2 cups flour to the milk mixture and beat well until smooth. Add yeast mixture and beaten eggs and continue to mix until smooth.

◆ Gradually add the 4½ to 5 cups flour (will probably have to knead the last cup or two on board).

◆ Knead lightly and put in a big (1½ to 2 gallon) greased bowl. Turn as you put in so top is greased.

◆ Let rise in warm place about 2 hours or double in size.

◆ Punch down and divide in quarters, work with a quarter at a time. Press flat and cover with a mixture of butter, sugar, cinnamon, nuts and raisins. Roll up like a jelly roll and slice off pieces and put in greased pans.

◆ Let rise about 1 hour, until double.

◆ Bake at **350°** for about 20 minutes. While still warm, drizzle with frosting.

CREAM CHEESE FROSTING:
⅛ cup milk
1 tablespoon margarine
½ tablespoon vanilla extract
  Confectioners' sugar
2 ounces cream cheese

CREAM CHEESE FROSTING:

◆ Cook milk and margarine over low heat until butter melts. Add vanilla and remove from stove.

◆ Add confectioners' sugar until you reach a smooth spreadable consistency.

◆ Beat in cream cheese and blend until smooth. Spread on cinnamon rolls.

CHIPS AND NUTS MUFFINS

Yield: 12 to 18 muffins

⅓ cup sugar
⅓ cup brown sugar, packed
2 cups flour
2 teaspoons baking powder
½ teaspoon salt
⅔ cup milk
½ cup butter, melted and cooled
2 eggs, lightly beaten
1½ teaspoons vanilla extract
6 ounces milk chocolate chips
6 ounces semi-sweet chocolate chips
½ cup walnuts, chopped

◆ In a large bowl, stir together sugars, flour, baking powder, and salt.

◆ In another bowl, combine milk, butter, eggs and vanilla until well-blended.

◆ Mix dry and wet ingredients together. Stir in chocolate chips and nuts.

◆ Spoon batter into greased muffin tins.

◆ Bake at **400°** for 15 to 20 minutes or until done. Remove from tins and cool for 5 minutes.

◆ May be served warm or cold.

These are good for brunch or for an evening snack.

SPICED APPLE MUFFINS

Yield: 1 dozen

2 cups flour
½ cup sugar
4 teaspoons baking powder
½ teaspoon salt
½ teaspoon cinnamon
1 egg
1 cup milk
¼ cup butter or margarine, melted
1 cup apples, chopped
TOPPING:
2 tablespoons sugar
½ teaspoon cinnamon

◆ Sift together flour, sugar, baking powder, and salt into large bowl. Add cinnamon.

◆ Beat egg and combine with milk and butter. Add to dry ingredients. Beat thoroughly.

◆ Fold in chopped apples and mix well.

◆ Drop by tablespoons into greased muffin tin. Sprinkle topping on dough.

◆ Bake in a preheated **425°** oven for 15 minutes.

Great for breakfast, brunch or after-school!

Variation: Substitute brown sugar for white sugar and add ¼ cup pecans for topping.

HIGH COUNTRY CARROT MUFFINS

Yield: 2 dozen muffins

1 ½ cups sugar
3 large eggs
1 cup vegetable oil
1 tablespoon vanilla extract
1 (7 ounce) can crushed pineapple, undrained
2 cups plus 2 tablespoons flour
1 ½ teaspoons cinnamon
2 teaspoons baking soda
1 teaspoon salt
2 cups carrots, grated
½ cup walnuts, chopped

◆ In a large bowl, combine sugar, eggs, oil and vanilla. Add pineapple and its juice.

◆ In another bowl, combine dry ingredients: flour, cinnamon, baking soda and salt.

◆ Stir flour mixture into egg mixture until just moistened (batter will be very moist). Add carrots and nuts.

◆ Grease 2 muffin tins liberally or use paper muffin cups.

◆ Fill cups about ¾ full of batter.

◆ Bake in a preheated 325° oven for 15 to 20 minutes or until wooden pick inserted in center comes out clean.

Variation: Substitute 1 cup applesauce for oil to make a low-fat snack.

REFRIGERATOR BUTTERMILK BRAN MUFFINS

Yield: 3 dozen muffins

1 cup bran nugget cereal
1 cup boiling water
2 cups buttermilk
½ cup margarine
¾ cup sugar
2 eggs
2½ cups flour
2½ teaspoons baking soda
1 teaspoon salt
2 cups bran flakes
   Cinnamon-sugar mixture

◆ Soak bran cereal in water and buttermilk for 10 minutes.

◆ Cream together margarine and sugar. Add eggs and mix well.

◆ Add the creamed mixture to the buttermilk mixture and then add dry ingredients.

◆ Fold in 2 cups bran flakes.

◆ Generously grease 2 muffin tins or use paper muffin cups. Fill cups ¾ full and sprinkle tops with cinnamon-sugar mixture.

◆ Bake at 400° for 15 to 20 minutes.

Variation: For a low-fat recipe, substitute ½ cup applesauce for the margarine.

Hint: The batter will keep for 4 weeks in the refrigerator; so you can make fresh muffins every morning.

BLACK-BOTTOM BANANA BREAD

Yield: 1 loaf

4 small, very ripe bananas
1 stick unsalted butter or margarine, softened
⅔ cup sugar
3 large eggs
¼ cup milk
1 cup cake flour
1½ teaspoons baking powder
1 teaspoon baking soda
¼ teaspoon salt (generous)
1¼ cups semi-sweet chocolate chips

◆ Preheat oven to 350°. Generously grease 9 x 5-inch loaf pan; dust lightly with flour. Set aside.

◆ Coarsely chop bananas in food processor or mash until lumpy with a fork (about 1⅓ cups). Set aside in large mixing bowl.

◆ Beat butter and sugar in food processor or electric mixer. Add eggs and mix until fluffy and smooth. Add milk and combine.

◆ Transfer batter to mixing bowl with bananas.

◆ Sift dry ingredients. Add to bowl along with chocolate chips. Use wooden spoon or rubber spatula to combine gently.

◆ Transfer to loaf pan. Bake until loaf is dark brown and toothpick inserted in center comes out clean, 55 to 60 minutes. Let rest on wire rack 10 minutes.

◆ Gently remove loaf from pan; cool completely on wire rack. Can be served then or wrapped in foil overnight.

Hint: Chocolate goes to bottom. Freezes well.

ST. JOHN'S BANANA BANANA BREAD

Yield: 1 rich loaf

1 ⅓ cups sugar
¾ cup butter or margarine
2 eggs, lightly beaten
1 teaspoon baking soda
6 tablespoons sour cream
3 very ripe bananas (about 2½ cups, mashed)
1 ½ cups flour
¼ teaspoon salt
1 teaspoon vanilla extract
1 teaspoon cinnamon
½ teaspoon nutmeg
1 ½ cups walnuts, chopped

TOPPING:
1 tablespoon butter or margarine, melted
Cinnamon-sugar mixture to taste

◆ Cream butter and sugar, and add lightly beaten eggs.

◆ In a separate bowl, sprinkle the soda over the sour cream to dissolve. Add to the butter mixture.

◆ Beat well and add banana pulp, flour, vanilla, spices and salt. Beat well.

◆ Add the walnut pieces, mixing again.

◆ Bake in a well greased bread pan at **350°** for 60 minutes. Bread is done when golden on top and when toothpick inserted in the center is clean when removed.

◆ While bread is still warm, pour melted butter over top and sprinkle with cinnamon-sugar.

ORANGE CRANBERRY BREAD

Yield: 1 loaf

2 cups flour
½ teaspoon salt
½ teaspoon baking soda
1 cup sugar
1 egg, beaten
2 tablespoons butter, melted
¾ cup orange juice
1 cup cranberries, cut in half
¾ cup chopped nuts

◆ Sift together flour, salt, baking soda and sugar.

◆ Add the beaten egg, melted butter and orange juice, mix well. Stir in cranberries and nuts last.

◆ Bake at **325°** in a greased loaf pan for 1 hour and 10 minutes.

Variation: This recipe lends itself well to mini-loaf pans. Decrease cooking time if using several smaller pans.

This bread has a wonderful texture and a sweet/tart taste.

CLASSIC POPPY SEED BREAD

Yield: 2 loaves

3 eggs
1⅛ cups vegetable oil
2¼ cups sugar
1½ teaspoons vanilla extract
1 teaspoon almond extract
1½ cups milk
3 cups flour, sifted
1½ teaspoons salt
1½ teaspoons baking powder
2 tablespoons poppy seeds

GLAZE:
¼ cup orange juice
¾ cup sugar
½ teaspoon vanilla extract
½ teaspoon almond extract

◆ Mix eggs, oil, sugar, extracts and milk in a large bowl.

◆ Combine remaining dry ingredients in another bowl. Add this mixture alternately with egg mixture.

◆ Grease two loaf pans. Pour in batter. Bake at 350° for 60 minutes.

◆ When loaves are completely cool, mix glaze ingredients together in a bowl and spoon over loaves.

Hint: This recipe can be halved as well as doubled. To ensure freshness, wrap cooled loaves first in plastic wrap and then with aluminum foil.

HOBO BREAD

Yield: 2 loaves

2 cups raisins
2 cups boiling water
4 teaspoons baking soda
2 tablespoons oil
4 cups flour
1 cup chopped nuts
½ cup sugar (optional)
½ teaspoon salt (optional)

◆ The evening before or in the morning, combine the raisins, boiling water and baking soda. Mix well and let stand at least 12 hours.

◆ Add the oil, flour and chopped nuts. If desired, add sugar and salt at this time.

◆ Mix well and put in 2 greased and floured bread pans.

◆ Bake at 350° for 1 hour and 15 minutes or until done (tested with a toothpick and comes out dry).

Note: These loaves freeze well.

PALISADE PEACH BREAD

Yield: 2 loaves

3	cups fresh peaches, peeled and sliced
6	tablespoons sugar, divided
2½	cups flour
1	teaspoon baking powder
1	teaspoon baking soda
¼	teaspoon salt
1	teaspoon ground cinnamon
1-1½	cups sugar
½	cup margarine or butter
2	eggs
1	cup pecans, finely chopped
1	teaspoon vanilla extract

◆ Purée the peaches and 6 tablespoons sugar in a blender. Combine the flour, baking powder, baking soda, salt and cinnamon and set aside.

◆ Combine the remaining sugar and butter or margarine with an electric mixer until creamy. Add eggs and mix again.

◆ Add peach purée and dry ingredients, mixing until all ingredients are well-combined. Stir in the pecans and vanilla extract.

◆ Pour batter into 2 greased and floured 9 x 5 x 3-inch bread pans.

◆ Bake in a preheated **325°** oven for 55 to 60 minutes.

Note: Don't hesitate to use very ripe peaches for this recipe. This bread freezes well for those winter mornings when you need a reminder of summer's peach harvest.

CORNBELT SPECIAL

Yield: 12 servings

1	(16 ounce) can creamed corn
1	(16 ounce) can whole kernel corn, drained
½	cup margarine or butter, melted
1	cup sour cream
2	eggs
1	(8½ ounce) package corn bread mix
2	tablespoons green chiles
½	cup onion, chopped
1½	cups Cheddar cheese, grated

◆ Mix all ingredients together, stirring as each is added. Pour into a greased 9 x 13-inch pan.

◆ Bake at **350°** for 45 to 50 minutes.

Note: Serve garnished with parsley or red pepper for color. A fast and easy side or main dish.

BUMPER CROP ZUCCHINI BREAD

Yield: 2 loaves

3   eggs
2   cups sugar
¾   cup vegetable oil
2   cups shredded zucchini
2   teaspoons vanilla extract
3   cups flour
1   teaspoon baking soda
3   teaspoons cinnamon
1   cup walnuts or pecans, chopped

◆ Beat eggs and sugar until smooth.

◆ Mix in oil, zucchini and vanilla extract.

◆ Stir in flour, baking soda and cinnamon. Fold in nuts.

◆ Spray 2 loaf pans with non-stick vegetable shortening spray. Divide batter between the 2 pans and knife through.

◆ Bake at **375°** for 1 hour.

Variation: Add 4 tablespoons cocoa and 1 cup mini chocolate morsels for "Chocolate Zucchini Bread".

No cook in the fertile Grand Valley can be without this recipe to use up all that summer garden zucchini.

IRISH SODA BREAD

Yield: 1 round loaf

2½   cups flour
½   cup sugar
1½   teaspoons baking powder
¾   teaspoon salt
½   teaspoon baking soda
½   cup (1 stick) unsalted butter
1   cup raisins
1   tablespoon caraway seeds
1   large egg
1¼   cups buttermilk
¼   cup sour cream

◆ Preheat oven to **350°**. Grease a 9-inch round cake pan.

◆ Sift together dry ingredients.

◆ Using a food processor with a steel blade or a pastry cutter, cut the butter into the flour mixture until it resembles small peas. Blend in raisins and caraway seeds.

◆ Beat the egg, buttermilk, and sour cream together until blended.

◆ Stir the egg mixture into the dry mixture just until blended.

◆ Transfer the batter to the pan and bake for about 50 to 55 minutes, until a toothpick inserted in the center comes out clean.

A rich version of a St. Patrick's Day treat!

94

DILLY CASSEROLE BREAD

Yield: 10 to 12 servings

1 package dry yeast (1 tablespoon)
¼ cup lukewarm water
1 cup cream style cottage cheese
1 tablespoon butter
2 tablespoons sugar
1 teaspoon salt
¼ teaspoon baking soda
1 teaspoon instant minced onion
2 teaspoons dill seed
1 egg
2¼-2½ cups flour

◆ Dissolve yeast in ¼ cup water.

◆ Heat cottage cheese in pan over low heat.

◆ In large bowl, combine all ingredients except flour. Gradually add flour to liquid mixture, stirring well.

◆ Cover with a cloth and let rise 1 hour.

◆ Stir down and pour into a greased 2-quart casserole dish.

◆ Bake at 350° for 35 to 45 minutes. Brush top with butter, cool 5 minutes before removing from dish.

Serve with beef stew or soup.

This recipe comes from the **Simply Colorado** *cookbook*

TOFFEE COFFEE CAKE

Yield: 10 servings

2 cups flour
1 stick margarine or butter
1 cup brown sugar
½ cup sugar
1 cup buttermilk
1 teaspoon baking soda
1 egg
1 teaspoon vanilla extract
6 ounces Enstrom's Toffee crumbs or any fine quality toffee candy (crumbled)

◆ Mix first 4 ingredients and reserve ½ cup of this mixture for topping.

◆ Combine buttermilk, baking soda, egg and vanilla extract. Add to flour and sugar mixture.

◆ Pour batter into a greased 9 x 9-inch baking pan.

◆ Combine reserved mixture with the Enstrom's crumbs and sprinkle on top of cake batter in pan. Lightly swirl the topping into the batter if you wish.

◆ Bake at 375° for 35 to 40 minutes or until done.

COLORADO COFFEE CAKE

Yield: 2 10-inch round cakes

4½   cups flour
1½   cups sugar
1½   cups butter or solid
      vegetable shortening
2   eggs, beaten
1½   cups sour cream
½   teaspoon salt
1   teaspoon baking powder
1   teaspoon baking soda
2   teaspoons almond extract

FILLING:
1   pound cream cheese,
      softened
¼   teaspoon vanilla
2   eggs, beaten
½   cup sugar

TOPPING:
1   cup raspberry preserves
1⅓   cups almonds, chopped

◆ Preheat oven to **350°**. Grease two 9- or 10-inch spring form or deep round foil pans.

◆ Combine flour and 1½ cups sugar. Cut in butter or shortening. Reserve 2 cups of this crumb mixture.

◆ To remaining crumb mixture, add 2 eggs, sour cream, salt, baking powder, baking soda and almond extract. Mix well.

◆ Spread mixture over bottom and up sides of pans.

◆ Filling: Combine cream cheese, vanilla, 2 beaten eggs and sugar. Spread half of this mixture over the batter in each pan.

◆ Topping: On top of the cream cheese mixture on each cake spread ½ cup of the raspberry preserves.

◆ Whirl almonds in processor until chunky. Combine with reserved crumb mixture and sprinkle over preserves on each cake.

◆ Bake cakes for 45 to 55 minutes until a toothpick inserted in center of cake comes out clean. Cool the cake at least ½ hour before serving.

Hint: This recipe is better to make ahead and refrigerate.

The following 3 recipes are for bread machines:

GRAPE NUT BREAD

Yield: One 1½-pound loaf

1⅓ cups water
2⅔ tablespoons vegetable oil
1¼ tablespoons sugar
2 teaspoons salt
⅔ cup natural wheat and barley cereal
1⅓ cups bread flour
1⅓ cups whole wheat flour
2¼ teaspoons yeast

◆ Put all ingredients as listed in order into the bowl of the bread machine.
◆ Add yeast as specified by your particular bread machine.
◆ Push button.

NORTH AFRICAN CORIANDER BREAD

Yield: One 1½-pound loaf

1⅛ cups milk
3 tablespoons margarine
3 tablespoons honey
1½ teaspoons salt
¾ tablespoon ground coriander
⅛ teaspoon ground ginger
¼ teaspoon cinnamon
⅛ teaspoon ground cloves
½ teaspoon orange rind
3 cups bread flour
2½ teaspoons yeast

◆ Place milk, margarine and honey in bread machine container. Then add all the dry ingredients.
◆ Add yeast as specified by your particular bread machine.
◆ Push button.

Hint: For best results, bring milk and margarine to room temperature.

PECAN AND RED ONION BREAD

Yield: One 1½-pound loaf

1 package dry yeast (1 tablespoon)
3 cups bread flour
2 teaspoons sugar
1½ teaspoons salt
1 cup plus 1 tablespoon warm milk
¼ cup butter or margarine
½ cup fresh red onion, chopped
¾ cup pecans, chopped

◆ Place all ingredients in order in the bowl of your bread machine. (Add yeast as specified by your particular bread machine).
◆ Push button.

The following 3 recipes are quick and easy topping recipes for commercially-prepared French baguettes:

FRESH TOMATO AND GREEN ONION GARLIC BREAD

Yield: 12 pieces

¼   cup olive oil
¼   cup canola oil
5   cloves garlic, diced
3-4 green onions, finely chopped
12   cherry tomatoes, quartered
     Salt and pepper to taste
     Parmesan cheese, freshly grated

◆ Slice baguette horizontally and slice each piece (not all the way through) into 6 pieces.

◆ Mix oils, garlic, green onions, salt and pepper together and brush onto bread.

◆ Arrange quartered tomatoes on top and sprinkle with Parmesan cheese. Broil and serve.

NEW MEXICAN CHILE BREAD

Yield: 10 to 12 servings

3   cloves garlic, minced
½   cup fresh cilantro, cut up
1   green onion, chopped
2-3 teaspoons chili powder
½   cup butter, melted
2-3 tablespoons olive oil
½   cup Parmesan cheese, grated
     Salt to taste

◆ Combine all ingredients, except the Parmesan. Spread on horizontally sliced baguette. Bake on cookie sheet at **350°** for 30 minutes. Sprinkle with Parmesan cheese.

Note: Serve with chili or soup.

GARLIC CHEESE LOAF

Yield: 12 slices

½   cup butter or margarine, softened
1   cup mozzarella or Swiss cheese, shredded
1   tablespoon parsley, chopped
1   garlic clove, minced

◆ Cut baguette horizontally and cut each side into 12 1-inch wide slices. Combine topping ingredients in small bowl. Spread 1 tablespoon cheese mixture on 12 of the cut slices. Place remaining 12 slices on top. Reassemble loaf and wrap securely in heavy foil.

◆ Bake at **375°** for 15 to 20 minutes or place on barbecue over medium coals for about 10 to 12 minutes or until cheese is melted. Turn often.

Eggstrordinary

• WHERE WILD HORSES RUN FREE... MT. GARFIELD •

ASPARAGUS GRUYÈRE QUICHE

Yield: 4 servings

1   9–inch unbaked pie shell
1½ cups asparagus, sliced
½   cup fresh cilantro, sliced
    and loosely packed
1   leek, thinly sliced
½   cup mushrooms, sliced
¾   Swiss Gruyère cheese,
cup grated
4   eggs, beaten
½   cup half and half cream
1   teaspoon salt

◆ Place unbaked pie shell into 9–inch glass pie plate or quiche dish.

◆ Slice vegetables and arrange in pie shell. Sprinkle grated cheese on top of vegetables.

◆ Beat eggs, cream, and salt. Pour over vegetables and cheese. Bake at 375° for 45 minutes, or until knife inserted in center comes out clean. Let stand 10 minutes before serving.

FIESTA BRUNCH

Yield: 12 to 15 servings

2   (7 ounce) cans chopped
    green chiles
6   corn tortillas, cut in strips
1   pound hot bulk sausage,
    cooked and drained
1   pound Monterey Jack
    cheese, grated
8   eggs, beaten
½   cup milk
½   teaspoon salt
½   teaspoon pepper
½   teaspoon ground cumin
½   teaspoon garlic salt
½   teaspoon onion salt
½   teaspoon paprika
2   large tomatoes, sliced

◆ Spread half of the chiles on the bottom of a greased 9 x 13 x 2–inch glass dish. Top with half of tortilla strips, half of sausage, and half of cheese. Repeat layers.

◆ Beat eggs, milk, and all spices except paprika. Pour over the layers of chiles, tortillas, sausage, and cheese. Lay sliced tomatoes over the top and sprinkle with paprika.

◆ Cover with plastic wrap and refrigerate overnight.

◆ Bake uncovered at 350° for 50–60 minutes. Let stand 10 minutes before serving.

Serve with sour cream and salsa on the side. This may be frozen after it has been baked and then reheated.

Pat Brinegar's National Award Winner in Land O' Lakes and Country Living Contest, Cheese Category, 1994.

FRENCH TOAST SANTA FE

Yield: 4 to 6 servings

6 slices of slightly stale, ¾–inch thick bread
4 eggs
1 cup cream
⅛ teaspoon salt
Dash nutmeg
½ cup cooking oil, as needed
Confectioners' sugar
Maple syrup

◆ Trim crusts from bread and cut diagonally into 2 pieces.

◆ In a bowl, beat eggs until light and frothy. Add cream, salt and nutmeg. Soak bread, a few pieces at a time, until they absorb egg mixture thoroughly.

◆ In skillet, heat 2 tablespoons cooking oil. Fry bread on both sides to a golden color. Add cooking oil as needed to fry all the bread. Remove bread from skillet and drain on paper towels to absorb excess oil.

◆ Place all pieces on baking sheet. Place in **400°** oven and allow toast to puff up, 3 to 5 minutes. Remove from oven and sprinkle with confectioner's sugar. Serve with syrup.

GOLD RUSH CASSEROLE

Yield: 12 to 15 servings

1 pound Monterey Jack cheese, grated
1 cup milk
1 cup flour
2 cups cottage cheese
6 eggs, lightly beaten
½ cup butter or margarine, melted and divided

◆ Combine grated cheese, milk, flour, cottage cheese in a large bowl. Add beaten eggs, and ¼ cup of melted butter.

◆ Brush remaining ¼ cup of butter over the bottom and sides of 12 x 7–inch baking dish.

◆ Pour cheese mixture into dish and bake at **375°** for 40 minutes, or until golden and set.

SCRAMBLED EGGS CONFETTI

Yield: 4 servings

4   ounces cream cheese
½   stick butter (4 tablespoons)
½   cup green bell pepper, chopped
½   cup red bell pepper, chopped
½   cup green onion, chopped
1   cup drained cooked corn
6   eggs, lightly beaten
    Salt and freshly ground pepper
    Pinch of ground red pepper
    Chopped green onion and crumbled cooked bacon for garnish

◆ Place cream cheese in top of double boiler and set over simmering water. Cook over low heat until cheese melts. Remove from heat and set aside.

◆ Melt 2 tablespoons butter in large skillet over medium–high heat. Add bell peppers and green onion and sauté until onion is translucent, about 3 to 5 minutes. Blend into cream cheese. Stir in corn, mixing thoroughly.

◆ Melt remaining 2 tablespoons butter in same skillet over medium–low heat. Blend eggs into cream cheese vegetable mixture. Season to taste with salt, pepper, and red pepper. Cook, stirring occasionally, until eggs are barely set.

◆ Transfer to heated platter. Sprinkle with green onion and bacon. Serve immediately.

VEGETABLE QUICHE

Yield: 4 to 6 servings

1   deep dish pie shell
2   medium zucchini, thinly sliced
4   green onions, sliced
8   ounces mushrooms, sliced
1   broccoli crown, cut in bite–sized pieces, (about ¼ cup)
¼   red or yellow bell pepper, chopped
2   tablespoons butter
3   eggs
½   pint whipping cream
¼   pound Cheddar cheese, grated
¼   pound Swiss cheese, grated

◆ Sauté zucchini, green onions, mushrooms, broccoli, and pepper in butter until tender, but still crisp. Cool fully.

◆ Place vegetables in pie crust. Mix the two cheeses together and sprinkle over the vegetables. Whisk eggs and whipping cream just enough to blend and gently pour mixture over the vegetables and cheese.

◆ Place pan on a baking sheet and bake at 350° for 45 minutes until quiche is set and golden. Check often after 40 minutes. Let stand 10 minutes before serving.

WESTERN–STYLE GRITS

Yield: 8 servings

3 cups water
1 teaspoon salt
¾ cup grits
4 tablespoons margarine or butter
½ pound sharp Cheddar cheese, grated (reserve ½ cup)
2 eggs, beaten
1 (4 ounce) can diced green chiles

◆ Combine the water, salt, and grits in saucepan. Cook over medium–high heat until thick, stirring constantly. Add the margarine, cheese, eggs, and green chiles. Mix well.

◆ Pour into greased 3 quart casserole. Cover and bake at **350°** for 45 minutes.

◆ Sprinkle the remaining ½ cup cheese on top and bake, covered, an additional 15 minutes.

BRUNCH EGGS WITH SPANISH SAUCE

Yield: 9 to 12 servings

1 loaf textured white bread, both sides buttered, cubed
1 pound Cheddar cheese, grated
3 cups milk
¾ teaspoon white pepper
¾ teaspoon dry mustard
6 eggs, beaten

◆ In 13 x 9 x 2–inch casserole dish layer half the buttered, cubed bread. Cover with half the cheese. Repeat the layers. Mix the milk, eggs, pepper, and mustard and gently pour over the bread and cheese.

◆ Cover and refrigerate overnight.

◆ Bake, uncovered, at **350°** for 45 minutes, or until center is set. Serve with freshly made Spanish Sauce.

SPANISH SAUCE:
⅓ cup onion, chopped
¼ cup green pepper, chopped
¾ cup mushrooms, thinly sliced
3 tablespoons olive oil
1 tablespoon cornstarch
1 (16–ounce) can whole tomatoes with liquid
1 teaspoon salt
Dash pepper
2 tablespoons sugar
Dash cayenne pepper

SPANISH SAUCE:
◆ Sauté onion, green pepper, and mushrooms in olive oil. Combine cornstarch with 2 tablespoons liquid from the canned tomatoes, and combine with sautéed vegetables. Add tomatoes, with liquid, salt, pepper, sugar, and cayenne.

◆ Cook over low heat, stirring often, until sauce is thickened. Serve over eggs.

SCRAMBLED EGGS WITH ASPARAGUS

Yield: 6 servings

6–8 ounces fresh asparagus
8 eggs
¾ teaspoon salt
½ teaspoon pepper
6 tablespoons unsalted butter

◆ Wash, trim, and cut asparagus into ½-inch pieces. In a pot of lightly salted water, cook asparagus until just tender, about 4 minutes. Drain and transfer to ice water to cool. Drain and pat dry.

◆ In medium bowl, whisk eggs, salt, and pepper. In large skillet melt butter over medium heat, add eggs and asparagus and cook, stirring often until eggs are done. Serve immediately.

Variation: Use any fresh vegetable such as broccoli, or substitute marinated artichoke hearts, or crab, shrimp, or chicken livers and mushrooms. Be creative with combinations.

OMELET OLÉ

Yield: 4 omelets

4 teaspoons margarine, divided
8 egg whites, whisked until frothy
1 cup Monterey Jack cheese, diced in small cubes
2 cups fresh spinach, cleaned and chopped
1 cup green chiles, roasted, peeled, seeded, and diced

◆ Heat a small non–stick omelet pan over medium–high heat until it is hot. Melt 1 teaspoon of margarine in the pan. Add ¼ of the egg whites. Cook the omelet 4 minutes. To cook evenly, pull the omelet from the sides of the pan with a spatula.

◆ Place ¼ of the cheese, spinach, and chiles on top. Reduce the heat to low and cover pan. Cook the omelet 2 minutes more, or until the ingredients are hot. Fold the omelet over in half and serve.

◆ Repeat for each omelet.

SWEET PEPPER AND BASIL FRITTATA
Yield: 6 to 8 servings

6   tablespoons balsamic
    vinegar
2   tablespoons olive oil (or
    more)
2   cups yellow or red onion,
    sliced
½   teaspoon salt
4   cups sweet bell peppers,
    sliced (combination of red,
    yellow, and green)
4   cloves garlic, minced
1   bay leaf
8   eggs
½   cup Jarlsberg cheese,
    grated
⅔   cup Parmesan cheese,
    grated
½   cup fresh basil leaves,
    thinly sliced

◆ In small saucepan, reduce balsamic vinegar by half over medium heat. Set aside to cool.

◆ Heat 1 tablespoon olive oil in large skillet, sauté onion over medium heat until limp.

◆ Add salt, peppers, garlic, and bay leaf. Cover and cook slowly over low heat, about 15 minutes, until peppers are soft and juicy. Set aside to cool. Remove bay leaf.

◆ Beat eggs and add onion and pepper mixture, the cheeses, and basil.

◆ In a 9–inch sauté pan, heat 1 tablespoon or more oil to almost the smoking point. Turn the pan to coat it with oil, turn the heat to low, then immediately pour in the frittata mixture (eggs will sizzle). Cook 1 to 2 minutes until the sides begin to set.

◆ Transfer the pan and ingredients to **325°** oven and bake uncovered 20–25 minutes until golden and firm. Loosen frittata with rubber spatula. Place plate over pan, flip it over, and turn out the frittata.

◆ Brush the bottom and sides of the cooked frittata with the reduced balsamic vinegar. Cut in wedges. Serve warm or at room temperature.

GARDEN BENEDICT

Yield: 4 servings of 2 muffins each

8   poached eggs
4   English muffins, split
1   tomato, sliced
1   avocado, peeled and sliced
    Alfalfa sprouts
    Paprika

HOLLANDAISE SAUCE:
4   egg yolks
2   tablespoons lemon juice
¼   teaspoon salt
    Dash cayenne pepper
1   stick melted butter

◆ Poach eggs. Toast English muffins and place on individual plates, two per serving.

◆ On each muffin, layer sliced tomato, then poached egg, topped with sliced avocado.

◆ HOLLANDAISE SAUCE: Whisk together egg yolks, lemon juice, salt, cayenne pepper. Place mixture in double boiler.

◆ Over hot water, slowly add the melted butter to the egg mixture while whisking constantly until sauce is thickened.

◆ Pour hollandaise over muffin, vegetables, and egg. Sprinkle with paprika and garnish with alfalfa sprouts according to taste.

PEACH PRESERVE FRENCH TOAST

Yield: 4 to 6 servings

1   small loaf French bread
4   ounces cream cheese
3   tablespoons peach preserves (do not substitute jam or jelly)
4   eggs
1   cup half and half
    Dash vanilla
⅓   cup cooking oil
    Confectioners' sugar
    Maple syrup

◆ Slice French bread in ¾-inch pieces. Cream together cream cheese and peach preserves.

◆ Spread 1 tablespoon cream cheese mixture between two slices of French bread. Repeat, making six "sandwiches" of cream cheese mixture.

◆ Whisk eggs with half and half, add a dash of vanilla. Soak each side of sandwich in egg mixture, allowing it to absorb .

◆ Heat 2 tablespoons oil in skillet. Fry each sandwich until golden on both sides. Remove and drain on paper towel. Add more cooking oil as needed.

◆ Sprinkle with confectioners' sugar. Serve with maple syrup.

SALMON STRATA

Yield: 8 servings

1   (15 ounce) can salmon
14 slices cocktail rye bread (or sourdough)
2   cups Swiss cheese, shredded
1   (10 ounce) package frozen chopped broccoli, thawed, drained, and uncooked
    Milk
6   eggs, beaten
1   teaspoon lemon juice
¾   teaspoon salt (or to taste)
¼   teaspoon dry mustard
    Pepper to taste

◆ Drain and flake salmon, reserving liquid in a measuring cup.

◆ Cut bread slices into triangles (halves). Grease a shallow 2 quart baking dish and cover bottom with half of the bread slices.

◆ Top with ⅓ of the cheese, all of the salmon, and all the broccoli. Arrange ½ of the remaining cheese on top. Arrange remaining bread triangles over top.

◆ Add enough milk to reserved salmon liquid to make 1½ cups. Beat together salmon liquid with eggs, lemon juice, salt, mustard, and pepper. Pour egg mixture over salmon, broccoli mixture.

◆ Refrigerate, covered, 1 hour or overnight. Uncover and place directly in preheated 325° oven. Bake 1 hour. Sprinkle remaining cheese on top and heat until cheese is melted.

ASPARAGUS AND BROCCOLI QUICHE

Yield: 6 servings

1 9 inch pastry shell
1 cup asparagus, cut in 1 inch pieces
1 cup broccoli flowerets, cut in bite–size pieces
8 slices bacon, cooked crisp
1 cup Swiss cheese, shredded
1 cup whipping cream
3 eggs, slightly beaten
1 teaspoon tarragon, dried or 1 tablespoon fresh
¼ teaspoon nutmeg
Dash pepper

◆ Prick pastry shell with fork. Bake in preheated **450°** oven for 7 minutes. Cool.

◆ Steam asparagus and broccoli until just crisp tender.

◆ Crumble bacon in pastry shell. Add asparagus, broccoli, then sprinkle cheese over vegetables.

◆ In bowl, mix the beaten eggs, whipping cream, tarragon, nutmeg, and pepper. Pour gently over vegetable and cheese mixture in pastry shell. Bake in preheated **350°** oven for 40 minutes, or until center is set and quiche is puffy and golden. Let it sit for 10 minutes before serving.

From Streams and Beyond

· FLY FISHING IN COLORADO'S GOLD MEDAL STREAMS ·

← ◆ →

GRILLED SALMON WITH DILL SAUCE

Yield: 6 to 12 servings

1   4 to 4½ pound whole salmon, leaving skins and bones intact
2   lemons, thinly sliced
1   teaspoon tarragon
1   teaspoon parsley, chopped
¼   teaspoon onion salt
    Guiltless Cucumber Dill Sauce (see below)
    Aluminum foil

◆ Prepare grill.

◆ Spray aluminum foil with non–stick vegetable spray.

◆ Wash and dry salmon. Sprinkle herbs and salt and place lemon slices on inside of salmon and place lemon on outside of each side of salmon. Fold foil over, sealing tightly at edges.

◆ Place salmon in foil on grill, keeping heat on medium. Grill for about 20 minutes per side. Check for flakiness after 40 minutes.

◆ Serve with Cucumber Dill Sauce.

CUCUMBER DILL SAUCE:

1   cup cucumber, peeled, seeded, and chopped
½   cup non fat plain yogurt
¼   cup non fat mayonnaise
1   tablespoon lemon juice
1   tablespoon dill weed (or to taste)
½   teaspoon salt
¼   teaspoon pepper

Yield: 1¼ cups

CUCUMBER DILL SAUCE:

◆ Combine all ingredients in a small bowl.

◆ Refrigerate until serving time.

Can be used with halibut.

BETTER BEER–BATTER FOR FISH FILLETS

Yield: ½ to ¾ pound per serving

1 cup all–purpose flour
1 teaspoon baking powder
¼ teaspoon white pepper (or to taste)
¼ teaspoon black pepper (or to taste)
¼ teaspoon cayenne pepper (or to taste)
½ teaspoon salt
1 egg
2 tablespoons vegetable oil
1 cup beer
Fish fillets, up to 3 pounds

◆ In a bowl, combine flour, baking powder, white, black, and cayenne peppers and salt. Stir with a fork to combine.

◆ In a separate bowl, stir together the egg and the oil. Add the beer and stir briefly.

◆ Add the beer mixture to the flour mixture until well-blended. Batter should be runny.

◆ Add fish fillets to batter and stir so they are completely covered. Heat 1 to 2 inches of oil in a skillet (cast iron preferred) to a temperature of 375°.

◆ Lift fillets from batter. Allow excess batter to drip off, then transfer immediately to hot oil. Do not overcrowd pan. Cook until browned on both sides. Remove to paper towels to drain, season with extra salt if desired and serve at once.

Batter can be used for onions or vegetables of your choice, but it is recommended that the oil be changed if preparing both vegetables and fish so as not to have fishy tasting vegetables.

SASSY SEAFOOD SALAD

Yield: Makes about 2¼ cups sauce and 4 to 6 salad servings

½ cup celery, finely chopped
4 ounces bay shrimp, cooked
6 ounces langostinos (small lobster), cooked
½ pound halibut steak, poached, boned and flaked
1 tablespoon chives, chopped
Sassy Sauce (see below)
Lemon juice
Curly endive
2 tomatoes, peeled and sliced
3 hard-boiled eggs, sliced
Lemon wedges
Pitted black olives, halved
Canned white asparagus
Belgian endive

◆ Combine celery, shrimp, langostinos, halibut and chives in large bowl.
◆ Add enough Sassy Sauce to moisten, season to taste with lemon juice and gently toss.
◆ Let stand in refrigerator 1 hour.
◆ Mound seafood mixture on large platter lined with curly endive. Surround edges with alternate slices of tomatoes and inverted lemon wedges. Top each tomato slice with slice of hard-boiled egg and half an olive.
◆ Garnish with asparagus and Belgian endive. If desired, garnish top of seafood mound with Belgian endive centered with tomato rose made from end slices of tomatoes.
◆ Serve with remaining sauce.

SASSY SAUCE:
1½ cups mayonnaise
4½ tablespoons ketchup
4½ tablespoons chili sauce
1½ teaspoons horseradish
4 anchovy fillets, minced
1½ teaspoons lemon juice
Salt, pepper
Worcestershire sauce

SASSY SAUCE:
◆ Combine mayonnaise, ketchup, chili sauce, horseradish, anchovies and lemon juice and season to taste with salt, pepper, and Worcestershire. Blend well.

This recipe can easily be multiplied to serve larger groups.

TELLURIDE SHRIMP JAMBALAYA

Yield: 3 to 4 servings

2   tablespoons olive oil
1   pint oysters (or 2 cups crab or chicken)
2   onions, chopped
1   garlic clove, pressed
1   small green pepper, minced
1   pound raw shrimp, shelled, deveined
1   cup rice (long grain), uncooked
2   cups tomatoes, chopped
2   cups chicken bouillon
1   bay leaf
1   teaspoon salt
⅛   teaspoon pepper
1   teaspoon sugar
    Minced parsley

◆ Heat oil in large skillet. Add oysters and cook over low heat until edges start to curl. Remove from pan; refrigerate.

◆ Cook onions, garlic, green pepper in skillet 2 to 3 minutes.

◆ Add shrimp, cook until shrimp turns pink, remove, and refrigerate.

◆ Put rice in skillet and heat, stirring constantly until rice is browned. Add tomatoes, bouillon and seasonings, cover and simmer until rice is tender and liquid absorbed.

◆ Add oysters and shrimp, heat through, stir gently.

◆ Garnish with minced parsley.

◎ GRILLED MARINATED SHRIMP

Yield: 6 servings

2   pounds large raw shrimp, shelled, deveined
½   cup dry sherry
1   clove garlic (or more), minced
½   cup olive oil
½   cup soy sauce

◆ Combine all five ingredients and marinate 3 to 4 hours.

◆ Grill over hot grill 2 to 3 minutes until just barely done.

◆ Serve with warmed Butter Sauce.

BUTTER SAUCE FOR DIPPING:
4   ounces butter, melted
1   small lemon, juiced
1   tablespoon soy sauce
1   tablespoon Worcestershire sauce
4   dashes hot pepper sauce

BUTTER SAUCE:
◆ Melt butter over low heat.
◆ Add remaining ingredients, stir well.

SMOKED SALMON CHEESECAKE

Yield: 12 to 16 servings

1 cup Parmesan cheese, freshly grated
1 cup bread crumbs (crumb in food processor)
½ cup unsalted butter, melted
1 tablespoon olive oil
1 cup onion, minced
½ cup green bell pepper, minced
½ cup red bell pepper, minced
½ teaspoons salt
12 turns freshly ground black pepper
1¾ pounds cream cheese, at room temperature
4 large eggs
½ cup heavy cream
1 cup smoked Gouda cheese, grated
1 pound smoked salmon, chopped (two cups)

◆ Preheat oven to 350°. Spray spring form pan with non–stick vegetable spray.

◆ Thoroughly combine Parmesan cheese, bread crumbs and butter. Press the mixture into the bottom of a 9–inch spring form pan.

◆ Heat the oil in a medium skillet over high heat. Add the onions and peppers and sauté, stirring and shaking skillet for 2 minutes. Stir in salt and pepper, sauté for 1 minute and remove from heat.

◆ Using an electric mixer, beat cream cheese with the eggs in a large bowl until very thick and frothy, about 4 minutes. Beat in the heavy cream, Gouda, sautéed vegetables and smoked salmon until well mixed, about 2 minutes.

◆ Pour the filling over the crust and bake until firm, about 1 hour and 15 minutes. Allow to cool to room temperature. If the cheesecake is refrigerated, allow to come to room temperature, 1 hour before serving.

Can be served as hors d'oeuvres or luncheon buffet.

CRAB CLAWS WITH MUSTARD SAUCE

Yield: 6 to 8 servings

4 pounds crab claws, cooked, cracked and chilled

MUSTARD SAUCE:
3½ teaspoons dry English mustard
1 cup mayonnaise
2 teaspoons Worcestershire sauce
1 teaspoon steak sauce
⅛ cup light cream
⅛ teaspoon salt

◆ Add mayonnaise to English mustard and beat for 1 minute.

◆ Add remaining ingredients and beat until mixture is smooth and creamy, chill.

◆ Dip crab claw in mustard sauce and enjoy.

Variation: Can be made with shrimp.

SEAFOOD LASAGNA

Yield: 8 servings

8 lasagna noodles
1 cup onion, minced
2 tablespoons margarine
1 (8 ounce) package cream cheese
1½ cups cream style cottage cheese
1 egg, beaten (or 2 egg whites)
½ teaspoon salt
⅛ teaspoon pepper
2 teaspoons basil, crushed
2 cans cream of mushroom soup
½ cup milk (can be skim)
⅓ cup cooking sherry
1 pound shrimp, boiled, peeled, deveined
1 (17½ ounce) can crab meat or imitation crab
¼ cup Parmesan cheese
½ cup Swiss cheese, grated

◆ Cook noodles, arrange half in bottom of 9 x 13 greased pan.

◆ Cook onion in margarine until tender. Blend in cream cheese, cottage cheese, egg, basil, salt and pepper.

◆ Spread half of mixture on noodles.

◆ Combine soup, milk, and wine. Stir in shrimp and crab. Spread half of mixture onto cheeses.

◆ Repeat layers of noodles, cheese and seafood.

◆ Sprinkle on Parmesan cheese.

◆ Bake 45 minutes at 350°. Top with Swiss cheese, heat until melted. Let stand 10 minutes before serving.

Note: Can make the night before, but increase baking time by 10 to 15 minutes.

Variation: Can use nonfat cheeses.

SOLE DEL MAR

Yield: 2 servings

2 fillets of sole (4 small fillets for larger appetites)
5-6 medium scallops
¼ cup crab meat
¼ cup salad shrimp
¼ cup mozzarella or Monterey Jack cheese, shredded
¾ cup hollandaise sauce (see index for recipe)
Garnish with paprika and parsley, minced

◆ Preheat oven to 450°.
◆ Place one sole fillet on bottom in individual casserole and layer with scallops, crab, shrimp and cheese. Top with second fillet and cover with hollandaise.
◆ Bake until fish flakes and sauce is bubbly, 10 to 15 minutes.
◆ Sprinkle with paprika and parsley as garnish.

Can increase ingredients if serving more people.

SHRIMP ON THE BAR-B

Yield: 4 to 5 servings

4-5 shrimp per person, uncooked, unshelled
1 cup olive oil
Juice of 2 lemons
¼ cup soy sauce
½ cup dry red wine
¼ cup parsley, chopped
1 tablespoon dill weed
1 tablespoon tarragon
1 tablespoon basil
1 clove garlic, pressed

◆ Cut through the back of the shrimp and remove the vein, but not the shell. Rinse.
◆ Combine the remaining ingredients and pour over the shrimp. Marinate, covered and refrigerated, for at least 2 hours.
◆ To grill, arrange in a basket grill or on a sheet of heavy-duty foil with holes poked through it. Cook on a rack over hot coals for 5 to 6 minutes. The shrimp should be pink, tender and moist, with slightly charred shells. Don't overcook!
◆ Remove shells or let each person peel his or her own.

SEAFOOD LA JOYA

Yield: 6 to 8 servings

2-2½ pounds scallops
2-2½ pounds medium shrimp, cleaned and deveined
2 cups Chablis wine
¼ cup fresh lemon juice
1 pound fresh mushrooms, sliced
2 green peppers, diced
6 tablespoons butter
¾ teaspoons salt
Dash pepper or to taste
6-7 tablespoons flour
3 cups Swiss cheese, grated
1 cup Romano or Parmesan cheese, grated (or ½ cup each)
½-1 pint heavy cream

◆ Wash and drain scallops. Clean and devein shrimp. Bring wine and lemon juice to boil. Add scallops, shrimp, mushrooms and green peppers. (If needed, use additional wine to be sure ingredients are just barely covered.) Simmer slowly for 6 to 8 minutes. Drain and save liquid.

◆ Melt butter. Blend in flour until bubbly and smooth. Gradually blend in 2 cups of reserved liquid. (Stir constantly). Cook over medium heat stirring constantly until sauce is smooth and thickened.

◆ Add salt, pepper, Swiss cheese and ½ cup Romano cheese. Stir over lowest heat until well blended. Cool.

◆ Whip cream until very stiff and fold into cooled sauce. Stir in shrimp and scallop mixture.

◆ Divide mixture into individual ramekins. Top with remaining Romano cheese. Sprinkle with paprika if desired.

◆ If serving immediately, brown under broiler until bubbly.

*Can be made earlier: heat at **350°** for 20 minutes.*

LEAF–WRAPPED STUFFED SALMON

Yield: 6 to 12 servings

3 heads lettuce, preferably butter type

1 5 to 8 pound salmon, dressed and boned
Salmon caviar or cooked crayfish for garnish (optional)
Stuffing (see below)

LEMON–ALMOND STUFFING:

1 cup fine fresh bread crumbs, processed from about (3 ounces) good–textured white bread, (preferably French)

1 cup almonds, unblanched

1 cup fresh parsley

1 tablespoon fresh tarragon or thyme leaves

3 tablespoons lemon zest, freshly grated

¼ cup lemon juice, freshly squeezed

¼ pound (1 stick) unsalted butter, softened
Salt
Black pepper, freshly ground
Cayenne pepper, ground

◆ Dip the lettuce in boiling water just until wilted, about 10 seconds. Remove immediately to a bowl of ice water, drain, and spread out on paper toweling; reserve.

◆ STUFFING: Combine the bread crumbs, almonds, and parsley in a food processor or blender and process just until coarsely chopped and mixed well. Add the tarragon or thyme, lemon zest and juice, and butter and mix thoroughly. Season to taste with salt, pepper and cayenne.

◆ Quickly rinse the salmon under running cold water and pat dry with paper toweling. To determine the cooking time, measure the fish across the back (hold ruler perpendicular to the spine) at its thickest point.

◆ Stuff the cavity of the salmon with the bread crumb mixture. Place the fish on a baking sheet.

◆ Drain the blanched lettuce and wrap the fish in the leaves, overlapping them as you work and covering the fish completely with several layers.

◆ Bake the salmon until the flesh is barely opaque throughout, about 10 minutes per inch of thickness. Garnish with caviar or crayfish and serve immediately. To serve, cut the fish crosswise into 1–inch thick slices.

◎ GINGERED SALMON

Yield: 4 to 6 servings

4½ tablespoons scallions, minced
3 tablespoons fresh ginger root, peeled and finely grated
3 tablespoons vegetable oil
¼ cup soy sauce
1 tablespoon sugar
1 teaspoon sweet rice wine
1 teaspoon oriental sesame oil
⅛ teaspoon pepper
4 pounds salmon fillets

◆ Prepare the marinade: In a small skillet cook the scallions and the ginger root in the vegetable oil over moderate heat stirring until the mixture is golden and remove the skillet from the heat. In a bowl, whisk together the soy sauce, sugar, sweet rice wine, sesame oil, pepper and the scallion mixture.

◆ Arrange the salmon in a large shallow glass dish, spoon the marinade over it and let the salmon marinate, covered and chilled for at least 1 hour or overnight. Transfer the salmon with tongs to the rack of a foil-lined broiler pan.

◆ Brush generously with marinade and broil about 4 inches from the heat for 5 minutes per ½ inch of thickness or until it flakes.

The marinade may be made 2 weeks in advance and kept covered and chilled.

REDSTONE FISH FILLETS

Yield: 6 servings

6 medium fish fillets (sole or flounder), about 2 pounds
⅓ cup and 2 tablespoons butter, divided
⅓ cup onion, chopped
½ cup celery, chopped
⅓ cup almonds, toasted and chopped
2 tablespoons parsley, snipped
½ cup and ⅓ cup stuffed olives, sliced, divided
Salt and pepper to taste
2 tablespoons lemon juice

◆ Prepare stuffing for fillets: Melt 2 tablespoons butter in a small skillet over low heat. Sauté onion and celery until golden. Stir in almonds, parsley, ½ cup olives and dash of pepper.

◆ Divide mixture into 6 parts. Place ⅙ at end of a fillet and roll up jelly roll fashion (secure with a toothpick). Sprinkle with salt and pepper and arrange seam side down in a shallow baking dish which has been sprayed with non–stick oil. Repeat with the rest of the fillets.

◆ Combine remaining ⅓ cup melted butter with the lemon juice and pour over the fillets.

◆ Bake at **350°** about 25 minutes. Distribute the remaining ⅓ cup of olives over the top of the fillets for the last 10 minutes of baking time.

SHRIMP AND ARTICHOKE CASSEROLE

Yield: 4 servings

2 (8½ ounce) cans artichoke hearts, quartered and drained
1½-2 pounds shrimp, steamed and shelled
1 pound fresh mushrooms, sliced
8 tablespoons butter or margarine, (or olive oil and margarine to equal 8 tablespoons)
5 tablespoons flour
2 cups evaporated milk
Salt and pepper to taste
2 tablespoons Worcestershire sauce
⅓ cup dry sherry
½ cup fresh Parmesan cheese, grated
Dash of cayenne
Sprinkle of paprika

◆ Arrange artichoke hearts in shallow, buttered 9 x 13-inch baking dish and layer with the shrimp.

◆ Sauté sliced mushrooms in butter in saucepan and stir in flour. When smooth, stir in evaporated milk, salt and pepper to taste. Add Worcestershire and sherry. Blend well.

◆ Pour the mushroom mixture over contents in baking dish, sprinkle with Parmesan and dust with paprika.

◆ Bake 20 minutes at 375°.

SZECHWAN SHRIMP

Yield: 2 to 4 servings

¼ cup fresh ginger, finely minced
1 small clove garlic, pressed
5-6 green onion bulbs, minced
¼ cup bamboo shoots, minced
¼ cup ketchup
3 tablespoon dry sherry
½ tablespoon dark soy sauce
1 teaspoon sesame oil
1 teaspoon monosodium glutamate (optional)
1 tablespoon sugar
1 tablespoon cornstarch
1½ tablespoons water
1 cup peanut or vegetable oil
½ pound shrimp, shelled

♦ In bowl 1, combine ginger, garlic, green onion bulbs, bamboo shoots. Set aside.

♦ In bowl 2, combine all remaining ingredients except peanut oil. 4 shrimp Mix thoroughly.

♦ Heat 1 cup peanut oil in a heavy skillet, add the shrimp, and cook, stirring constantly until they turn pink, 1 to 2 minutes. Drain through a sieve.

♦ Pour off all the oil except about 2 tablespoons. Add the ingredients from bowl 1 and stir about 1 minute. Add the shrimp and cook ½ minute.

♦ Finally add the ingredients from bowl 2. Bring to a boil, stirring and cook for 1 minute exactly.

By Bob Sammons, M.D., a Grand Junction physician, and author of **The Longhorn Dragon.**

ROARING FORK OVEN CRISP TROUT

Yield: 6 servings

6 trout, cleaned
Salt and pepper to taste
¼ cup butter, softened
½ cup parsley, finely chopped
¼ cup milk
1 egg
1 teaspoon salt
¾ cup fine bread crumbs, toasted
½ cup Swiss cheese, shredded
2 tablespoons butter
Lemon wedges

♦ Wash and pat fish dry with paper towel. Sprinkle inside of fish with salt and pepper.

♦ Combine butter and parsley, spread in cavity of each fish.

♦ Beat together milk with egg and salt.

♦ Combine bread crumbs with cheese.

♦ Dip each fish in egg mixture and roll in crumb and cheese mixture to coat each side.

♦ Put fish in a well buttered shallow pan. Dot with lots of butter.

♦ Bake at 500° 15 to 20 minutes until tender and brown. Serve with lemon wedges.

 FISH D'LISH

Yield: 4 servings

4 pounds halibut fillets, cut
   in approximately 2 x 2–inch
   squares

MARINADE:

¾ cup pure vegetable oil
¼ cup red wine vinegar
¼ cup Chablis wine
½ teaspoon salt
½ package onion soup mix
2 tablespoons soy sauce
2 tablespoons Worcestershire
   sauce
1 tablespoon lemon juice
2 cloves garlic, pressed

BREADING:

1½ cups bread or cracker
   crumbs
½ cup flour
1 teaspoon wheat germ
   (optional)
   Parmesan cheese, grated
   Butter
   Paprika to taste

◆ Add halibut to marinade, turning
  occasionally so marinade flavors
  all of the fish. Be sure the lid is
  tight and keep turning for at least
  6 hours.

◆ When ready to cook, remove fish
  from marinade and roll in breading mixture.

◆ Pour leftover marinade in shallow
  9 x 13 x 2–inch baking dish, add
  fish, sprinkle with grated Parmesan cheese, generously dot with
  butter and sprinkle with paprika.

◆ Bake at 400° for 20 to 25 minutes. Serve immediately.

ORANGE HORSERADISH CRUSTED SALMON FILLET WITH A LIGHT ORANGE DILL SAUCE

Yield: 4 servings

Flour
4 (7 ounce) salmon fillets
2 tablespoons olive oil
Salt and pepper to taste

CRUST:
1 cup dry bread crumbs, unseasoned
1 tablespoon grated horseradish
1 tablespoon butter, melted
Zest from one orange, minced
Salt and pepper to taste

SAUCE:
2 tablespoons shallot or onion, minced
1 tablespoon olive oil
½ cup white wine
2 cups orange juice, freshly squeezed
1 teaspoon cornstarch
1 tablespoon fresh dill, chopped

◆ For Sauce: In small saucepan, heat olive oil and sauté shallots or onions until soft and clear. Add wine and reduce until nearly dry, then add orange juice and reduce by half. Mix cornstarch with enough water to form a paste and whisk into sauce to thicken slightly. Cook gently for 5 minutes. Add dill and salt and pepper to taste. Keep warm.

◆ For Crust: Combine ingredients thoroughly.

◆ For Salmon: Preheat oven to 400°. Season salmon with salt and pepper, then dredge in flour and shake off excess. Heat oil in sauté pan large enough to hold all 4 salmon fillets. Cook fish on one side for about 4 minutes, turn over and place about one fourth of the crust mixture on each fillet. Place in oven until crust is browned and fish is flaky, about 6 to 7 minutes.

◆ Serve immediately drizzled with the sauce and a little fresh dill.

From Chef Rand Morgan of G.B. Gladstone's Restaurant

124

SALMON SPINACH PASTY

Yield: 3 dozen

1 (7 ounce) can salmon
2 pieces bacon, cooked, drained and crumbled
2 cups fresh spinach, chopped and wilted
½ cup cheddar cheese, shredded
1 tablespoon green onion, finely chopped
1 tablespoon Greek black olives, chopped
¼ teaspoon nutmeg
Salt and pepper to taste
Pastry recipe for 3 crusts
1 egg white (for glaze)

◆ Drain salmon and flake, removing bones and skin.

◆ Roll fresh spinach leaves a few at a time and slice diagonally, continuing this process until you fill a 2 cup measuring cup. Steam the spinach until just wilted.

◆ Cook, drain and crumble bacon.

◆ Combine the salmon, spinach, bacon, cheese, olives, onions, nutmeg, salt and pepper and set aside.

◆ Roll out pastry and cut into 3½–inch rounds with a glass or cookie cutter (roll left over dough for additional rounds).

◆ Place a rounded measuring teaspoon of the salmon mixture on half of each round, moisten edges, fold pasty over and seal by pressing tines of fork along the rounded edges.

◆ Prick the top of each pastry. Brush with egg white and bake at 350° to 375° on a greased cookie sheet for 20 minutes or until golden brown.

 SAUTÉED TROUT

Yield: 6 servings

2¾ pounds trout, whole, boned
¼ cup skim milk
¼ cup flour
Salt and pepper to taste
1½ tablespoons margarine
1 tablespoon almonds, sliced
3 tablespoons lemon juice
2 tablespoons parsley, fresh and chopped

◆ Rinse and dry trout. Open fish flat, dip into milk. Season flour with salt and pepper. Dip trout into flour, making sure both sides are completely covered, shake off excess.

◆ Heat margarine in non–stick skillet large enough to hold fish in one layer. Sauté fish two minutes, turn and sauté other side two minutes.

◆ Remove to a plate and keep warm.

◆ Add almonds to pan and sauté until slightly golden (about one minute).

◆ Sprinkle fish with lemon juice, almonds and parsley.

SHRIMP NEW ORLEANS

Yield: 8 servings

1 pound shrimp, steamed, medium size
¼ cup canola oil
1 tablespoon prepared mustard
2 tablespoons lemon juice
2 green onions, thinly sliced
¼ cup celery, finely chopped
½ teaspoon salt
¼ teaspoon pepper

◆ Remove shells down to the tail and clean shrimp.

◆ Steam or poach shrimp until they turn pink all over, (you may need to stir the mixture to be sure the shrimp are pink all over). Be sure not to overcook, it takes only 2 minutes or so to cook shrimp.

◆ Combine other ingredients and marinate shrimp in that mixture overnight.

Serve on a bed of chopped greens as an appetizer.

The Grand Event

• SPECTACULAR MT. SOPRIS •

♠BEEF TENDERLOIN

Yield: 1 tenderloin serves 4

1   or more whole beef
tenderloins, depending on
the amount of people you
intend to serve (1½ to 2
pounds tenderloin should
serve 4)
Olive oil
Bottled brown bouquet
sauce
Chef's salt (see below)

◆ Rub the tenderloins all over with
olive oil

◆ Then rub all over with the
bottled brown bouquet sauce (to
close pores and for color).

◆ Sprinkle the Chef's salt over the
surface of the tenderloin.

◆ Bake at 450°, 25 minutes for
smaller tenderloins or up to 35
minutes for thicker pieces.

◆ This will be fairly rare.

◆ Serving slices should be ¼–inch
to ½–inch thick.

CHEF'S SALT:
1   cup salt
1   tablespoon paprika
1   teaspoon black pepper
1   teaspoon white pepper
¼   teaspoon celery salt
¼   teaspoon garlic salt

◆ To make the Chef's Salt, mix all
ingredients thoroughly and store
in an airtight container.

Hint: Makes enough for future
tenderloin meals. Easy and
wonderful. Can also be used for
pork tenderloin.

*Bake at **425°** for 20 minutes*

STEAK ORE HOUSE

Yield: 6 servings

1	6 to 9–ounce filet mignon
	Smoked bacon
2-3	ounces crab meat (not imitation)
3-4	ounces sautéed mushrooms
1-1½	ounces Béarnaise sauce

◆ Trim all excess fat from steak. Wrap slice of bacon around perimeter of steak and secure with a large wooden pick. Grill filets over hot mesquite coals until desired doneness. Meat is best if cooked hot and fast.

◆ While filets are cooking, heat crab meat. To serve, top steaks with crab meat, surround with sautéed mushrooms and apply a good scoop of Béarnaise sauce (see index) over the works. Serve with steamed broccoli or another green vegetable and a fresh baked russet potato.

A wonderful recipe from
Steamboat Entertains.

◎ COMPANY BRISKET

Yield: 8 to 12 servings

4-5 pounds beef brisket, fat
trimmed
Seasoned salt, salt, pepper
and paprika to taste
3 onions, thinly sliced
¼ cup celery, chopped
½ cup carrots, thinly sliced
2 cups hot water
¼ cup vinegar
1 cup beef broth, optional
Cornstarch or flour

DO THE DAY BEFORE:

♦ Season brisket with salts, pepper and paprika.

♦ Place in roaster uncovered.

♦ Bake at 350° for one hour to brown.

♦ Remove from the oven and add onions, celery, carrots, water and vinegar.

♦ Return to the oven and bake covered at 300° for 3 to 4 hours or until tender.

♦ Remove meat and strain juices. Discard vegetables.

♦ Cool and refrigerate overnight.

THE DAY OF SERVING:

♦ Remove fat from the juices and make gravy to desired thickness using canned beef broth if you want more gravy.

♦ Slice meat against the grain into thin slices.

♦ Place meat in a roaster or serving casserole with a little of the gravy on top for moisture.

♦ Place in the oven and cover.

♦ Bake at 325° for 45 minutes or until hot.

♦ Heat the gravy and serve on the side.

Delicious with mashed potatoes or potato casserole.

 # PEPPERED BEEF

Yield: 8 servings

¼ cup coarsely ground black pepper
1 teaspoon ground cardamom
1 3 to 4 pound boneless brisket of beef
Tomato–Soy Marinade (see below)
Thinly sliced rye bread
Mustard Horseradish Sauce (see below)

◆ Combine pepper and cardamom and spread evenly on a sheet of waxed paper. Place beef over mixture and press down. Turn beef over.

◆ With heel of hand, press pepper mixture firmly down into the meat. Cover both sides evenly and thoroughly, using all the pepper mixture.

◆ Place meat in shallow dish and add Tomato–Soy Marinade. Cover and refrigerate overnight, turning meat occasionally.

◆ When ready to bake, remove meat from marinade and wrap securely in aluminum foil. Place in a shallow pan and bake at 300° for 3 hours or until meat is quite tender.

◆ Slice very thin and serve hot or cold on thin–sliced rye bread with Mustard Horseradish Sauce.

TOMATO–SOY MARINADE:
⅔ cup soy sauce
½ cup vinegar
¼ cup tomato paste
1 teaspoon paprika
3 cloves garlic, crushed

TOMATO–SOY MARINADE
◆ Combine ingredients and pour over meat.

This is also delicious with pork or chicken. Allow meat to marinate overnight, refrigerated.

Yield: 1½ cups

MUSTARD HORSERADISH SAUCE:
3 ounces cream cheese
½ cup mayonnaise
Salt to taste
2 teaspoons dry mustard
1½ tablespoons prepared horseradish

MUSTARD HORSERADISH SAUCE:
◆ Blend all ingredients until smooth. Refrigerate for several hours or overnight before serving.

Yield: 1 cup

This recipe was contributed by
Colorado Cookbook

242-7225

ITALIAN MEATLOAF

Yield: 8 to 10 servings

2 pounds ground beef or turkey
2 eggs
1 cup bread crumbs
1 teaspoon salt
1 teaspoon pepper
3 cloves garlic, minced
1 tablespoon Italian seasoning
  Dash Worcestershire
  Dash hot pepper sauce
¼ cup Parmesan cheese
½ onion, diced
¼ cup celery, chopped

◆ Mix all ingredients together with hands and place in a loaf pan.
◆ Bake at **350°** for one hour.

This recipe contributed by 7th Street Cafe.

ANNIVERSARY MEATLOAF

Yield: 6 to 8 servings

2 eggs, beaten
2 tablespoons whipping cream (or low–fat evaporated milk)
2 tablespoons milk
2 slices bread, torn up
1 tablespoon dried minced onion
1½ teaspoons salt
2 teaspoons prepared horseradish
¼ teaspoon black pepper (preferably freshly ground)
¼ teaspoon dried thyme
½ teaspoon dry mustard
2 pounds lean ground beef
½ cup ketchup

◆ Mix eggs with cream and milk, then add torn up bread, onion, salt, horseradish, pepper, thyme, and dry mustard. Stir well, let stand for 10 minutes, then stir well again, until all is well moistened and the bread is no longer in pieces. Add ground beef and mix well.
◆ Shape into loaf.
◆ Put ketchup on top.
◆ Bake at **375°** for one hour.

BONELESS BARBECUE BEEF RIBS

Yield: 6 servings

4 pounds boneless beef ribs (or beef brisket cut in 2–inch wide strips)
3 cups barbecue sauce (see below)

BARBECUE SAUCE:
14 ounces ketchup
½ cup water
2 tablespoons liquid smoke
3 tablespoons brown sugar
4 tablespoons Worcestershire sauce
3 teaspoons dry mustard
2 teaspoons celery seed
3 tablespoons butter
Salt and pepper to taste
2 tablespoons instant coffee granules
2 cloves garlic, finely minced

◆ Brown ribs and place in large casserole
◆ Pour sauce over ribs.
◆ Cover and bake at 325° for 3 to 4 hours.
◆ To make the Barbecue Sauce, combine all ingredients and bring to a boil, stirring occasionally.

MOUNTAIN MAN MUSTARD SAUCE

Yield: 3 cups

1½ cups yellow mustard
3 tablespoons Dijon mustard
2 tablespoons beef extract
½ teaspoon seasoned salt
1 teaspoon white pepper
½ teaspoon black pepper
1 tablespoon honey
2 tablespoons onion, minced
1 tablespoon parsley, finely minced
1 teaspoon garlic powder

◆ Mix all ingredients for sauce.
◆ Brush onto roast or beef ribs about 1 hour before cooking.
◆ Cook ribs over medium coals until the ribs are cooked to desired doneness (about 10 minutes per side for rare).
◆ Cook standing rib roast according to taste.

This is a yummy sauce for standing rib roast or BBQ beef ribs. Serve with lots of napkins!

STEAK ROLLS WITH MUSHROOMS *Yield: 6 to 8 servings (2 rolls each)*

2 pounds top round as thin as possible (⅛–inch is ideal)

⅔ cup onion, chopped, divided, reserve 2 heaping tablespoons

2 cups bread crumbs (preferably Italian)

12-13 slices bacon, diced and precooked to remove the fat, drain

16 ounces fresh mushrooms or 1 (16 ounce) can of sliced mushrooms

4 cups beef broth, reserve 1 cup for deglazing

6 cups water

2 to 3 cloves garlic, finely minced

Salt and pepper to taste

♦ Cut steak into 2½–ounce pieces, if necessary pound to ⅛–inch pieces.

♦ Salt and pepper each serving piece lightly.

♦ Combine bacon, bread crumbs, and onions (reserve 2 tablespoons) and place about 1 heaping tablespoon of this mixture on each serving of meat.

♦ Roll and secure each roll with toothpicks.

♦ Brown all sides in a little oil in a medium sized skillet.

♦ Place meat in baking pan at least 3 to 4 inches deep.

♦ Pour broth and water over the rolls, save 1 cup for deglazing.

♦ Discard any excess fat in the skillet and deglaze with some of the beef broth and add the drippings to the steak pan. Add remaining onions and garlic.

♦ Bake 1½ hours at 350°, covered.

♦ Turn top layers and add mushrooms with juice if using canned. Bake another 30 minutes.

♦ Remove rolls and put on serving platter and keep warm.

♦ Thicken remaining juices with flour or cornstarch mixed with about 2 tablespoons water to thin it out.

♦ Serve with mashed potatoes.

Can be made a day ahead or frozen for a short time. Worth the time! Men love it!

BRACCIOLE

Yield: 4 per round steak

1 round steak (thin, ¼–inch to ⅜–inch thick)
  Dash salt and pepper
4 bacon strips
2 cloves garlic thinly slivered
¼-½ cup fresh green pepper, chopped
¼-½ cup fresh parsley, chopped
¼ cup fresh sweet basil, chopped
¼ cup fresh grated Parmesan cheese
  String
  Your favorite tomato sauce

◆ Trim round steak of fat. The round will likely break into 2 separate pieces.

◆ Season with salt and pepper.

◆ Lay bacon strips over face of round steak.

◆ Evenly scatter pieces of garlic, green pepper, parsley, and basil over bacon.

◆ Roll up steak over long dimension like a jelly roll with all ingredients inside.

◆ Tie well with string.

◆ In a large saucepan, brown meat slowly on all sides over medium temperature, being careful not to burn.

◆ Add Your Favorite Tomato Sauce (see index) to pot, enough to completely cover meat rolls on all sides and top. Meat will flavor sauce as it cooks.

◆ Bring sauce to a boil, reduce heat to medium low for a slow, easy boil.

◆ Cook for 2 hours.

◆ Remove meat rolls from sauce, removing string. Slice like jelly roll (½ to 1–inch pieces).

◆ Arrange meat cuts on platter. Cover with tomato sauce and dress with Parmesan cheese.

◆ Serve remaining sauce over favorite pasta, such as spaghetti.

Very forgiving. Always comes out great. Can also be made with veal, but produces less flavor to sauce.

FALL RIVER RIB ROAST

Yield: 10 to 12 servings

½ cup minced fresh parsley
3 tablespoons freshly grated lemon peel
4 teaspoons dried thyme, crumbled
8 juniper berries, crushed
6 cloves garlic
1 teaspoon freshly ground black pepper
4-8 drops hot pepper sauce
1 cup olive oil
¼ cup fresh lemon juice
1 10 pound standing rib roast of beef

◆ Combine parsley, lemon peel, thyme, juniper berries, garlic, pepper and hot pepper sauce in blender. Add oil 1 tablespoon at a time, blending until a smooth paste is formed. Add lemon juice and blend. Rub mixture over surface of roast. Cover and refrigerate for at least 24 hours.

◆ Bring roast to room temperature before proceeding. Place roast in large, heavy roasting pan and roast in preheated oven at 500° for 15 minutes. Reduce temperature to 350° and continue roasting for 15 minutes per pound for rare, 20 minutes per pound for medium, or 25 minutes per pound for well done. Let roast rest for 10 minutes before carving. Serve with Hunters' Horseradish Sauce.

Yield: 4 cups

HUNTERS' HORSERADISH SAUCE:
6 egg yolks
2 tablespoons fresh lemon juice
Salt and freshly ground black pepper to taste
1 cup butter, melted and hot
1½ cups heavy cream, whipped
6-8 tablespoons prepared horseradish
2-4 drops hot pepper sauce
3 tablespoons minced onion
3 tablespoons minced fresh parsley

HUNTERS' HORSERADISH SAUCE:
◆ Combine egg yolks, lemon juice, salt and pepper in blender. Mix until well blended. While machine is running, add hot butter in a slow stream. Transfer to a large bowl and fold in whipped cream. Add horseradish and hot pepper sauce to taste. Fold in minced onion and parsley and transfer to serving bowl.

This recipe was contributed by **Crème de Colorado**. *The best prime rib recipe ever!*

BOLICHE ASADO DE COLORADO
Yield: 6 servings

4-5 pound eye of round roast
2 chorizos
½ pound slab bacon
¼ cup stuffed olives
¼ cup olive oil
2 large onions
  String
1 celery rib, chopped
½ small green pepper, chopped
1 large apple, chopped
1 large ripe tomato, quartered and seeded
½ teaspoon crushed oregano
1 bay leaf
  Salt and pepper to taste
½ cup good red wine
12 small new potatoes, peeled
1 pound baby carrots
3 tablespoons lemon juice

◆ When you order your roast, have the butcher make a pocket through the center lengthwise. Put chorizos, bacon and olives through food processor or chopper and stuff mixture into pocket, distributing it evenly throughout length of roast. Tie with the string.

◆ Using a roasting pan with cover, heat olive oil on range top. Sear roast on all sides, making sure it is browned (15 minutes). To the roasting pan (without removing meat) add chopped vegetables and apples, oregano, salt and pepper and bay leaf. Sauté until onion is transparent, add wine and cover. Place in 300° oven and cook approximately 2½ to 3 hours or until roast is fork tender. Uncover every hour to baste and turn roast. When done, cool meat completely on cutting board before carving.

◆ While meat is cooling, strain pan sauce through a sieve. Skim fat. Return sauce to roasting pan. Add ½ cup water and bring to a boil and then let simmer.

◆ Slice roast into thin slices and replace in sauce, in pan, to form whole roast. Surround with potatoes and carrots, sprinkle with lemon juice. Baste roast with sauce, cover and continue cooking at 325° until potatoes and carrots are done (approximately 45 minutes to 1 hour).

 Osso Buco with Orzo Milanese

Yield: 6 servings

6   1½ to 2–inch thick veal shanks (about 1 pound each)
    All–purpose flour
3   tablespoons olive oil
1   cup diced carrot
1   cup chopped celery
1   cup chopped onion
1   large clove garlic, minced
1   (28–ounce) can plum tomatoes undrained and chopped
1   cup Chablis or other dry white wine
½   cup water
¼   cup minced fresh parsley
1   bay leaf
1½ teaspoons beef–flavored bouillon granules
1   teaspoon dried basil
½   teaspoon salt
½   teaspoon dried oregano
¼   teaspoon garlic powder
⅛   teaspoon coarsely ground pepper
    Orzo Milanese (see below)
¼   cup water
2   tablespoons all–purpose flour
2   tablespoons minced fresh parsley
1   teaspoon grated lemon rind

ORZO MILANESE:

¼   cup chopped onion
1   teaspoon butter or margarine, melted
1   cup water
1   cup Chablis or other dry white wine
2   teaspoons beef–flavored bouillon granules
¼   teaspoon ground saffron
1   cup uncooked orzo

♦ Using kitchen twine, tie each veal shank in 2 places (package fashion) to keep shape. Dredge shanks in flour; brown in hot oil in a Dutch oven. Remove veal from Dutch oven, reserving drippings. Add carrot, celery, onion, and minced garlic to drippings.

♦ Cook, uncovered, until vegetables are tender. Drain off drippings. Return veal to Dutch oven with vegetables.

♦ Add tomatoes and next 10 ingredients. Bring mixture to a boil; cover, reduce heat, and simmer 2 to 2½ hours or until veal is tender. Remove and discard bay leaf.

♦ Arrange veal over Orzo Milanese on a serving platter; remove and discard twine. Combine ¼ cup water and 2 tablespoons flour, stirring well; add to tomato mixture, and cook until thickened. Pour over veal; sprinkle with 2 tablespoons parsley and lemon rind.

ORZO MILANESE:

♦ Sauté chopped onion in butter in a medium saucepan over medium heat until tender. Add water, wine, bouillon granules, and saffron; bring to a boil. Add orzo; return mixture to a boil. Cover, reduce heat to medium low, and simmer 10 minutes or until orzo is tender. Drain if necessary, and serve immediately.

Apple–Stuffed Veal Rolls

Yield: 6 servings

6 tablespoons butter, divided
1 onion, finely chopped
1 clove garlic, minced
1 cup soft bread cubes
2 cups peeled apple, coarsely chopped
1 teaspoon salt
½ teaspoons poultry seasoning
12 thin veal scallops
Flour
¾ cup apple cider or juice
2 tablespoons Calvados or applejack
Crabapples or sautéed apple slices (garnish)

◆ Melt 4 tablespoons of the butter in a large skillet and sauté onion, stirring often, until golden.

◆ Add garlic, bread cubes, apple, salt, and poultry seasoning.

◆ Stir over low heat until ingredients are thoroughly mixed.

◆ Pound veal scallops until very thin.

◆ Divide stuffing among veal slices; roll up and secure with toothpicks.

◆ Coat veal rolls with flour.

◆ Heat remaining butter in skillet.

◆ Brown veal rolls well on all sides.

◆ Add cider and Calvados or applejack.

◆ Simmer, covered for 25 to 30 minutes or until tender.

◆ Remove toothpicks and place veal on a heated platter. Spoon sauce over veal and garnish with crabapples or apple slices.

A salad of hearts of palm, tomatoes and lettuce in a vinaigrette dressing and buttery hot rolls would round out this menu.

SAUSAGE AND MUSHROOM STRUDEL

Yield: 3 to 4 servings
(2 strudels)

FILLING:

- 4 tablespoons unsalted butter
- ½ cup minced shallots
- 1½ pounds mushrooms, trimmed and chopped medium fine
- 2½ teaspoons salt, divided
- ½ teaspoon freshly ground black pepper, divided
- 9 tablespoons dry sherry, divided
- 4 slices bacon, cut into 1–inch pieces
- 1 very large onion, chopped medium fine
- 1 tablespoon safflower oil
- ¾ pound sausage meat
- 2 tablespoons fresh parsley, minced
- 1 cup sour cream

STRUDEL DOUGH:

- 8 sheets strudel or phyllo dough
- 8 tablespoons (1 stick) unsalted butter, melted

◆ To make the filling, melt the butter in a large skillet and add shallots. Sauté for a few minutes to wilt. Add mushrooms and cook over medium high heat for a few minutes, stirring constantly. Add 1½ teaspoons salt and ¼ teaspoon pepper, and continue to cook until the liquid evaporates. Add 6 tablespoons sherry and cook a few minutes until it evaporates. Remove from skillet, put in a bowl, and set aside.

◆ Wipe out the skillet and add the bacon. Fry until crisp. Drain and crumble. Add to mushroom–shallot mixture.

◆ Pour out all but 1 tablespoon of the rendered fat in the skillet. Add onion and sauté until wilted. Add to mushroom mixture.

◆ Wipe out the skillet once more and add the safflower oil, heat and add the sausage. Break up the sausage with a wooden spoon and cook until it turns light and most of the liquid has evaporated. If any fat has rendered out, drain it off. Add the remaining 1 teaspoon salt, ¼ teaspoon pepper, and 3 tablespoons sherry. Cook over fairly high heat, stirring constantly, until liquid evaporates. Remove from pan when it begins to stick to the bottom, add to the mushrooms, and mix. At this point, the mixture can be refrigerated for up to 4 or 5 days. When ready to use, heat until just warm and add the parsley and sour cream. Mix.

◆ To assemble: Immerse a fresh dish towel in cold water and

Continued on next page

Sausage and Mushroom Strudel (continued)

wring dry. Spread out flat on your work surface, narrow end toward you. Smooth out wrinkles. Have ready a pot of melted butter and a very fine brush. (The best kind is made of goose feathers.) Carefully spread a sheet of dough on the cloth, narrow end toward you, and quickly (and gently) coat well with melted butter, using the fine brush. Repeat with three more sheets. If sheets are packaged two together, do not separate, but spread them both out and fold the top one halfway down to allow you to butter the sheet underneath. Repeat on the lower half, then butter the top one.

◆ Turn on oven to **375°** and liberally oil a cookie sheet.

◆ Place half the filling in a line at the bottom end of the dough facing you, leaving a space about 2 inches from the sides and the bottom end. Fold this 2 inches of dough over the sides and then on the end. Lift the dish towel with both hands and gently roll the stuffing forward until it is encased, sausage– like, in the dough. When this is completed, carefully lift the end of the towel onto the cookie sheet and roll the finished strudel onto it, seam side down. Do not handle with your hands if you can avoid it. Repeat with the second strudel. Brush generously with butter and bake for 20 minutes.

This freezes well (thaw before baking).

If you would prefer, you can make three thinner strudels out of this amount of filling. This will require 4 more sheets of dough. See Special Guide Section for phyllo hints.

PLUM–MARINATED SPARERIBS

Yield: 8 servings

⅓ cup plum jam
1 cup dry red wine
¼ cup olive or salad oil
¼ cup red wine vinegar
¼ cup low sodium soy sauce
2–3 cloves garlic, minced
1 medium onion, finely chopped
½ teaspoon thyme
6-8 pounds lean pork spareribs, left in slabs

♦ Combine first eight ingredients in a small pan and cook over medium heat until bubbling, then cool.

♦ Remove thin membrane from underside of rib slabs to enhance absorption of marinade.

♦ Place the rib slabs in rimmed baking pan lined with a plastic bag. Pour marinade in bag and close bag with a twist tie. Turn bag to coat rib slabs with marinade.

♦ Refrigerate overnight, turning the bag occasionally.

♦ Before cooking, remove rib slabs from marinade and allow to drain (reserve marinade for basting).

♦ Grill rib slabs 4 to 6 inches above low–glowing coals or indirect heat on a gas grill for approximately 1 hour or until meat near bone is no longer pink when cut with a knife.

♦ Turn and baste the rib slabs frequently with the reserved marinade.

♦ Cut into individual ribs for serving.

This marinade is also good with boneless pork steaks or beef ribs.

Spareribs Hawaiian

Yield: 6 servings

3   pounds country–style pork ribs
3   tablespoons brown sugar
2   tablespoons cornstarch
½   teaspoon salt
¼   cup vinegar
½   cup ketchup
1   (9–ounce) can crushed pineapple and juice
1   teaspoon soy sauce

◆ Cook brown sugar, cornstarch, salt, vinegar, ketchup, and pineapple and juice together in medium pan until thick over very low heat, stirring constantly.

◆ Brush on spare ribs and bake at 350° for 1½ to 2 hours.

Super easy and tasty. Great with rice.

Baked Ham with Spicy Mustard Sauce

Yield: 8 to 10 servings

1   (5 pound) smoked ham
1   (18–ounce) jar orange marmalade
½   cup stone–ground mustard
2   tablespoons dry mustard
1   clove garlic, minced
½   teaspoon ground ginger

◆ Preheat oven to 350°.

◆ Place ham, fat side up, on rack in a roasting pan.

◆ Mix remaining ingredients until well blended.

◆ Brush ½ of the sauce on the ham.

◆ Bake 2 hours, brushing on more sauce about every 15 minutes.

An easy and different way to have ham. Would be great with potato salad. The leftovers would make great sandwiches!

BUFFET HAM

Yield: 8 to 10 servings

1 (5 pound) canned ham
1 loaf frozen honey wheat bread dough, thawed
Garnish of your choice

◆ Bake ham to melt any jellied sauce. Drain and wipe with paper towel.

◆ Pat out unfrozen honey wheat bread dough and spread around the ham evenly.

◆ You can cut out special detail, i.e. leaves and apply to the surface of the ham with egg white, for a special occasion.

◆ Bake at **350°** until the bread is golden and thoroughly baked, check at about 20 to 25 minutes.

◆ Remove from oven and let cool.

◆ Place on serving platter and garnish with parsley, pineapple, etc.

◆ Slice and serve for a buffet.

MARINATED GRILLED PORK CHOPS

Yield: 4 servings

4 1 to 1½–inch boneless loin pork chops
2 cloves garlic, crushed
1 tablespoon coriander
1 teaspoon brown sugar
3 tablespoons soy sauce (low sodium)

◆ Start grill.

◆ Combine all ingredients except pork chops.

◆ Marinate chops in mixture for 30 minutes turning once or twice.

◆ Grill over medium coals 11 to 15 minutes per side, turning once (more time if thick, less time if thinner).

This is a moist and delicious pork chop.

144

MEDALLIONS OF PORK TENDERLOIN WITH TARRAGON

Yield: 4 servings

½ pound boneless pork tenderloin, sliced in ¼–inch pieces and pounded thin
2 tablespoons butter or margarine, divided (can substitute olive oil)
Salt and pepper to taste
⅓ cup tarragon vinegar
⅓ cup beef broth
1 tablespoon fresh (or 1 teaspoon dried) tarragon
1½ tablespoon Dijon mustard
½ cup evaporated milk, divided

◆ Pound ¼–inch slices of pork between sheets of waxed paper (can be done ahead of time and refrigerated or frozen with paper between slices).

◆ In a small bowl, combine vinegar and broth.

◆ In a large skillet, melt butter and sauté pork in small batches until browned on both sides, adding remaining olive oil as needed.

◆ Remove pork to serving platter, sprinkle with salt and pepper and keep warm.

◆ Stir vinegar mixture into skillet, scraping up browned bits. Cook over medium heat until reduced by half (about 5 minutes). Lower heat, stir in mustard and ¼ cup evaporated milk.

◆ Over medium high heat, reduce liquid by half.

◆ Add remaining ¼ cup evaporated milk and cook until slightly thickened.

◆ Add tarragon.

◆ Stir and pour over pork medallions.

RACK OF LAMB DIJON

Yield: 2 to 4 ribs to person

1 large clove garlic, minced
½ teaspoon salt
½ teaspoon thyme
2½ tablespoons Dijon mustard
3 tablespoons olive oil
6-8 rib rack of lamb

◆ Preheat oven to **500°**.

◆ Mix all ingredients into a paste.

◆ Slash rack of lamb diagonally every 1½ inches.

◆ Brush mixture over entire rack, top and sides included.

◆ Cook 10 minutes at **500°**.

◆ Reduce oven temperature to **400°** and continue to bake 15 minutes more.

Note: Increase time if rack is over 6 ribs and increase ingredients.

LAMB BURGERS

Yield: 4 servings

1 pound lean ground lamb
½ cup fresh parsley, chopped
½ teaspoon dried rosemary leaves, crumbled
1 teaspoon dried (or 1 tablespoon fresh) mint leaves crumbled or chopped fine
3 tablespoons green onions, minced
1–2 cloves garlic, minced
¼ teaspoon black pepper
1 pinch allspice

◆ Mix thoroughly all ingredients in a mixing bowl.

◆ Form 4 equal sized patties.

◆ Barbecue over hot coals or on high on a gas grill for approximately 5 to 6 minutes on each side. Do not overcook.

◆ Serve immediately on traditional or whole wheat buns with your favorite condiments.

This recipe is from a lamb–raising family and they love chutney on it. Try it!

BUTTERFLIED LEG OF LAMB WITH HERB–WINE MARINADE

Yield: 8 *servings*

FOR THE HERB–WINE MARINADE:

- 2 cups dry red wine
- ¼ cup lemon juice
- ¼ cup red wine vinegar
- 4 cloves garlic, minced
- 2 teaspoons salt (optional or less)
- 1 teaspoon tarragon
- 1 teaspoon rosemary, crumbled
- ⅓ cup salad or olive oil
- 5-7 pound butterflied leg of lamb (weight after bone has been removed)

◆ Have butcher butterfly (bone) the leg of lamb. Before marinating the lamb, remove as much of the outer membrane and fat as possible. Slice away tendons or membrane on the underside so that the leg of lamb lies flat.

◆ Combine the marinade ingredients in a mixing bowl.

◆ Pour half the marinade in the bottom of a large baking dish (10 x 15 x 2½–inch). Place the leg of lamb in the baking pan and pour remaining marinade over the top.

◆ Cover with plastic wrap and aluminum foil and refrigerate for 24 hours, turning occasionally.

◆ Grill the leg of lamb 4 to 6 inches above glowing coals or over medium-high heat on a gas grill for 30 to 35 minutes.

◆ Turn the leg of lamb every 4 minutes to prevent charring and baste frequently with the remaining marinade.

◆ Do not overcook the lamb. The above cooking time is for medium rare. There will be thicker portions of the leg that will cook more slowly. If a portion of the leg is becoming overdone, remove it to a platter and keep warm in the oven until you are ready to slice. Do not hesitate to slice into the thicker pieces to check cooking progress.

◆ Slice lamb into ¼–inch slices and arrange on a serving platter. Serve immediately.

Wonderful with fresh tossed salad, steamed broccoli, and red wine.

LEG OF LAMB SWEDISH STYLE

Yield: 4 to 6 servings

1 whole leg of lamb
1 clove garlic
1 teaspoon salt
1 teaspoon dry mustard
COFFEE MIXTURE:
  1 cup strong coffee
  2 teaspoons sugar
  2 teaspoons cream
  1 pony brandy
CURRANT JELLY MIXTURE:
  ¾ cup cream
  2 tablespoons currant jelly

◆ Preheat oven to **350°**.

◆ Wipe leg of lamb with damp cloth.

◈ Insert slivers of garlic into flesh of lamb.

◆ Rub outside with the mixed salt and dry mustard.

◆ Place in roasting pan and bake for 1 hour and 20 minutes at **350°**. (Remove from the oven and refrigerate at this point if it is to be finished later.)

◆ 1½ hours before serving: Put meat back in oven at **350°** and baste with coffee mixture for approximately 1 more hour. (Will have to gauge the size of lamb and desired doneness.)

◆ Remove leg of lamb to serving platter and keep warm.

◆ Add to the pan juices the currant jelly mixture and cook until bubbling.

◆ Season to taste and strain gravy if desired. Add more cream or water if needed, thicken with flour.

Sauce is wonderful! Serve with brown rice or new potatoes.

LAMB CURRY

Yield: 4 servings

1 onion, chopped
¼ cup olive oil
3 pounds lamb shoulder, cut into 1–inch cubes
2 tablespoons flour
2 tablespoons curry powder
1 quart chicken broth
¼ pound celery root, peeled and diced
4 tomatoes, peeled, seeded and diced
½ pint heavy cream
2 Golden Delicious apples, peeled, cored, and diced

◆ In a 3 quart Dutch oven or heavy pan, sauté onion in oil until tender. Add lamb and sauté until it is slightly browned on all sides.

◆ Stir in flour and cook the mixture stirring frequently for about 7 to 8 minutes.

◆ Mix in the curry powder and enough of the chicken broth to cover the meat.

◆ Add ¾ of the celery root and tomatoes, bring the liquid to a boil.

◆ Reduce heat and simmer, covered for 1½ hours.

◆ Transfer meat to a bowl, add the cream to remaining sauce in the pan.

◆ Simmer 2 minutes, add meat, remaining celery, and tomatoes.

◆ Add the apples and heat through, adjusting the seasonings to taste.

◆ Serve with rice and other condiments.

Note: Condiments that could be served with the curry: chopped apples, nuts, chutney, grated coconut, etc.

BUD'S GREEK BASTING SAUCE

Yield: 1½ cups

½ cup plus 2 tablespoons lemon juice
½ cup plus 2 tablespoons olive oil
1 tablespoon parsley
1 tablespoon oregano
1 tablespoon garlic powder
2 tablespoons Greek seasoning

◆ Combine all ingredients.
◆ Be sure to baste meat often during cooking.
◆ For lamb: Add several garlic cloves to the meat roast.

You may use more lemon juice and olive oil if desired.

Excellent for lamb or dove.

CHICKEN & WINE

Yield: 6 servings

8 chicken breasts
1 cup flour
2 teaspoons salt
¼ teaspoon pepper
1 bunch green onions, sliced
½ cup mushrooms, sliced
3-4 tablespoons butter
1 cup dry wine or dry vermouth
2 tablespoons parsley, chopped
Pinch of thyme
Pinch of marjoram
Dash Worcestershire sauce
1 bay leaf, crumbled
Salt and pepper to taste

◆ In paper bag combine flour, salt, and pepper.
◆ Place chicken breasts, a few at a time, in bag and shake.
◆ Melt butter in frying pan and brown chicken.
◆ Place chicken in a 13 x 9-inch casserole.
◆ Add onions and mushrooms to pan and lightly brown.
◆ Add wine, parsley, thyme, marjoram, Worcestershire sauce, bay leaf, and salt and pepper to taste.
◆ Simmer gently for a few minutes to blend flavors, pour over chicken.
◆ Cover and bake at **325°** until tender, about 1 hour to 90 minutes.

Freezes well.

KOREAN CHICKEN

Yield: 4 servings

⅓ cup flour
1 pint oil
8 chicken thighs, boned
½ cup soy sauce
6 tablespoons sugar
1 clove garlic
1 green onion, chopped (onion & green top)
1 small red chile, diced, or ½ teaspoon crushed red pepper

♦ Coat chicken with flour.
♦ Deep fry chicken in oil at medium-high temperature until golden brown and tender, about 15 minutes.
♦ Combine soy sauce, sugar, garlic, onion, and chile to make sauce.
♦ As chicken is removed from fryer, coat with sauce.

PERFECT GRILLED CHICKEN

Yield: 8 servings

3 pounds whole chickens, split
½ cup orange juice, freshly squeezed
3 tablespoons olive oil
3 cloves garlic, minced
3 tablespoons rosemary, fresh
1 tablespoon thyme, fresh

♦ Prick skin and meat of chicken.
♦ In a glass bowl or a large sealable plastic bag, combine orange juice, olive oil, garlic, rosemary, and thyme.
♦ Add chicken, turning to coat.
♦ Refrigerate 3 hours (or overnight).
♦ To grill, place chicken bone-side down and cook 12 minutes; turn and baste with marinade and cook 10 minutes more (or until juices run clear when meat is pricked).

Chicken could be prepared inside, under the broiler.

Variation: For a change in flavor, substitute lemon juice for the orange juice and use tarragon instead of rosemary and thyme. Or, use lime juice with cilantro and minced jalapeño peppers!

CHICKEN AND ARTICHOKES ITALIAN

Yield: 6 to 8 servings

3   tablespoons olive oil
2-3 pounds chicken, skinned and cut up
1   cup onion, chopped
1   cup fresh mushrooms, sliced
¼   cup green pepper, chopped
¼   cup carrots, chopped
1   large clove garlic, minced
¼   cup flour
1   (14 ounce) can stewed tomatoes
1   (14 ounce) can artichoke hearts, drained and halved
1   (8 ounce) can tomato sauce
½   cup dry white wine (or apple juice)
1   teaspoon dried Italian seasonings, crushed
    Pepper to taste

◆ Heat oil in a large skillet and sauté onion, mushrooms, green pepper, carrot, and garlic until tender but not brown.

◆ Remove vegetables from pan and set aside.

◆ Coat chicken with flour and brown over medium-heat 10 minutes, turning occasionally.

◆ Return vegetables to skillet, add undrained tomatoes, tomato sauce, drained artichoke hearts, wine, and Italian seasonings.

◆ Heat to a boil, reduce heat and simmer 35-40 minutes or until chicken is tender, stirring occasionally.

◆ Transfer chicken to platter and keep warm.

◆ Boil sauce gently, uncovered, 5 minutes or to desired consistency.

◆ Serve over chicken.

Good with pasta or rice.

CORNISH HENS FLAMED IN COGNAC

Yield: 6 to 8 servings

6-8	hens
6-8	shallots, diced
4	tablespoons olive oil
½	stick butter
	Salt, pepper, and basil to taste
2-3	tablespoons cognac
1	pound fresh mushrooms, sliced
½	cup whipping cream or canned evaporated milk

◆ Loosen skin of hens by inserting fingers over the breast meat, carefully tearing any connecting tissue, and place one shallot per bird under skin.

◆ Melt oil and butter in a large pan and brown all sides of the hens.

◆ Sprinkle hens with salt, pepper, and basil.

◆ Cover and bake slowly in a 300° oven for about ½ hour.

◆ Take out of oven and pour cognac over hens to flame.

◆ Increase oven to 325°.

◆ After flaming, scrape down the juices and bake slowly for an additional 1-½ to 2 hours, uncovered, in 325° oven.

◆ After cooking, set aside hens, keeping them warm.

◆ Stir juices, adjust seasonings, and add the mushrooms.

◆ Add enough whipping cream to thicken juices, stirring frequently.

◆ When mushrooms are cooked and juice is creamy, serve over hens.

Wonderful with wild rice or pilaf.

SPANISH PAELLA

Yield: 12 to 14 servings

⅓ cup olive oil
4 pounds chicken pieces, skin removed (thighs work well)
1 pound chorizo, Italian or other spicy sausage cut in bite-size pieces
12 cloves garlic, minced
2 medium onions, chopped
1 cup dry vermouth
4 (8 ounce) bottles of clam juice
2 (13 ounce) cans chicken broth
1 teaspoon saffron (see below)
2 teaspoons paprika
4 bay leaves
3 teaspoons oregano
2 teaspoons thyme
24 mussels, scrubbed
2 pounds shrimp (41-50 count)
8 ounces stuffed green olives
4 cups long-grain rice
2 (9 ounce) packages frozen artichoke hearts (canned may be substituted)
2 (10 ounce) packages frozen peas

ONE DAY OR A FEW HOURS BEFORE SERVING:
♦ Heat oil in a large roasting pan over medium heat.
♦ Add chicken and sausage, and brown on all sides.
♦ Add garlic and onion. Cook until onion is translucent.
♦ Pour in vermouth, clam juice, and chicken broth. Bring to boil.
♦ Add saffron, paprika, bay leaves, oregano, and thyme. Reduce heat. Cover pot and simmer 15 to 20 minutes.
♦ (If doing this step ahead, remove stock mixture and refrigerate in pot until ready to proceed with next step.)

TWO HOURS BEFORE SERVING:
♦ Soak mussels in cold water to remove sand.
♦ Shell and devein shrimp. Set aside.
♦ Remove stock from refrigerator and bring to room temperature.

ONE HOUR BEFORE SERVING:
♦ Drain mussels, discarding dead ones (any open ones) prior to cooking.
♦ Drain olives. Set aside.
♦ Remove frozen vegetables from freezer to partially thaw.

30 MINUTES BEFORE SERVING:
♦ Bring stock mixture to a boil. Sprinkle rice evenly over all, mixing it down into the liquid with a wooden spoon. Boil rapidly, uncovered, for 15 minutes until rice begins to swell and absorb liquid. Stir occasionally to prevent rice from

Continued on next page

Spanish Paella (Continued)

sticking.

◆ Add shrimp and mussels. Cover and reduce heat. Simmer 4-5 minutes.

◆ Add artichokes and peas. Cover and simmer 8-10 minutes or until mussels open.

◆ Before serving sprinkle in the olives.

Recipe may be cut in half.

Saffron is the dried stigmas of a fall-flowering crocus grown primarily in Mediterranean countries such as Spain. It looks like tiny threads of orange string and is expensive.

The recipe calls for 24 mussels. Buy 30 mussels because a few invariably die. Ask the attendant at the seafood counter how to store the mussels until you are ready to use them.

SWEETWATER'S CHICKEN MONTE CRISTO

Yield: 4 servings

4 chicken breasts
4 eggs, beaten lightly
1 cup flour
1 cup bread crumbs
½ pound sliced Danish or honey ham
4 slices Swiss cheese, sliced thickly
Lingonberry jam or raspberry preserves

◆ Dip chicken breasts in flour, then egg, then bread crumbs.

◆ Deep fry in vegetable oil until done (should be golden brown and firm to the touch).

◆ Layer ham on each breast and top with Swiss cheese.

◆ Bake until cheese is melted at 350° (10-15 minutes).

◆ Heat Lingonberry or raspberry preserves in microwave until hot. (If done on top of stove, just until it bubbles).

◆ Serve over chicken.

Sweetwater's chef serves rice as a side dish for this meal.

Variation: Instead of frying chicken, bake for ½ hour until golden and firm to the touch.

155

WEEKEND CHICKEN

Yield: 5 to 7 servings

1   7 pound capon
5   slices white bread
½   cup water
½   cup parsley, finely chopped
4   eggs, lightly beaten
1   teaspoon salt
¼   teaspoon pepper
1   teaspoon thyme or sage
    leaves, crumbled
1   small onion, grated
½   cup butter, softened

◆ Loosen skin of capon by inserting hand over the breast meat and down around the thighs, carefully tearing any connecting tissue.

◆ Cut crusts from bread. Sprinkle with water and let soak for 3 minutes. Squeeze out excess moisture and mix the bread with chopped parsley, eggs, salt, pepper, thyme, and grated onion.

◆ Preheat oven to 375°.

◆ Stuff the dressing between the skin and meat of the capon, over the breast, and forcing it into the leg pockets, as well.

◆ Place capon breast side up on a rack in a shallow roasting pan. Spread with the soft butter and sprinkle with salt and pepper.

◆ Roast for 45 minutes, basting frequently. Reduce oven temperature to 350° and cook for 1 hour longer, basting every 20 minutes. Turn capon over onto breast and cook for 15 minutes longer.

◆ Serve hot or at room temperature.

RIDGEWAY CHICKEN BREASTS

Yield: 8 to 10 servings

6 whole chicken breasts, boned, skinned, and quartered
½ cup flour
1 cup butter or margarine, melted
Salt and pepper to taste
½ cup dry white wine
1½ cups mushrooms, sliced
¾ cup chicken stock
½ cup (2 ounces) mozzarella cheese, shredded
½ cup Parmesan cheese, grated
½ teaspoon salt
⅛ teaspoon pepper

◆ Place each piece of chicken between 2 sheets of waxed paper and pound to ⅛ inch thickness.
◆ Dredge chicken lightly with flour.
◆ Place 4 pieces at a time in 2 tablespoons melted butter in a large skillet; cook over low heat 3 to 4 minutes on each side.
◆ Place chicken in a greased 13 x 9 x 2-inch baking dish, overlapping edges; sprinkle with salt and pepper to taste.
◆ Repeat procedure with remaining chicken, adding 2 tablespoons butter to skillet each time.
◆ Reserve drippings in skillet.
◆ Sauté mushrooms in ¼ cup melted butter until tender. Drain. Distribute over chicken.
◆ Stir wine and chicken stock into drippings in skillet. Simmer 10 minutes, stirring occasionally.
◆ Stir in ½ teaspoon salt and ⅛ teaspoon pepper.
◆ Spoon sauce evenly over chicken.
◆ Combine cheeses and sprinkle over chicken.
◆ Bake at **450°** for 10 to 12 minutes.
◆ Place under broiler 1 to 2 minutes or until lightly browned.

PUFFERBELLY POT PIE

Yield: 6 servings

1 3-pound whole fryer chicken, boiled and boned
4 cups chicken broth
2 medium-sized carrots cut in large pieces
2 onions, peeled and cut in large pieces
6 ounces small fresh mushrooms, halved
2 medium-size ribs celery, cut in large pieces
1 bay leaf
3 tablespoons butter or margarine
¼ cup plus 2 teaspoons all-purpose flour
½ cup heavy cream or evaporated milk
1 teaspoon poultry seasoning
1 teaspoon salt
¼ teaspoon pepper
1 cup frozen green peas (optional)
   Biscuit dough (see below)
   Deep 2-quart casserole dish

BISCUIT DOUGH:
1½ cups all-purpose flour
2 teaspoons baking powder
1¼ teaspoons granulated sugar
¼ teaspoon salt
¼ cup plus 2 teaspoons solid vegetable shortening
½ cup milk

♦ Place 4 cups of chicken broth in large Dutch oven.

♦ Add all of the vegetables and bay leaf. Cover and simmer for 20 minutes.

♦ Place a colander in a large bowl and drain vegetables, reserving liquid.

♦ Melt butter in same Dutch oven over low heat.

♦ Stir in flour until smooth. Let mixture bubble about 3 minutes, stirring often to prevent browning.

♦ Gradually stir in 2 cups of cooled chicken broth and the cream. Cook over medium heat, stirring constantly, until thickened.

♦ Add seasonings, green peas, vegetables, and chicken. Stir to mix.

♦ Pour into a greased casserole.

♦ For Biscuits: Preheat oven to 400°.

♦ Mix flour, baking powder, sugar, and salt in medium bowl.

♦ Cut in shortening with pastry blender or 2 knives until mixture resembles coarse crumbs.

♦ Stir in milk and beat with wooden spoon until soft dough forms.

♦ Turn out onto a lightly floured surface and roll or pat dough to ½ inch thickness.

♦ Cut dough with floured biscuit cutter and place biscuits on top

Continued on next page

Pufferbelly Pot Pie (Continued)

of the casserole.

◆ Bake in a preheated 400° oven for 18-20 minutes until biscuits are golden brown.

Hint: Can use refrigerator biscuits

An old-fashioned recipe like Grandma used to make.

This recipe could be doubled for heartier appetites.

CHICKEN AND SAUSAGE JAMBALAYA

Yield: 4 servings.

½ pound Cajun-style andouille or other hot smoked pork sausage
1 2½ to 3½ pound fryer, cut into serving pieces
Salt to taste
Freshly ground black pepper to taste
1 cup chopped onion
1 cup chopped celery
1 teaspoon garlic, minced or pressed, or to taste
2 cups long-grain brown or white rice
2 cups homemade chicken stock, canned low-sodium broth, or water
Minced fresh parsley for garnish

◆ Slice the sausages into bite-sized pieces and place in a cast-iron Dutch oven or other deep heavy pot, with water to a depth of about 1 inch.

◆ Cook over medium-high heat until the water boils away, about 10 minutes. Continue cooking until sausage slices are lightly browned and fat is rendered, about 8 minutes more.

◆ Remove sausage slices with a slotted spoon and reserve. Leave rendered fat in pot.

◆ Salt and pepper the chicken pieces to taste. Cook in the rendered sausage fat over medium heat until browned, about 5 minutes. Remove and reserve.

◆ Add the onion and celery to the pot and sauté until soft, about 5 minutes.

◆ Add the garlic, reserved sausage and chicken, rice, and chicken stock or water. Bring to a boil, reduce the heat to low, cover, and simmer until the water evaporates and the rice is tender, about 30 minutes.

◆ Garnish with minced parsley.

CHICKEN AND WILD RICE CASSEROLE

Yield: 6 servings.

1   chicken, cooked (reserve liquid)
½   cup butter or margarine
¾   cup fresh mushrooms, sliced
¼   cup celery, sliced
¼   onion, sliced
¼   cup dry sherry
¼   cup flour
3   tablespoons fresh parsley, snipped
½   teaspoon curry powder
1   (5 ounce) can evaporated milk
1   (4.2 ounce) package long grain and wild rice
    Salt and pepper to taste

◆ Place chicken in deep pan, cover with water and simmer 1½ to 2 hours.

◆ Remove chicken, cool and remove bones and skin. Reserve liquid (strain).

◆ Dice chicken and refrigerate while making sauce.

◆ Cook rice in reserved broth following instructions on package.

◆ Meanwhile, melt the butter and sauté mushrooms, celery, and onions briefly.

◆ Add flour and stir until absorbed.

◆ Add 1¾ cups reserved broth and ¼ cup sherry all at once and stir until mixture is blended and begins to thicken.

◆ Add parsley, curry powder, and salt and pepper to taste. Simmer 5 minutes.

◆ Add evaporated milk and blend completely.

◆ Combine chicken, cooked rice and mushroom mixture in a casserole and bake at 350° (or 325° if container is glass) for 30 minutes. Sprinkle with toasted almonds.

On the Wild Side

PHEASANT IN ELEGANT ORANGE SAUCE   *Yield: 4 servings*

2   pheasant breasts, halved, boned, skin removed
2   tablespoons butter or margarine
4   teaspoons flour
¼   teaspoon ground cinnamon
½   cup orange juice
2   tablespoons orange marmalade
¾   teaspoon instant chicken bouillon
4   tablespoons orange liqueur
½   cup white seedless grapes
1   medium orange peeled, cut into sections
¼   cup toasted sliced almonds
4-6 cups cooked rice

♦ Preheat oven to 325°. Line a 13 x 9 x 2-inch rectangular pan with aluminum foil, leaving a 1½-inch foil collar. Place pheasant breasts in pan in a single layer.

♦ Melt butter in a small saucepan. Stir in flour and cinnamon until smooth.

♦ Blend in orange juice, marmalade and bouillon. Bring to a boil and stir until thickened. Stir in liqueur (you may want to add more than called for).

♦ Spoon sauce over pheasant. Cover with a sheet of foil the size of the pan plus the 1½-inch collar to allow for heat expansion. Fold edges together and seal tightly. Bake 30 minutes or until tender.

♦ Spoon grapes and orange sections over the pheasant. Bake uncovered for 5 minutes longer, or until fruit is heated through. Sprinkle with almonds. Serve with rice.

Breasts may stay more tender if left on the bone, just increase the cooking time accordingly. Don't spare the sauce, it's the best part.

CHILLED PHEASANT SALAD VINAIGRETTE

Yield: 4 to 6 servings

2-3   pheasant breasts, boneless
2   tablespoons butter or margarine
1   cup heavy cream
1   teaspoon basil
  Salt and pepper to taste
1   (14 ounce) can artichoke hearts, in brine
  Fresh greens

VINAIGRETTE DRESSING:
½   cup olive oil
1   teaspoon mustard
2   tablespoons red wine vinegar
½   garlic clove, minced

◆ To poach pheasant breasts, first toss the breasts in melted butter until they just turn white on the outside. Place in a buttered baking dish. Butter a piece of wax paper that has been cut to fit the pan, and press over the pheasant. Bake 5 minutes at 450° or until meat is just springy to the touch. Do not overcook as meat will continue to cook after removing from heat. Remove breasts from pan, saving any juice (skim off fat).

◆ Reduce the cream by bringing to a boil over a high heat. Reduce to simmer. Add basil, salt and pepper to taste. Stir often to avoid sticking. Cook until thick and about half in volume. Mix in leftover juices and cool.

◆ Slice breast meat on the diagonal.

◆ Drain artichoke hearts and soak in cold water, changing water 3 times to remove metallic taste. Cut in quarters.

◆ Combine dressing ingredients in a blender for 30 seconds.

◆ Mix vinaigrette dressing with the reduced cream mixture and pour over meat and artichoke hearts. Toss. Serve on bed of fresh greens with your choice of fresh bread.

HONEY BOURBON BIRDS

Yield: 6 servings

3   (20 ounce) game hens
2   cloves garlic
1   teaspoon salt
½   teaspoon black pepper
¼   cup honey
¼   cup bourbon
½   cup butter or margarine, melted
6   cups cooked rice

◆ Place game hens in shallow baking pan.

◆ Crush garlic with salt, then combine with pepper, honey, bourbon and melted butter or margarine.

◆ Brush hens with sauce and bake at 350° for 35 or 40 minutes, basting often with remaining sauce. Cut hens in half. Serve with rice.

COLD SPRINGS MOUNTAIN GROUSE

Yield: 4 servings

4   blue grouse or small sage grouse breasts
3   cloves of garlic sliced into slivers
½   cup soy sauce
¼   cup wine, any type
¼   cup olive oil
½   teaspoon black pepper
½   teaspoon cayenne (optional)
1   tablespoon orange zest

◆ With tip of knife, poke holes into breasts. Insert garlic slivers into holes.

◆ Combine remaining ingredients into marinade. Add breasts and let marinate 4 hours or longer.

◆ Grill breasts over medium hot coals, basting frequently with marinade. Turn once. Cook until done, approximately 15 to 20 minutes.

GRAND VALLEY HEARTY GOOSE GUMBO

Yield: 12 servings

1	wild goose, cut up
4	quarts water
2	ribs celery, whole
1	teaspoon salt
1	teaspoon pepper
1	bay leaf
1	onion, chopped
1	clove garlic
½	cup flour
¼	cup hot bacon drippings
3	medium onions, finely chopped
4	ribs celery, finely chopped
2	cloves garlic, crushed
1	(8 ounce) can tomato sauce
2	tablespoons Worcestershire sauce
1	teaspoon salt
1	package frozen okra, chopped while frozen
½	teaspoon hot pepper sauce
2	teaspoons gumbo filé
	Cooked and chopped goose meat
1	(6 ounce) box long grain and wild rice mixture (do not use seasoning packet)

◆ Make stock with first 8 ingredients by simmering goose with water and seasonings for 1½ to 2 hours in a 5 quart stock pot.

◆ Remove goose from stock. Strain and save. Cut up goose meat and chop in food processor.

◆ In heavy 5 or 6 quart stock pot, brown ½ cup flour slowly added to ¼ cup hot bacon drippings, stirring constantly until walnut colored. When roux is brown, quickly add the 3 medium onions, 4 ribs celery and 2 cloves garlic. Cook over medium heat for 5 minutes, stirring occasionally.

◆ Add stock a little at a time at first, stirring until smooth, then add last 8 ingredients.

◆ Simmer for 1 hour. If gumbo becomes too thick, add water.

This gumbo is best when made ahead, and it freezes well.

QUAIL WITH WILD RICE AND ROASTED SHALLOTS

Yield: 8 servings

8   whole quail
    Salt and pepper
1   teaspoon dried thyme, finely chopped
4   cups cooked wild rice
8   shallots, peeled and left whole
1   cup dry sherry
½   cup white wine vinegar
1   cup heavy cream
    Fresh herbs for garnish

◆ Preheat oven to **425°**.

◆ Season the cavities of the quail with a pinch of salt, pepper and thyme. Using a small spoon, fill with wild rice so the quail plump slightly.

◆ Place them in a shallow roasting pan with the peeled shallots, taking care that none of the birds touches another.

◆ Add the sherry, vinegar and any remaining thyme to the pan.

◆ Roast until the birds and the shallots are golden brown, 20 to 30 minutes. The quail are ready when a joint is pricked and the juices run pink to clear.

◆ Remove birds from the pan and arrange on a serving platter with the shallots.

◆ Pour the pan juices into a small saucepan and reduce by simmering to ¼ the original volume.

◆ Add the heavy cream and continue simmering to reduce until the sauce thickens, 5 to 10 minutes. Season to taste with salt and pepper.

◆ Serve the sauce around the birds and shallots on the platter, and garnish with fresh herbs.

M.E.'s DUCK CHORIZO

Yield: 1½ pounds

1 pound duck meat (not breast meat) or other game bird meat
½ pound pork fat or suet
4 green chilies, seeded and ground (add more if desired)
½ teaspoon oregano
½ teaspoon cilantro, chopped
½ teaspoon coriander
½ teaspoon ground cloves
½ teaspoon black pepper
4 cloves garlic, minced
2 tablespoons paprika
1½ teaspoons salt
¼ cup vinegar

◆ Chop duck meat and pork into small chunks.

◆ Use a food processor to process the fat first, then add the duck meat until you have a coarse pate' consistency.

◆ Remove from processor and add remaining ingredients.

◆ Refrigerate sausage in a plastic bag for several hours before cooking.

◆ Chorizo can be grilled, or fried in patties.

Great for breakfast or used as a stuffing. Add to cheese for con queso dip. You can also add jalapeños to make a more spicy blend.

CRISP DUCK WITH PALISADE PEACHES

Yield: 10 servings

5 5 pound ducks
Salt and pepper
½ cup honey
⅓ cup cider vinegar
2 cups veal or chicken stock
4½ cups fresh Palisade peaches (or canned peaches, in syrup)
¼ cup butter or margarine
2 pounds fresh spinach, blanched
Zest of 5 limes, lightly blanched

◆ Preheat oven to 400°.

◆ Roast ducks by seasoning them with salt and pepper and placing them breast side down in a hot roasting pan.

◆ Cook approximately 45 minutes, then turn over and cook for 20 more minutes.

◆ Remove from oven and take out breast bone (optional).

◆ To prepare sauce, boil together honey and vinegar to a light syrup, add stock and peach juice. Reduce to thicken.

◆ At serving time, quickly blend in butter or margarine.

◆ For each serving, slice duck and arrange with peaches on a bed of blanched spinach. Garnish with blanched lime zest. Serve the sauce on the side.

BRAISED DUCK PULLMAN STYLE

Yield: 4 servings

STUFFED DUCK:

1	5-6 pound duck
	Salt and pepper
3	tablespoons butter or margarine
¼	cup onion, chopped fine
1	cup rice, uncooked
2½	cups chicken broth
¼	cup butter
½	teaspoon salt
1	large celery stalk, whole
1	large carrot, whole
1	small onion, whole
1	cup water

SAUCE:

1	teaspoon flour
1	cup duck or chicken stock
1	large navel orange
⅓	cup Burgundy wine
¼	teaspoon English mustard
1	teaspoon Worcestershire sauce
1	tablespoon currant jelly
	Dash of cayenne

◆ Preheat oven to **325°**.

◆ Sprinkle cavity of duck with salt and pepper and wipe to distribute evenly.

◆ For stuffing, melt butter in 1 quart saucepan over medium heat and sauté chopped onion until tender.

◆ Add rice and continue cooking until rice turns yellow.

◆ Meanwhile, bring chicken broth to a boil. Add broth, ¼ cup butter and salt to sautéed onion-rice mixture. Cover and simmer until moisture is absorbed by rice, about 30 minutes.

◆ Stuff and truss duck and place on a wire rack in roasting pan, breast up.

◆ Add celery, carrot, whole onion and water.

◆ Place in oven and bake 25 minutes per pound (about 2½ hours) basting occasionally.

◆ Remove baked duck from roasting pan, place on a platter, and keep warm. Drain excess fat off remaining liquid. Sprinkle flour in pan, stirring constantly to mix.

◆ Meanwhile, in a small saucepan, heat duck stock and add to drippings, stirring constantly. Simmer for 20 minutes, stirring occasionally.

◆ Peel orange and remove white membrane from peel. Cut the peel into narrow strips and place in small saucepan with water to cover. Bring peel and water to a boil and continue boiling for 5

Continued on next page

Braised Duck Pullman Style (Continued)

minutes.

◆ Drain peeled strips and add to hot mixture.

◆ Add wine, mustard, Worcestershire sauce, jelly and cayenne and heat through.

◆ Separate orange into sections, removing all white membrane.

◆ Place the duck on a serving platter. Arrange orange sections in two rows over the duck. Ladle a few spoonfuls of sauce over the duck and serve remaining sauce with individual portions.

SWEET AND SOUR DUCK

Yield: 4 servings

MEAT:
2 ducks, meat cubed
½ cup flour
¼ cup cornstarch
¼ teaspoon baking powder
¼ teaspoon salt
¾ cup water
Oil

SAUCE:
¾ cup ketchup
¼ cup white vinegar
3 tablespoons sugar
1 cup juice from canned pineapple
½ cup white onion, chopped
1 cup green pepper, chopped
1 (15 ounce) can pineapple chunks, reserve juice
4 cups cooked rice

◆ Mix together flour, corn starch, baking powder, salt and water to make a batter.

◆ Dip the meat cubes in the batter and fry in oil until browned. Make ahead and keep warm in the oven.

◆ Combine ketchup, vinegar, sugar and pineapple juice. Bring to a boil and thicken.

◆ Add onion and green pepper and cook over high heat for 1 minute.

◆ Add pineapple, stir to mix.

◆ Remove from heat, add meat and serve with rice.

◎ ORIENTAL BARBECUE DUCK SALAD

Yield: 4 servings

2 cloves garlic, minced
3 tablespoons soy sauce
2 tablespoons dry sherry
1 teaspoon fresh grated ginger
½ tablespoon brown sugar
½ tablespoon sesame oil
¼ teaspoon cinnamon
¼ teaspoon ground fennel
¼ teaspoon anise
¼ teaspoon ground cloves
1 tablespoon ketchup
4 duck breasts, deboned
Salad greens, Bibb lettuce (or personal favorite)
Quartered cherry tomatoes for garnish
Red wine for sauce (optional)

SAUCE:

◆ Combine all ingredients except duck, greens, tomatoes and wine.

◆ Coat meat with sauce in a plastic bag or container. Refrigerate 2 hours or more.

◆ Grill duck breasts five minutes on each side until duck is just pink in the middle. Chill.

◆ Slice duck breasts and arrange on a bed of greens. Garnish with quartered cherry tomatoes.

◆ Leftover sauce can be heated and diluted with red wine to taste. After cooking, cool sauce mix and use as a dressing for the salad.

ELK TERIYAKI

Yield: 2 to 4 servings

1 pound elk round steak, sliced thin
3 tablespoons olive oil
½ large onion, diced
1 clove garlic, diced
1 Anaheim pepper, diced (mild)
¼ cup soy sauce
¼ cup teriyaki sauce
¼ cup Burgundy wine
Pepper to taste
4 cups cooked rice

◆ Fry sliced round steak in olive oil. When it starts to juice, cover and cook over low-medium heat until juice is gone and it starts to fry.

◆ Add onion, garlic, and Anaheim pepper; cook until soft.

◆ Add soy sauce, teriyaki sauce, wine and pepper; cook until absorbed into meat on medium heat, and it starts to fry again. Serve with rice.

WEST SLOPE ELK STROGANOFF

Yield: 4 to 6 servings

2 pounds elk round steak
  Salt and pepper to taste
3 tablespoons butter or margarine
2½ tablespoons flour
1 cup beef stock
1 teaspoon Dijon mustard
2 tablespoons olive oil
1½ cups sliced fresh mushrooms
2 cloves garlic, minced
⅓ cup red Burgundy wine
1 pound egg noodles
2 teaspoons butter or margarine
⅓ cup sour cream
  Freshly chopped parsley

◆ Cut elk into ½-inch to 2-inch cubes. Season to taste with salt and pepper, then refrigerate covered for 1 hour.

◆ In a small saucepan, melt butter or margarine over medium low heat. Add flour and whisk constantly until it comes away from the pan and is slightly browned.

◆ Warm the beef stock in a separate pan, then add it to the flour mixture slowly, whisking constantly until mixture is thick and smooth. Add mustard, stir, and remove from heat.

◆ In a large skillet, heat oil over high heat and brown the cubed meat. Add mushrooms and stir until mushrooms are browned, then turn down heat to medium low.

◆ Add stock and flour mixture to meat mixture; stir in garlic and wine. Simmer over low heat.

◆ Meanwhile, cook egg noodles according to package instructions. Drain and add 2 teaspoons butter, stir until melted.

◆ Fold sour cream into meat mixture just before serving.

◆ Serve meat over a nest of buttered noodles. Garnish with fresh parsley.

WESTERN COLORADO ELK CURRY

Yield: 8 servings

4-5 pounds elk sirloin, cubed
4 tablespoons olive oil
1½ large onions, finely sliced
2-3 cloves garlic, chopped fine
2 cardamom seeds
1 2-inch stick cinnamon
1 tablespoon ground coriander
1 tablespoon curry powder
1 (30 ounce) can tomatoes
Salt to taste
1 tablespoon vinegar
2 teaspoons sugar
6 cups cooked rice

CONDIMENTS:
Minced tomatoes
Chopped green peppers
Chopped hard boiled eggs
Sliced green onions
Chopped peanuts
Chutney
Bacon bits

◆ Brown elk cubes in oil, adding onions to sauté until just limp.
◆ Add garlic and spices.
◆ Add tomatoes and juice, simmer 5 minutes.
◆ Add enough water to just cover meat and simmer uncovered until meat is tender, about 2½ hours. Add water if necessary during this time.
◆ Just before serving, stir in vinegar and sugar.
◆ Serve over rice. Place separate bowls with condiments on table and have diners sprinkle a little of each on top of the meat mixture.

Note: Meat mixture may be made ahead of time, and it freezes well. Do not add vinegar and sugar for freezing. Follow the recipe.

COLORADO VENISON CHILI

Yield: 10 servings

½ pound venison hamburger (elk hamburger may be substituted)
1 pound venison bulk sausage (pork sausage may be substituted)
1 large onion, chopped
1 clove garlic, diced
1 (32 ounce) can tomato sauce
2 tablespoons chili powder
1 teaspoon oregano
½ teaspoon thyme
1 bay leaf
1 (32 ounce) can red kidney beans, drained
½ green pepper, chopped

◆ Brown hamburger and sausage in a 5 quart pot. Drain.
◆ Add onions and garlic and sauté with meat.
◆ Add tomato sauce, chili powder, oregano, thyme, bay leaf, kidney beans and green pepper. Simmer, covered, for 1 hour or longer.

Variation: For a more spicy chili, use green chilies or jalapeños instead of green pepper. Serve with warm flour tortillas or corn bread.

GRILLED VENISON WITH APRICOT AND GREEN PEPPERCORN GLAZE

Yield: 4 servings

GRILLED VENISON:

1½ pounds boneless venison loin, cut into medallions, if desired

¼ cup olive oil

2 tablespoons mixed herbs (rosemary, thyme, marjoram, etc.), finely chopped

6 whole cloves garlic, split in half

◆ Marinate the venison with the olive oil, fresh herbs and garlic in a shallow dish. Cover with plastic wrap and refrigerate for at least 3 hours (overnight is preferable, if time allows).

APRICOT GREEN PEPPERCORN GLAZE:

¼ cup garlic, finely minced

½ cup shallots, finely minced

2 tablespoons olive oil

2 cups Marsala wine

¼ cup balsamic vinegar

¼ cup canned green peppercorns, drained

1 cup dried apricots, julienned

2 quarts game stock or mixture of beef and chicken stocks
Salt and pepper

◆ In a large saucepan over medium heat, sauté the minced garlic and shallots in the olive oil, stirring frequently as the mixture begins to brown (3 to 5 minutes).

◆ When evenly golden brown, add the wine, vinegar, peppercorns and apricots. Allow the mixture to reduce slightly.

◆ Add the stock and reduce by about ½, or until the sauce will coat a spoon (30 minutes or more). Lower the heat to warm and season to taste with salt and pepper.

◆ Charcoal grill or pan fry the venison to your preference (3 to 5 minutes per side). Serve on a bed of Apricot-Peppercorn glaze.

VENISON WITH STONE FRUITS AND BERRY SAUCE

Yield: 4 servings

BERRY SAUCE:

2 cups cranberry juice
2 cups pineapple juice
1 teaspoon shallots, chopped
2 quarts venison stock, or combination of chicken and beef stock
1 bay leaf
1 sprig fresh thyme
Salt and pepper to taste

VENISON:

4 2 ounce venison medallions
2 tablespoons butter
2 peaches, cut in wedges
2 apricots, cut in wedges
¼ cup raspberries
¼ pound butter or margarine

◆ For sauce: slightly reduce fruit juices and shallots in a large saucepan over medium-high heat.

◆ Add stock, bay leaf and thyme. Reduce by ½ (about 30 minutes) and strain, season with salt and pepper to taste.

◆ Sauté venison medallions quickly in 2 tablespoons butter (cook to medium rare).

◆ Remove medallions and add sauce to pan. Add fruit (raspberries last).

◆ Over low heat, warm sauce. Add butter and stir to melt. Season with salt and pepper.

◆ To serve, pass sauce to use for dipping.

JUNG'S BEST BIRD MARINADE

Yield: 3 cups

1 cup gin
1 cup olive oil
1 cup soy sauce (low sodium is best)
Sugar and grated ginger root to taste

◆ Combine gin, olive oil and soy sauce.

◆ Add sugar and ginger root to taste.

◆ Marinate game birds several hours or overnight, then grill.

Large batches can be made by using equal parts of gin, olive oil and soy sauce. This marinade works extremely well on all types of game birds; grouse, sage hen, pheasant, duck and dove.

Farmers' Market

• HIGH MOUNTAIN PASTURE ON DALLAS DIVIDE •

ROASTED GREEN BEANS, ONION AND GARLIC

Yield: 4 servings

3-4 tablespoons olive oil
1 pound fresh green beans, cleaned, trimmed and patted dry
1 medium red onion, cut in thin rings or slices
6-8 medium-sized garlic cloves, peeled and cut in half lengthwise
½ teaspoon salt
1-2 tablespoons balsamic vinegar (or other fruity vinegar)
Freshly ground black pepper

◆ Preheat oven to 400°. Brush large baking sheet with 2 tablespoons of the olive oil.

◆ Spread beans, onions, and garlic on sheet. Salt lightly and drizzle with rest of oil.

◆ Bake vegetables 20 to 30 minutes. While baking, stir or shake pan several times.

◆ Remove when all vegetables are tender. Transfer to bowl.

◆ Drizzle immediately with vinegar. Add fresh ground pepper to taste.

Note: Can serve hot, warm or cold.

GREEN BEANS ELEGANT

Yield: 8 servings

2 (16 ounce) cans green beans (may also be fresh or frozen)
¼ cup Italian dressing
½ cup mayonnaise
2 tablespoons Parmesan cheese, grated
Fresh tomato for garnish (wedged)

◆ Drain green beans. Place in 2-quart casserole dish.

◆ Combine Italian dressing with mayonnaise and pour over beans.

◆ Garnish with fresh tomatoes. Sprinkle with Parmesan cheese.

◆ Bake in 350° oven for 10 to 15 minutes.

HERBED GREEN BEANS

Yield: 6 servings

1½ pounds fresh green beans
4 tablespoons olive oil
2-3 cloves garlic, minced
¼ cup onion, chopped
¾ cup green pepper, diced
¼ cup boiling water
¾ teaspoon salt
1 teaspoon dried basil
½ cup Parmesan cheese, grated

◆ Cut beans into 1-inch pieces.

◆ Heat oil in heavy pan. Add onion, green pepper, and garlic and cook slowly 3 to 6 minutes.

◆ Add green beans, water, salt, and basil. Cover and simmer 10 to 12 minutes, until beans are tender.

◆ Stir in half of cheese. Sprinkle with remaining cheese and serve.

SHERRIED ONION GRATIN

Yield: 8 to 10 servings

4 cups onions, thinly sliced (about 2 very large onions)
3 tablespoons vegetable oil
¼ cup cooking sherry
2 tablespoons unsalted butter
2 tablespoons flour
¼ teaspoon white pepper
½ teaspoon salt
Pinch of nutmeg
⅔ cup chicken broth
French bread, sliced
1½ cups Swiss or Gruyère cheese, grated
3 tablespoons unsalted butter

◆ Cook onions in oil over moderate heat until golden, but not browned (about 20 to 30 minutes). Stir frequently.

◆ Add sherry and cook the mixture, stirring until most of the liquid is evaporated.

◆ While onions are cooking, melt 2 tablespoons butter in saucepan over moderately low heat. Add flour, salt, pepper and nutmeg.

◆ Cook roux, whisking about 3 minutes. Add broth gradually, whisking for about 2 minutes more.

◆ Combine sauce with onions.

◆ Spread mixture in buttered 14- to 15-inch oval gratin dish (or 2-quart baking dish).

◆ Butter 1 side of each slice of bread with softened butter. Arrange buttered side up, overlapping slightly, on the onion mixture. Layer grated cheese on top.

◆ Bake in preheated 425° oven for 10 to 15 minutes, or until cheese is melted and bubbling.

Note: The sherried onion part of this recipe may be prepared 2 days in advance and kept covered in baking dish in the refrigerator. Before adding bread, reheat mixture, covered with foil, in a preheated 425° oven for 20 minutes, or until thoroughly heated through.

BAKED ACORN SQUASH WITH CRANBERRY-ORANGE COMPOTE

Yield: 12 servings

3 small acorn squash
6 ounces butter, melted
4 ounces brown sugar (or honey or maple syrup)
Salt and pepper to taste

COMPOTE:
1 pound cranberries
6 ounces orange juice
2 ounces orange zest, blanched
Water and sugar as needed

◆ Cut squash into quarters and remove seeds.

◆ Combine butter and brown sugar. Brush the glaze on the squash. Season squash with salt and pepper. Reserve any excess butter and sugar.

◆ Bake the squash quarters at 300° in oven until they are tender. Baste them periodically with the reserved butter and sugar mixture.

◆ COMPOTE: Combine the cranberries, orange juice and water as needed to barely cover the berries. Add sugar to taste. Simmer the berries over medium heat until they soften and thicken. Add the orange zest.

◆ To serve, spoon the hot cranberry mixture over the squash.

This recipe comes from Eric Flatt (the son of a charter Junior Service League member), the owner and executive chef of the Tonto Bar and Grill at Rancho Mañana Golf Course in Cave Creek, Arizona.

YAMS AND APPLES

Yield: 10 to 12 servings

1 cup sugar
3 tablespoons cornstarch
1¾ cups water
1 teaspoon salt
½ cup butter or margarine
5 yams, par-boiled and sliced
5 apples, cored, peeled and sliced
Cinnamon to taste

◆ Combine sugar, cornstarch, water, salt and butter. Cook until thick.

◆ Layer yams and apples in 9 x 13-inch baking dish.

◆ Sprinkle cinnamon between layers. Pour sauce over all and bake 1 hour at 350°.

This is a great Thanksgiving dish!

THANKSGIVING SQUASH

Yield: 8 to 10 servings

2 pounds yellow crookneck squash
4 eggs, beaten
1 cup Cheddar cheese, grated
4 tablespoons butter
⅓ cup onion, chopped
⅓ cup green pepper, chopped
⅓ cup red pepper, chopped
½ cup pecans, chopped
1 cup bread crumbs
Dash of hot pepper sauce
Salt to taste

◆ Slice squash. Cook in boiling water until tender, about 5 minutes. Drain well.

◆ Mash squash. Add beaten eggs and cheese.

◆ Sauté onion and peppers in butter.

◆ Combine squash mixture, vegetables, pecans, bread crumbs, hot pepper sauce, and salt.

◆ Put in 1 quart casserole and bake at 350° for 35 to 40 minutes, or until casserole sets.

GRILLED GARLIC SQUASH

Yield: 4 servings

1 clove garlic, minced
1 teaspoon olive oil
1 teaspoon water
1 teaspoon basil
¼ teaspoon lemon pepper
¼ teaspoon salt
2 medium zucchini, cut in half lengthwise
2 medium yellow squash, cut in half lengthwise

◆ Combine garlic, oil, water and seasonings.

◆ Brush cut surfaces of squash with half of garlic mixture.

◆ Place vegetables on clean, preheated grill, cut side down.

◆ Grill for 4 minutes. Turn and brush with remaining mixture.

◆ Cook for 4 more minutes, or until tender.

CRANBERRY RED CABBAGE

Yield: 4 to 6 servings

1 red cabbage, shredded
½ cup onion, chopped
½ cup fresh cranberries
½ cup brown sugar, packed
3 tablespoons oil
1 cup red wine

◆ Combine all ingredients in a sauté pan and cook until tender but still crisp.

This unusual recipe comes from one of our Southern cooks.

COLCANNON

Yield: 4 servings

½ cup onion, leek or scallions, finely chopped
¼ cup butter
¼ cup milk
1 pound potatoes, cooked and mashed
1½ cups cabbage, cooked

♦ Gently fry onion in melted butter until soft.

♦ Add milk and mashed potatoes and stir until heated through.

♦ Finely chop cabbage and beat into mixture in pan over a low heat until all the mixture is pale green and fluffy.

A real comfort food!

ROASTED PARMESAN POTATO WEDGES

Yield: 6 to 8 servings

½-¾ cup margarine
Crushed garlic to taste (or use 1 to 2 teaspoons garlic powder)
6 baking potatoes
1 cup Italian bread crumbs
½ cup Parmesan cheese, grated
Salt and pepper to taste

♦ Melt butter and add garlic.

♦ Peel potatoes and slice lengthwise into quarters.

♦ Mix bread crumbs and cheese.

♦ Roll potatoes in butter, then in the bread crumb mixture. Sprinkle with salt and pepper.

♦ Roast at 350° on a baking sheet until golden brown, about 45 minutes.

POTATO BACON CASSEROLE

Yield: 4 servings

5 medium potatoes, leave skins on and cut in ½-inch cubes
5 slices uncooked bacon, diced
1 teaspoon lemon pepper
1 teaspoon dried parsley flakes
½ teaspoon garlic powder
¼ teaspoon onion powder
4 tablespoons margarine or butter

♦ Spray a 2-quart casserole with non-stick vegetable spray.

♦ Mix ingredients and top with the margarine.

♦ Cover and bake at 325° for 1½ hours. (May need to stir during baking.)

FARMERS' MARKET VEGETABLE ROAST

Yield: 8 servings

4 tomatoes
1 medium eggplant
4 small zucchini
1 red onion
3 tablespoons olive oil
2 garlic cloves, very thinly sliced
½ cup fresh basil leaves (or 1 tablespoon dried)
¼ cup parsley, chopped
2 tablespoons fresh thyme leaves (or 2 teaspoons dried)
Salt
Freshly ground pepper

◆ Heat oven to 400°.

◆ Cut tomatoes, eggplant, and zucchini into ¼-inch slices. Cut onion into thin wedges.

◆ Sprinkle 1 tablespoon olive oil over bottom of a 9 x 13-inch glass baking dish.

◆ Layer half the eggplant, tomatoes, and zucchini. Tuck in half the onion wedges. Scatter with half the garlic and herbs. Sprinkle on salt, pepper, and 1 tablespoon oil.

◆ Repeat with remaining ingredients. Cover with foil and bake 20 minutes.

◆ Uncover and baste with accumulated juices; replace foil and cook 20 minutes longer.

◆ Remove foil and cook about 10 more minutes.

Variation: Substitute mushrooms and asparagus for the eggplant.

TOFU, HERBS AND VEGETABLES

Yield: 4 to 5 servings

2 cups onions, chopped
4 large garlic cloves, minced coarsely
1 tablespoon olive oil
3-4 cups broccoli flowerets, cut into 1½-inch pieces
10 mushrooms, sliced
½ pound firm tofu, cut into ½-inch cubes
1 small red pepper, minced coarsely
2 tablespoons fresh basil (or 2 teaspoons dried)
¼ teaspoon dried thyme
  Pepper to taste
¾ cup cooked brown rice
½ cup Cheddar or Monterey Jack cheese
  Soy sauce (optional)

◆ In wok or large heavy skillet, sauté onions and half of garlic in the oil for 5 minutes over medium heat.

◆ Add broccoli and mushrooms and sauté 5 minutes more.

◆ Add tofu, red pepper, herbs, and black pepper. Cook another 8 to 10 minutes, until ingredients are just tender.

◆ During last 2 minutes of cooking time, add rest of garlic and cooked rice.

◆ Sprinkle with cheese and stir until melted, or broil lightly.

◆ Serve with soy sauce, if desired.

CALICO BEAN BAKE

Yield: 10 to 12 servings

½ pound hamburger
½ cup ketchup
1 cup onion, chopped
1 teaspoon salt
½ pound bacon, fried, drained and crumbled
¾ cup brown sugar
1 teaspoon mustard
2 teaspoons vinegar
1 (26 or 27 ounce) can pork and beans
1 (15 ounce) can lima beans
1 (15 ounce) can kidney beans

◆ Brown hamburger in skillet. Add ketchup, onion and salt. Sauté until onions are tender.

◆ Combine meat mixture with remaining ingredients in an oven-proof 2-quart casserole dish and bake for 40 minutes at **350°**.

Variation: This can also be done in a crock pot. Cook for 4 hours on high.

VEGETABLE MELANGE

Yield: 4 servings

DRESSING:
1 cup mayonnaise
1 cup plain yogurt
1 clove garlic, crushed
1 tablespoon fresh parsley, chopped
1 teaspoon dried basil
1 teaspoon onion, chopped
¼ teaspoon salt
3 teaspoons dried thyme

VEGETABLES:
2 tablespoons oil
¼ cup onion, chopped
¾ cup pearl onions, peeled and cooked
1 clove garlic, crushed
¾ cup zucchini, sliced with skin on
½ cup green pepper, diced
¼ teaspoon salt
¼ teaspoon pepper
1 (7.25 ounce) can small whole carrots
¾ cup tomatoes, cubed
4 cooked artichokes

◆ DRESSING: Combine dressing ingredients and chill.

◆ VEGETABLES: Heat oil in a large skillet. Add onions and garlic. Sauté onions until tender, approximately 2 minutes.

◆ Add zucchini, green pepper, salt and pepper. Sauté for 2 minutes more. Remove from heat.

◆ Add carrots and tomatoes. Cover and chill.

◆ Pull out centers of artichokes gently. Scoop out all "choke" until clean.

◆ Spoon vegetable mixture into artichokes. Chill.

◆ Serve artichokes with dressing on the side.

BEST BEETS

Yield: 6 to 8 servings

¾ cup sugar
2 teaspoons cornstarch
⅓ cup vinegar
⅓ cup beet liquid (reserved from cooking beets)
1 teaspoon dry mustard
4 cups beets, cooked and sliced (can be canned)
3 tablespoons butter
¼ teaspoon salt
Pepper to taste
1 teaspoon onion powder

◆ Combine sugar and cornstarch in saucepan.

◆ Add vinegar and beet juice; bring to a boil.

◆ Add remaining ingredients; reduce heat and simmer until heated through.

BROCCOLI, PEPPERS AND FETA

Yield: 4 servings

1 large bunch broccoli
1-2 tablespoons olive oil
2 garlic cloves, thinly sliced
10 Kalamata olives, chopped
3 tablespoons roasted** peppers, diced
2 teaspoons fresh marjoram, chopped (or ½ teaspoon dried)
1 tablespoon parsley, finely chopped
2 ounces feta cheese
Salt and pepper to taste
Lemon wedges for garnish

◆ Cut broccoli into fairly large flowerets. Set aside stalks for another purpose.

◆ Steam broccoli to desired firmness. While steaming, prepare rest of ingredients.

◆ When broccoli is cooked, heat oil in large heavy skillet with the sliced garlic.

◆ Remove garlic when browned. Add broccoli, olives, peppers, marjoram, and parsley. Sauté over medium heat until all is warm.

◆ Scatter cheese over vegetables. Season with salt and pepper. Serve warm with lemon wedges.

**Hint: To roast peppers, char with oven broiler or gas burner. When uniformly charred, place in bowl, cover with a plate and let steam for 10 minutes. (Some people put peppers in a paper bag instead of a covered bowl.) Then carefully scrape away charred peel, cut open and scrape out seeds.

BROCCOLI AND CREAM CHEESE

Yield: 8 servings

1½-2   pounds broccoli, cut
   5   tablespoons margarine, divided
   2   tablespoons flour
  ¼   teaspoon salt
     Dash pepper
   1   cup milk
   3   ounces cream cheese
  ½   cup onions, chopped
  ½   cup sharp American cheese, shredded
   1   cup soft bread crumbs

◆ Boil water in a large saucepan. Add broccoli and cook until tender but firm (5 to 10 minutes). Drain.

◆ In a small saucepan over medium heat, melt 2 tablespoons margarine. Blend in flour, salt and pepper.

◆ Add milk and cook, stirring constantly until bubbly. Reduce heat to low.

◆ Blend in cream cheese until smooth.

◆ Place broccoli and onion in 1½-quart casserole, pour sauce over and mix lightly. Top with shredded cheese.

◆ Melt 3 tablespoons margarine, toss with bread crumbs and sprinkle on top of casserole.

◆ Bake at **350°** for 40 minutes.

This is a nice accompaniment to almost any entrée.

ASPEN CARROTS

Yield: 8 servings

   8   carrots
   1   large onion, minced
  ½   green pepper, minced
   3   tablespoons butter
   1   large clove garlic, minced
   3   sprigs parsley, minced
  ½   teaspoon salt
  ⅛   teaspoon pepper

◆ Peel and cut carrots into matchstick-size pieces. Cook in boiling water until almost tender, about 10 minutes. Drain.

◆ Melt butter in frying pan over low heat. Add onion, garlic, green pepper and parsley.

◆ Cover and sauté gently until soft, 10 to 15 minutes. Stir frequently. Do not brown.

◆ Add carrots. Cover and cook until carrots are tender, 8 to 10 minutes. Season with salt and pepper.

BRAISED CARROTS WITH MUSHROOMS AND ARTICHOKES

Yield: 6 servings

1½ pounds carrots, peeled and sliced into 1-inch chunks (about 5½ cups)
1 tablespoon sugar
1½ cups water
1½ tablespoons butter
½ teaspoon salt
Fresh ground pepper to taste
½ pound fresh mushrooms, quartered
1 tablespoon oil
1½ tablespoons butter
1 (10 ounce) package frozen artichoke hearts, thawed
½ cup chicken bouillon

◆ In a 2-quart saucepan, combine carrots, sugar, water, butter, salt and pepper.

◆ Cover and boil slowly for 30 to 40 minutes or until carrots are tender and liquid has evaporated. Set aside while preparing mushrooms and artichokes.

◆ Sauté mushrooms in oil and butter until lightly browned. Add artichokes.

◆ Combine mushrooms and artichokes with carrots.

◆ Add bouillon and boil slowly for 4 to 5 minutes until the stock has almost completely evaporated.

◆ Correct seasoning; place in 2-quart casserole to serve.

GLAZED CARROTS

Yield: 4 servings

1 pound carrots, pared, sliced, cooked and drained
½ cup orange marmalade
2 teaspoons cornstarch
1 tablespoon margarine
⅛ teaspoon ground nutmeg
2 tablespoons slivered almonds, toasted

◆ In medium saucepan, stir together marmalade and cornstarch.

◆ Add carrots, margarine and nutmeg.

◆ Cook over medium heat until slightly thickened and heated through, stirring occasionally for about 8 to 10 minutes.

◆ Turn into serving bowl and garnish with almonds.

RUBY CARROTS

Yield: 8 servings

2 pounds carrots, peeled and cut into slices
1 cup seedless red grapes, halved
¼ cup honey
2 tablespoons butter
⅛ teaspoon ground ginger

- Preheat oven to **250°**.
- Steam carrots until tender, about 20 minutes.
- Combine carrots with other ingredients in a covered casserole. Warm in oven for 15 minutes.

SCALLOPED SPINACH

Yield: 8 to 10 servings

1 (10 ounce) package frozen chopped spinach, thawed, drained and squeezed dry
2 cups milk
2 eggs, beaten
2 cups bread, broken in small pieces (white bread is best), divided
4 tablespoons butter or margarine, melted
2 tablespoons minced dry onion
½ cup bacon, cooked (not too crisp) and chopped (optional)
Salt and pepper to taste

- Combine spinach, milk, eggs, 1½ cups of the bread pieces, melted butter, salt, pepper, and dry onion, mixing well.
- Pour into greased 1½-quart casserole.
- Sprinkle remaining ½ cup bread pieces and chopped bacon on top.
- Bake at **350°** for 45 minutes until set.

Variation: Substitute English muffins cut in little squares for bread pieces

SPINACH CRÊPES

Yield: 12 crêpes

CRÊPES
- 1 cup flour
- 3 tablespoons sugar
- ¼ teaspoon salt
- 4 eggs
- ½ cup milk
- ½ cup heavy cream
- ⅛ cup slivered almonds
- 2 tablespoons maple syrup
- 1 teaspoon butter

SPINACH FILLING:
- 1½ cups fresh spinach, cooked
- 1 cup ricotta cheese
- 2 tablespoons onion, minced
- ½ teaspoon salt
- ½ teaspoon pepper
- 12 slices Gruyère cheese

CHEESE AND CREAM SAUCE:
- 2 tablespoons butter
- 2 tablespoons flour
- 1 cup milk, scalded
- 2 tablespoons Gruyère cheese
- ⅓ cup heavy cream
- ½ teaspoon salt
- ½ teaspoon white pepper

◆ Preparing the combination: Begin with the Spinach Filling and the Cream and Cheese Sauce. Place them on low heat while preparing the crêpes.

◆ SPINACH FILLING: Heat all filling ingredients (except Gruyère slices) in a saucepan.

◆ CREAM AND CHEESE SAUCE: Prepare white sauce in saucepan using flour, butter, and milk. Heat until boiling, blend in cream and cheese until melted. Add salt and pepper.

◆ CRÊPES: Mix all crêpe ingredients in blender. Butter crêpe pan with about one teaspoon of butter and then fry crêpes.

◆ To assemble the crêpes: Place a slice of Gruyère cheese in the center of each crêpe, cover with the spinach filling, fold the crêpe, and then heat in 350° oven until the cheese melts, about 5 minutes.

◆ Top with cheese and cream sauce, and serve immediately. Grated Parmesan cheese may be sprinkled on top if desired.

Variation: As an alternative to the spinach filling, cooked crab meat can be added to the cheese and cream sauce and used as a filling. Remember to save some of the cheese and cream sauce for topping.

This recipe won first prize in a culinary contest sponsored by a Boulder newspaper.

SAUTÉED MUSHROOMS AND SPINACH WITH SHALLOTS

Yield: 6 servings

3 bunches fresh spinach, stemmed
4 large shallots, peeled
2 tablespoons olive oil
2 tablespoons butter or margarine
1½ pounds fresh mushrooms (shiitake, morels, or button), thinly sliced
½ teaspoon salt
¼ teaspoon ground nutmeg
¼ teaspoon pepper

- Rinse spinach. Drain thoroughly.
- Chop spinach coarsely. (A food processor works well using on/off turns - do in 3 batches).
- Transfer to heavy large saucepan or sauté pan. Using only water clinging to leaves, cook spinach over high heat until just wilted, stirring often, about 5 minutes.
- Wrap spinach in towel to squeeze out moisture. (Can be prepared 1 day ahead. Refrigerate in towel).
- Mince shallots. Heat olive oil and butter or margarine in a heavy large skillet and cook until soft but not brown, stirring frequently, about 3 minutes.
- Add mushrooms, salt, pepper, and nutmeg. Cook until mushrooms begin to soften, stirring frequently, about 6 minutes.
- Add spinach. Toss until vegetables are combined and heated through, about 4 minutes.
- Do not overcook. Season to taste.

SPINACH ARTICHOKE CASSEROLE

Yield: 6 servings

3 (10 ounce) packages frozen chopped spinach, thawed, drained, and squeezed dry
2 (6 ounce) jars marinated artichoke hearts, drained
1 (8 ounce) package cream cheese
4 tablespoons margarine
6 tablespoons milk
⅓ cup Parmesan cheese, grated

- Combine spinach and artichoke hearts.
- In a separate bowl, combine remaining ingredients.
- Place artichoke-spinach mixture in a 1½-quart casserole and spread cheese mixture on top.
- Refrigerate for 24 hours.
- Bake at **375°** for 40 minutes.

SPINACH, PEA, AND RED PEPPER TIMBALES

Yield: 8 timbales

1 large red pepper, cut into ¼-inch pieces
1 tablespoon unsalted butter
1 (10 ounce) package frozen chopped spinach, thawed, drained, and squeezed dry
1 (10 ounce) package frozen peas, thawed and drained
1 teaspoon dried chervil
¾ cup canned chicken broth
1 tablespoon sugar
Freshly ground pepper and salt to taste
3 eggs, slightly beaten

♦ In a small skillet, cook the red pepper in butter over moderately low heat, stirring, until soft.

♦ Remove skillet from heat, and let mixture cool.

♦ In a food processor, purée the spinach, peas and chervil with broth, sugar, black pepper and salt to taste.

♦ In a bowl, combine the purée, pepper mixture, and eggs and divide the mixture among 8 buttered ½ cup timbale molds.

♦ Put the molds in a baking pan, add enough hot water to the pan to reach halfway up the sides of the molds, and bake timbales in a preheated **400°** oven for 35 minutes, or until a knife comes out clean.

*Note: The timbales can be made 1 day in advance and kept covered and chilled. To reheat the timbales, unmold them into a glass baking dish large enough to just hold them, add about 2 tablespoons hot water to the dish, or enough to barely cover the bottom, and reheat the timbales, covered with foil, in a preheated **500°** oven for 15 minutes. Invert the timbales onto a platter or individual plates.*

Anything's Pastable

CHICKEN AND SHRIMP FETTUCCINE

Yield: 6 servings

1 whole, large chicken breast
½ pound large raw shrimp
½ pound fresh spinach
1 pound mushrooms
1 (12 ounce) package fettuccine
2 tablespoons dry sherry
1 tablespoon cornstarch
1 teaspoon ginger root, grated or ¼ teaspoon ground ginger
½ teaspoon salt
Salad oil
3 tablespoons soy sauce
Red pepper strips for garnish

◆ Remove skin and bone from chicken breast. Cut each breast in half crosswise into ½-inch strips. Shell and devein shrimp. Coarsely slice spinach, and cut mushrooms in quarters if large.

◆ Prepare fettuccine according to label. Drain and keep warm.

◆ Meanwhile, in bowl, toss chicken, shrimp, sherry, cornstarch, ginger, and salt. Set aside.

◆ Heat 2 tablespoons oil in 2–quart saucepan over high heat. Add mushrooms and soy sauce and heat to boiling, stirring occasionally. Reduce heat to low; cover and simmer 5 minutes.

◆ In 4–quart saucepan over high heat, in ¼ cup very hot salad oil, cook shrimp–chicken mixture 2 minutes or until shrimp is tender and chicken loses its pink color, stirring quickly and constantly.

◆ Spoon fettuccine onto platter; top with spinach and shrimp–chicken mixture. Spoon mushroom sauce over shrimp–chicken mixture. Garnish with red pepper strips. Toss before serving.

GREEN GROCER LASAGNA

Yield: 6 to 8 servings

8 ounces lasagna noodles
2 cups ricotta cheese
2 eggs
8 ounces asparagus, trimmed
  and sliced ½-inch thick
1 (6 ounce) jar marinated
  artichoke hearts, drained
¾ cup parsley, chopped
⅔ cup green onions, sliced
  (with tops)
2 tablespoons butter
1½ tablespoons flour
1 cup milk
¼ teaspoon nutmeg
  Salt and pepper to taste
  Dash cayenne pepper
3 cups medium Cheddar
  cheese, thinly sliced
2 tablespoons Parmesan
  cheese, grated

◆ Cook lasagna noodles as package directs. Drain and keep warm. Steam asparagus lightly, about 3–4 minutes. Cut artichoke hearts in quarters.

◆ In large bowl thoroughly mix ricotta cheese and eggs. Stir in asparagus, artichoke hearts, all but 1 tablespoon parsley, and green onions. Season with salt and pepper; set aside.

◆ Melt butter over medium–low heat in 1–quart saucepan. Whisk in flour; cook 1 minute. Gradually whisk in milk. Cook and stir until thickened, 4–5 minutes. Season with salt, pepper, nutmeg, and cayenne.

◆ Line bottom of oiled 11 x 7 x 2–inch baking dish with ⅓ of the noodles. Top with ½ the ricotta and ⅓ of the Cheddar cheese; repeat. Top with the remaining noodles and cheddar cheese. Pour the sauce evenly over the top. Sprinkle with Parmesan cheese and cover with foil.

◆ Bake at **375°** for 40 minutes. Uncover and bake 10 minutes longer. Sprinkle with reserved parsley. Let sit for 10 to 15 minutes and cut into squares to serve.

← ◆ →

GARLIC RICE WITH PIÑONS

Yield: 4 servings

1 small green pepper, cut in strips
1 small red pepper, cut in strips
¼ cup piñons (pine nuts)
1 large garlic clove, minced
2 tablespoons butter or margarine
2 cups cooked Arborio rice (cooked in chicken broth)
Salt and pepper to taste
Parsley

◆ In large skillet heat butter over medium–high heat. Sauté peppers, piñons, and garlic until peppers are tender crisp and nuts are lightly browned.

◆ Add cooked rice and season to taste. Garnish with chopped parsley.

Can be prepared, kept in casserole dish, and reheated.

PASTA AL LIMON

Yield: 8 servings

4 tablespoons butter
1 cup heavy cream
2 tablespoons fresh lemon juice
Rind of 4 lemons, grated
14–18 ounces of fettuccine, linguine, or pasta of your choice
½ cup grated Parmigiano–Reggiano cheese
Lemon slices

◆ Melt butter in large skillet (large enough to accommodate pasta later). Add cream. Turn heat to medium high and bring cream and butter to boil. Add lemon juice. Thoroughly stir while adding lemon rind. Reduce cream mixture to ½ its volume while stirring constantly.

◆ Meanwhile, cook pasta in boiling water until it is cooked, but still firm to bite (al dente). Drain pasta.

◆ Transfer pasta to the skillet with the lemon cream sauce. Toss thoroughly while reheating over medium heat, 30 seconds to one minute.

◆ Add grated Parmesan cheese, toss several times. Garnish with lemon slices.

RED MOUNTAIN SHELLS

Yield: 8 to 10 servings

1 package jumbo pasta shells
1 (16 ounce) carton lowfat cottage cheese, drained
8 ounces mozzarella cheese, shredded
8 ounces Cheddar cheese, shredded
½ cup mayonnaise
1 onion, chopped
1½ pound ground beef or mild Italian sausage
1 (30 ounce) jar spaghetti sauce
Oregano and Parmesan cheese

◆ Cook pasta shells according to directions on label. Drain.

◆ Brown ground meat or sausage and drain. Crumble in bite–sized pieces.

◆ Combine cottage cheese, mozzarella cheese, cheddar cheese, mayonnaise, onion, and meat. Stuff cooled shells with mixture. Place in 9 x 13 x 2–inch oiled baking dish and cover with the prepared spaghetti sauce. Sprinkle with oregano and Parmesan.

◆ Bake uncovered at **350°** for 30 to 35 minutes.

STIR–FRY SEAFOOD PASTA

Yield: 6 to 8 servings

2 tablespoons oil for wok
2 (14½ ounce) cans diced tomatoes, juice included
3 stalks celery, diagonally sliced
2 onions, sliced in thin wedges
1 tablespoon basil
1 tablespoon oregano
1 red bell pepper, thinly sliced
1 yellow bell pepper, thinly sliced (or green pepper)
1 cup frozen peas
1 pound fresh mushrooms, sliced
1 pound shrimp, shelled and deveined
1 pound crab, shelled
1 pound linguine, cooked

◆ Add all vegetables and seasonings to hot wok and stir until crisp tender. Remove vegetables to warm platter and quickly stir–fry shrimp and crab until pink. Do not overcook.

◆ Mix quickly with vegetables and serve over cooked linguine.

Recipe doubles and triples easily.

WHOLE WHEAT PASTA WITH VEGETABLES   *Yield: 4 servings*

1   pound whole wheat pasta, uncooked
¾   cup vegetable stock (or chicken stock)
1   tablespoon shallots, minced
3   cloves garlic, minced
2   cups mushrooms, thickly sliced
½   lemon, juiced
½   teaspoon red pepper flakes
24 spears of asparagus, cut in large pieces
3½ cups broccoli, cut in large pieces
3   cups plum tomatoes (or one 28–ounce can of pear tomatoes with juice)
8   black olives, chopped
1   tablespoon lite soy sauce

◆ Cook pasta al dente.

◆ Heat stock and add shallots, garlic, mushrooms, lemon juice and red pepper flakes. Reduce stock by half. Steam or micro-wave asparagus and broccoli until barely tender.

◆ Ten minutes before serving add vegetables, pasta and tomatoes to stock. Serve garnished with chopped olives and soy sauce.

From **Viva la Mediterranean, A Cultural Feast from HealthMark**

◎ LINGUINE WITH BASIL   *Yield: 4 to 6 servings*

4   large tomatoes, cut into ½–inch cubes
1   pound Brie cheese, cut into cubes
1   cup fresh basil leaves, cut into strips
3-5 cloves garlic, minced
1   cup + 1 tablespoon olive oil
2½ teaspoons salt
    Spinach
1½ pounds linguine
    Parmesan cheese

◆ Combine tomatoes, Brie, basil, garlic, olive oil, and salt in bowl. Marinate at least 2 hours in the refrigerator. Sauce will be served at room temperature, so remove from refrigerator ahead of serving time.

◆ Prepare pasta according to package directions. Drain.

◆ Line large bowl with spinach leaves. Put linguine over spinach; pour sauce over pasta. Sprinkle with Parmesan cheese.

SAUCE ALLA PUTTANESCA

Yield: 4 to 6 servings

2 tablespoons olive oil
3 large garlic cloves, minced
4 cups Italian plum tomatoes, peeled and chopped (or one 28–ounce can of Italian plum tomatoes), coarsely chopped (juice included)
¼ cup fresh Italian parsley, chopped
2 tablespoons fresh basil, finely chopped (or 1 tablespoon dried)
1 teaspoon dried oregano
¼ teaspoon red pepper flakes
3 tablespoons bottled capers, well–drained
1 cup oil–cured Greek black olives, pitted and halved
16 ounces spaghetti, cooked

◆ Heat olive oil in a large saucepan over medium heat. Add the garlic and sauté until pale gold, 3 to 5 minutes. Add the tomatoes and cook uncovered, stirring frequently, until slightly thickened, about 10 minutes.

◆ Add parsley, basil, oregano, red pepper flakes, capers, and olives. Cook for an additional 10 minutes. Serve over hot spaghetti.

WILD RICE WITH PIÑONS AND BRANDIED RAISINS

Yield: 6 servings

1 cup uncooked wild rice
Hot water
½ cup golden raisins
¼ cup brandy
2 tablespoons butter
4 green onions, finely chopped
½ teaspoon salt
Dash of freshly ground pepper
3 cups chicken stock
½ cup piñon nuts

◆ Wash rice and soak in very hot water for 1 hour. Drain well.

◆ Soak raisins in brandy. Melt butter in ¾–quart saucepan. Add green onions and sauté for 1 minute. Add wild rice and cook for 3 minutes, stirring constantly. Add salt, pepper, and chicken stock. Cover and cook for 30 minutes.

◆ Add raisins, brandy, and piñon nuts. Cover and continue cooking another 15–30 minutes, until rice is soft.

THREE CHEESE ZITI WITH ITALIAN SAUSAGE

Yield: 10 to 12 servings

TOMATO SAUCE:

2 tablespoons olive oil
3 tablespoons unsalted butter
4 cloves garlic, minced
2 small onions, minced
1 carrot, minced
1 stalk celery, thinly sliced
¼ teaspoon pepper, freshly ground
½ cup dry white wine
2 (35 ounce) cans Italian plum tomatoes, drained
1 (6 ounce) can tomato paste
1 cup canned beef broth
1 tablespoon sugar
1 tablespoon fresh basil, chopped (or 1 teaspoon dried)
1 tablespoon thyme (or 1 teaspoon dried)
¼ cup fresh parsley
2 bay leaves
5 cloves, tied in cheesecloth square
½ teaspoon fennel seed, crushed

LAYERED PASTA:

1¼ pounds mild Italian sausage
1 pound ricotta cheese
1 pound mozzarella cheese, grated
1½ ~~pounds~~ *cups* Parmesan cheese, freshly grated
1 pound ziti (tubular pasta)
1 large egg
¼ cup fresh parsley leaves, minced

◆ SAUCE: In very large pan sauté the garlic, onions, carrot, and celery in butter and olive oil over medium heat, until onion is softened. Add the white wine and stir for 1 minute. Add remaining ingredients, bring the sauce to a boil, reduce heat, and simmer covered for 1 hour, stirring occasionally. Remove and discard the bay leaves and cloves.

◆ PASTA: Brown the Italian sausage, drain, and crumble.

◆ Cook ziti according to package directions until pasta is al dente. Drain and rinse under cold water and rinse again. Combine the ricotta cheese, egg, and parsley in a bowl.

◆ Coat the bottom of a 10½ x 15 x 2½-inch pan with 2 cups of tomato sauce. Layer half the ziti, half the ricotta cheese mixture, half the sausage, half the mozzarella, and half the Parmesan cheese, and cover with 2 more cups of the tomato sauce.

◆ Repeat layers in same order. Cover the mixture with the remaining tomato sauce and top it with the remaining Parmesan cheese. Bake at **325°** for 1¼ hours, or until bubbling.

May be assembled the day before and baked before serving. Freezes well.

RICE FANDANGO

Yield: 4 to 6 servings

1 (4 ounce) can diced green chiles
3 cups sour cream
1 (4 ounce) can ripe olives, sliced
¼ teaspoon marjoram
3 cups rice, cooked
8 ounces Monterey Jack cheese, sliced
Salt and pepper
½ cup Cheddar cheese, grated
Paprika

◆ Mix chiles, sour cream, olives, and marjoram in bowl. In 9 x 9 x 1½–inch greased casserole layer half rice, all the sour cream mixture, all the Jack cheese, remaining rice.

◆ Sprinkle with salt and pepper.

◆ Bake at 350° for 25 minutes. Remove and cover with grated cheddar cheese, sprinkle with paprika. Return to oven for 5 minutes or until cheese is melted.

VERY EASY FRIED RICE

Yield: 4 servings

4 cups rice, cooked
3 tablespoons soy sauce
½ teaspoon sugar
Salt and pepper to taste
2 beaten eggs
3 tablespoons oil
1 cup cooked shrimp, pork, or beef, finely shredded
6 green onions, sliced

◆ Set rice aside to cool.

◆ Mix together the soy sauce, sugar, salt and pepper to taste. Set aside.

◆ Fry egg in oil until firm, cut in shreds. Return to frying pan. Add meat and onion. Cook over medium heat, stirring constantly, 3 to 4 minutes. Add rice. Drizzle soy mixture over rice mixture, and stir until rice is hot. Serve as a side dish or as a main dish with egg rolls.

CRAB TETRAZZINI

Yield: 6 servings

BÉCHAMEL SAUCE:
- ¼ cup butter
- ¼ cup flour
- 1½ cups well–seasoned chicken stock
- 1 cup milk
- Salt and white pepper

TETRAZZINI:
- 4 ounces spaghetti
- ¼ cup hot whipping cream
- 3 egg yolks, lightly beaten
- 2 cups hot béchamel sauce
- 2 tablespoons butter
- 2 tablespoons Parmesan or Swiss cheese, grated
- ½ teaspoon lemon juice
- ¾ pound crab meat
- 2 large sliced mushrooms
- 2½ teaspoons black olives, chopped
- ¾ teaspoon parsley, finely chopped
- 1½ teaspoons sherry
- ½ teaspoon onion juice (or ½ teaspoon onion salt)
- Salt
- Additional Parmesan, grated
- Paprika

◆ SAUCE: Melt butter. Stir in flour and cook, stirring, 1 minute. Gradually stir in chicken broth until smooth. Add milk and cook and stir until thickened. Season to taste with salt and pepper. Makes 2 cups.

◆ PASTA: Cook spaghetti according to package directions. Drain and keep warm.

◆ Gradually beat hot cream into egg yolks, then gradually add hot béchamel sauce, beating well. Turn into saucepan and cook and stir until boiling. Add butter and 2 tablespoons cheese.

◆ Combine lemon juice with crab. Add mushrooms, olives, parsley, sherry, and onion juice and season to taste with salt. Add crab mixture to béchamel and combine.

◆ Place spaghetti in generously buttered 2–quart baking dish. Add crab mixture, making sure spaghetti is completely covered. Sprinkle generously with Parmesan cheese. Dust with paprika.

◆ Bake at 350° until bubbly and heated through, about 20 minutes.

SPINACH STUFFED SHELLS

Yield: 8 to 10 servings

1 (12 ounce) package jumbo shells
½ pound ground beef or Italian sausage
1 (30 ounce) jar prepared spaghetti sauce
2 (9 ounce) packages frozen creamed spinach
15 ounces ricotta cheese
8 ounces shredded mozzarella cheese
1 teaspoon salt
¼ teaspoon pepper

◆ Prepare shells according to package directions. Drain well. Meanwhile, in skillet, brown ground beef or sausage. Drain. Stir in prepared spaghetti sauce, and leave on low heat.

◆ Prepare creamed spinach as directed. Pour into large bowl and cool slightly. Stir in ricotta cheese, mozzarella cheese, salt, and pepper. Stuff each shell with the cheese mixture.

◆ Arrange 4 shells in each of 8 to 10 individual casseroles, or place all shells in 9 x 13 x 2-inch casserole dish. Spoon scant ½ cup spaghetti sauce evenly over each individual casserole, or all of sauce over large casserole. Bake casseroles in 350° oven for 30 minutes or until bubbly.

Individual casseroles may be covered with foil before baking. May be frozen.

SESAME NOODLES

Yield: 8 servings

¼ cup tahini (sesame seed paste)
¼ cup warm water
¼ cup tamari
¼ cup vegetable oil
2 tablespoons sugar
2 tablespoons cider vinegar
2 cloves garlic, minced
1½ tablespoons chili oil, regular or hot, depending on taste
2 teaspoons sesame oil
½ cup green onions, sliced
1 pound udon (Japanese) noodles

◆ Thoroughly combine tahini with water with a whisk. Whisk in tamari, oil, sugar, garlic, chili oil, and sesame oil.

◆ Boil udon noodles about 9 minutes and drain. Lightly coat noodles with tahini sauce, tossing gently. Sprinkle green onions over top and serve either hot or at room temperature.

Chinese egg noodles may be substituted for udon noodles.

VEGETABLE FETTUCCINE ALFREDO

Yield: 8 servings

24 ounces fettuccine, cooked
3 tablespoons cooking oil
½ cup zucchini, sliced
½ cup summer squash, sliced
½ cup mushrooms, sliced
½ clove garlic, minced
½ shallot, minced
1½ cups whipping cream
¼ cup white wine
2 chicken broth cubes
   Salt and pepper to taste
¼ cup Parmesan cheese, grated

◆ Prepare fettuccine according to package directions. Drain and keep warm. In large sauté pan heat oil and sauté zucchini, squash, mushrooms, garlic, and shallots over medium–high heat until barely tender crisp.

◆ Add cream, wine, and chicken broth cubes. Bring to boil and reduce mixture by one–half. Add salt and pepper to taste. Add cooked fettuccine, bring back to boil, add cheese and stir all ingredients until cheese melts. Serve immediately.

Rockslide Restaurant and Brewery, Grand Junction

AVALANCHE MANICOTTI

Yield: 7 servings

SAUCE:
- 1 large onion, chopped
- 4 garlic cloves, pressed (pressed is preferable to chopped)
- 2 tablespoons olive oil
- 2 (6 ounce) cans tomato paste
- 4 tomato paste cans of water
- 2 tablespoons fresh oregano leaves, finely chopped
- 1 small bay leaf
- 1 teaspoon salt
- ½ teaspoon freshly ground black pepper

PASTA:
- 1 teaspoon olive oil
- 14 manicotti noodles

FILLING:
- 1½ cups ricotta cheese
- 6 eggs
- ¾ pound Fontina cheese, grated
- ¼ pound mozzarella cheese, grated
- ⅓ cup Parmesan cheese, freshly grated
- 6 tablespoons soft butter
- 1 teaspoon salt
- ¾ teaspoon black pepper, freshly ground
- 2 tablespoons fresh basil leaves, finely chopped Parmesan cheese, freshly grated to sprinkle on top

◆ SAUCE: Gently sauté onion and garlic in olive oil in a saucepan over medium heat until the onion is translucent, about 5 minutes. Add the tomato paste and stir. Slowly add 4 tomato paste cans of water and stir. Add the seasonings and allow the sauce to simmer.

◆ PASTA: Bring a large pot of water to boil, add the olive oil, and drop in manicotti. Cook just until al dente, about 10 to 15 minutes. Drain and run cold water over the manicotti in a colander. Set aside.

◆ FILLING: In large bowl, beat ricotta cheese and eggs with an electric mixer. Add the grated cheese and softened butter; beat until combined. Add salt, pepper, and basil. Beat on low just until everything is combined.

◆ Gently fill the manicotti shells with cheese mixture. Arrange in 2 buttered 9 x 13 x 2-inch pans.

◆ Cover pasta in each pan with half the sauce; sprinkle on additional Parmesan.

◆ Bake at 350° for 20 minutes, until the cheese is thoroughly melted and the sauce is bubbling.

ORZO WITH MOZZARELLA AND KALAMATA OLIVES

Yield: 8 to 10 servings

1 pound orzo (rice–shaped pasta)
2 cups onion, chopped
2 tablespoons olive oil
2 tablespoons unsalted butter
2 cups celery, chopped
2 tablespoons all–purpose flour
1 cup chicken broth
1 quart canned tomatoes, drained well or 1 (35 ounce) can plum tomatoes
1 teaspoon dried basil or 1 tablespoon fresh basil, chopped
½ pound mozzarella cheese, cut in ¼-inch cubes
½ teaspoon black pepper, or to taste
¼–½ pound Kalamata olives, pitted and thinly sliced
¼ pound mozzarella, thinly sliced

◆ Cook orzo in kettle of boiling salted water until it is al dente, drain well, and transfer to a large bowl. Set aside.

◆ In a large skillet cook the onion in the oil and butter over moderately low heat, stirring, until onion is softened. Add the celery and cook the mixture for 5–7 minutes, stirring periodically. Stir in flour and cook 2 minutes.

◆ Add the broth and the tomatoes, chopping them with a spoon. Add the basil, and the pepper. Simmer the mixture, stirring, for 5 minutes.

◆ Stir the mixture into the orzo with the olives, add the cubed mozzarella, and transfer the mixture to a 4 quart baking dish. Place the thin strips of mozzarella on top of orzo mixture.

◆ Bake in preheated oven for 30 minutes, or until heated through and lightly browned on top.

Unbaked casserole may be prepared ahead one day in advanced and kept covered and chilled.

Clean Livin'

CHOOSING A HEALTHIER ALTERNATIVE

If the recipe calls for: | Choose:

baking chocolate (1 ounce) — 3 tablespoons unsweetened cocoa powder plus 1 tablespoon vegetable oil

ground beef — ground turkey (no skin)

1 cup butter — 1 stick margarine with no more than 2 grams saturated fat per tablespoon OR ¾ cup polyunsaturated oil

cheeses — use lowfat, part–skim milk cheeses

1 cup cream or milk (for cooking) — 1 cup non–fat milk OR 1 cup evaporated skim milk OR 1 cup non–fat buttermilk

cream cheese — dry cottage cheese, blended OR blended lowfat ricotta

1 whole egg — 2 egg whites OR ¼ cup fat free egg substitute

ice cream — sorbet, sherbet, ice milk or lowfat frozen yogurt

sour cream — plain, lowfat yogurt OR lowfat blended cottage cheese mixed with a little lemon juice

What is "a serving", as recommended by those health–promoting letters, magazines, newspaper articles, etc. who recommend five to nine "servings" of fruit and/or vegetables per day?!

"A serving" is each of the following:

- 1 cup raw leafy greens or
- ½ cup other kinds of vegetables or
- 1 medium orange, apple, banana or

- ½ cup small (like grapes) or diced fruit (like pineapple) or
- ¼ cup dried fruit (like raisins) or
- ¾ cup pure fruit or vegetable juice

What are sources of vitamin C other than an orange or a pill?

- sweet red bell peppers
- kiwi
- grapefruit juice
- cantaloupe

- brussels sprouts
- strawberries and raspberries
- broccoli
- tomato juice

At a loss as to how to take in 800 milligrams of calcium per day? Trust the following to help:

- lowfat fruit yogurt
- skim milk
- Swiss cheese
- navy beans
- canned salmon (with bones)
- canned sardines (in tomato sauce)

- broccoli
- dried figs
- medium orange
- ice cream
- raw tofu

BLACK CANYON BEAN SALAD

Yield: 8 servings

2 (16 ounce) cans black beans, drained and rinsed
10 ounces frozen corn, thawed
1 whole red bell pepper, chopped fine (about 1 cup)
2 jalapeño peppers, seeded and chopped fine (use gloves)
1 Serrano pepper, seeded and chopped fine (use gloves), optional
½ cup cilantro, chopped
1⅓ tablespoons vegetable oil
½ cup lime juice
Salt to taste
Pepper to taste
1 clove garlic, minced

◆ Prepare ingredients and mix together!

Nutrition (per serving): 225 calories; total fat 3 g; protein 12 g; carbohydrates 38 g; cholesterol 0 mg; fiber 3 g; vitamin A 2539 IU; sodium 321 mg; iron 3 mg; vitamin C 66 mg.

CREAMY CAESAR SALAD

Yield: 8 servings

14 cups Romaine, washed, dried and torn
½ cup nonfat mayonnaise dressing
4 tablespoons Parmesan cheese, freshly grated
2 tablespoons fresh lemon juice
2 tablespoons water
½ teaspoon fresh ground black pepper
½ teaspoon garlic, minced
¾ teaspoon anchovy paste
1 teaspoon Dijon mustard
1 teaspoon Worcestershire sauce (preferably white wine variety)

◆ Place the prepared lettuce in a large salad bowl.
◆ Whisk together the mayonnaise, cheese, lemon juice, water, pepper, garlic, anchovy paste, mustard and Worcestershire sauce.
◆ Pour the dressing over the lettuce and toss lightly.

Note: Croutons are a perfect topping for this salad, but will add calories — your choice.

Nutrition (per serving): 25 calories; total fat 1 g; protein 1 g; carbohydrates 3 g; cholesterol 2 mg; fiber 0 g; vitamin A 18 IU; sodium 239 mg; iron 0 mg; vitamin C 2 mg.

MOLDED GAZPACHO SALAD

Yield: 8 servings

1 envelope gelatin, unflavored
2 cups tomato juice, divided
1 cup tomatoes, finely chopped
½ cup green bell peppers, ✱ finely chopped
½ cup celery, finely chopped
¼ cup green onions, sliced (include part of green)
2 teaspoons fresh chives, snipped
2 cloves garlic, minced
1 tablespoon tarragon vinegar
2 teaspoons olive oil
½ teaspoon Worcestershire sauce
½ teaspoon salt
Pepper, freshly ground to taste

◆ Soak gelatin in ½ cup cold tomato juice.

◆ Then dissolve in 1½ cups hot tomato juice and set aside to cool.

◆ Combine remaining ingredients, stirring gently to coat the mixture with the vinegar and oil.

◆ Add the tomato juice mixture and mix thoroughly.

◆ Coat a mold with non-stick spray. Pour ingredients into mold and chill 6 hours or overnight.

Note: If you use a tube type mold, fill the center with your favorite guacamole recipe. It looks beautiful and the flavors are very compatible!

Nutrition (per serving): 39 calories; total fat 1 g; protein 2 g; carbohydrates 5 g; cholesterol 0 mg; fiber 1 g; vitamin A 555 IU; sodium 374 mg; iron 1 mg; vitamin C 24 mg.

✱ add ½ cup cucumber finely chopped

SHANGHAI CHICKEN SALAD

Yield: 8 servings

2 chicken breasts, skinless, boneless
2 teaspoons canola oil
2 cups Romaine lettuce, washed, dried and torn
3 cups fresh spinach, washed, dried and torn
½ cup water chestnuts, sliced
½ cup carrots, sliced thin
½ cup red bell pepper, julienne
1½ cups bean sprouts
1 tablespoon sesame seeds, toasted

Dressing:
1 cup yogurt, plain, nonfat
¼ cup soy sauce, low-sodium
1 tablespoon sesame oil
2 tablespoons red wine vinegar

◆ Brush chicken with canola oil and grill about 7 to 8 minutes on each side (or until juice runs clear when pierced).

◆ In the meantime, prepare lettuce and spinach, tearing into bite-size pieces and placing in a large bowl. Toss together with water chestnuts, carrots and red pepper.

◆ Arrange on dinner plates and surround with bean sprouts.

◆ When chicken is cooked, slice diagonally into strips and place on top of salad.

◆ Sprinkle with toasted sesame seeds.

◆ Prepare dressing by whisking together yogurt, soy sauce, sesame oil and red wine vinegar.

◆ Serve with dressing on the side.

Nutrition (per serving): 140 calories; total fat 5 g; protein 17 g; carbohydrates 6 g; cholesterol 38 mg; fiber 1 g; sodium 588 mg; iron 2 mg; vitamin A 4116 IU; vitamin C 25 mg.

From **Delitefully HealthMark Cookbook**

SLICED AND DICED VEGETABLES

Yield: 10 servings

½ cup carrots, sliced in ½-inch pieces

1 cup radishes, sliced in ½-inch pieces

2 cups sweet green peppers, sliced in ½-inch pieces

1¼ cups celery, sliced in ½-inch pieces

1 cup onions, diced

½ cup cucumbers, peeled, seeded, and diced

2½ cups tomatoes, seeded and diced

1 cup cauliflower, separated into small flowerets

½ cup black olives, sliced

2 teaspoons lemon juice

2 tablespoons canola oil

½ teaspoon fresh mint leaves, snipped

¼ teaspoon black pepper

1 cup tomatoes, minced (including juice)

◆ Soak onion in cold water for 10 minutes before dicing.

◆ Combine all the ingredients except the tomato.

◆ Marinate at least one hour (and even overnight), stirring several times to blend the flavor thoroughly.

◆ Add tomato and mix gently.

Nutrition (per serving): 74 calories; total fat 4 g; protein 1 g; carbohydrates 8 g; cholesterol 0 mg; fiber 1 g; vitamin A 2123 IU; sodium 91 mg; iron 1 mg; vitamin C 47 mg.

HEALTH BREAD

Yield: 3 loaves of bread or 36 sandwich buns

2 packets fast-acting dry yeast
½ cup water, heated to 110°
2 cups boiling water
1½ cups cottage cheese, cream style
2 tablespoons margarine
2 teaspoons salt
¼ cup sugar
½ cup honey (or molasses)
1 cup bran (ready to eat cereal)
1 cup oatmeal, uncooked, quick cooking
6 cups white flour
1 cup whole wheat flour
1 cup raisins
½ cup sunflower seeds, unsalted (optional)

◆ Dissolve yeast in ½ cup tepid water for 5 minutes.
◆ Mix next 8 ingredients together.
◆ Microwave margarine until it melts.
◆ Pour into mixer and add 1 cup whole wheat flour, add yeast, add 1 cup white flour at a time and mix until dough is stiff.
◆ Turn dough out on a floured surface.
◆ Knead until smooth and elastic (about 8 minutes).
◆ Let rise in a warm place (45 minutes to an hour).
◆ Divide dough into 3 portions.
◆ Place into greased pans and cover with a cloth and place in a warm area until double in pan.
◆ Bake at 375° for 40 minutes or until golden brown. Remove from pan and cool.

Variation: This recipe also makes great sandwich buns. Make a small ball and roll flat with a rolling pin. Place onto a greased cookie sheet, cover with a cloth, place in a warm area and let rise until double in size. Bake at 375° for 10 minutes or until golden brown. Remove from cookie sheet to cool.

Nutrition (per serving): 165 calories; total fat 3 g; protein 5 g; carbohydrates 30 g; cholesterol 1 mg; fiber 0 g; vitamin A 45 IU; sodium 178 mg; iron 1 mg; vitamin C 0 mg.

GREEK-STYLE POCKETS

Yield: 6 servings

1 pound turkey, ground
1 (14 ounce) can stewed tomatoes, undrained
½ teaspoon cinnamon
1 teaspoon garlic, minced
Pepper to taste
1 (10 ounce) package refrigerated pizza dough
½ cup yogurt, plain
2 tablespoons green onions, sliced
Paprika to taste

◆ Brown turkey in skillet (sprayed with non-stick spray) until it is no longer pink. Drain if necessary.

◆ Stir in UNDRAINED tomatoes, cinnamon, garlic, pepper to taste. Bring to a boil, reduce heat, cover and simmer 15 minutes. Uncover and simmer until most of the liquid has evaporated (about 10 minutes), stirring often.

◆ Meanwhile, cut pizza dough into 6 portions. On lightly floured surface, roll each piece into a 10-inch round (or leave it in a square shape if you are not a "pita purist").

◆ Spray cold skillet with non-stick spray. Cook pitas, one at a time, until light brown (over medium-low heat) on each side.

◆ Combine yogurt and onion (for the topping). Set aside for a moment.

◆ Spoon filling into dough. Top with the yogurt mixture and sprinkle with paprika.

Nutrition (per serving): 149 calories; total fat 7 g; protein 17 g; carbohydrates 5 g; cholesterol 54 mg; fiber 1 g; vitamin A 550 IU; sodium 65 mg; iron 2 mg; vitamin C 18 mg.

PORK CHOPS NORMANDY

Yield: 6 servings

6 pork chops about 1-inch thick, boneless and trimmed
Salt and pepper to taste
2 cups apple cider
1 apple, (tart cooking variety) sliced thin
Ground cloves to taste
Ground cinnamon to taste
Ground nutmeg to taste
1 bay leaf

♦ Spray glass baking dish with non-stick spray.
♦ Place pork chops in dish, season with salt and pepper.
♦ Pour apple cider over chops until just covered.
♦ Arrange apple slices on the chops.
♦ Sprinkle apple slices with ground clove, cinnamon and nutmeg.
♦ Place the bay leaf in the cider.
♦ Bake at 325° (350° if not using a glass dish), for about 1 hour until lightly browned on top and internal temperature reaches 170°.

Nutrition (per serving): 223 calories; total fat 7.7 g; protein 23 g; carbohydrates 16 g; cholesterol 87 mg; fiber 0 g; vitamin A 50 IU; sodium 135 mg; iron 1 mg; vitamin C 3 mg.

Bran Muffins

Yield: 20 servings

2 cups bran buds
1 cup boiling water
2 cups buttermilk
½ cup applesauce
¾ cup sugar
½ cup egg whites (otherwise known as egg substitute)
2½ cups flour
2½ teaspoons baking soda
1 teaspoon salt
2 cups bran flakes cereal

◆ Combine bran buds, boiling water, and buttermilk and soak for 10 minutes.
◆ In the meantime, combine applesauce and sugar.
◆ Add egg whites (egg substitute) and mix.
◆ Add to the buttermilk-bran bud mixture.
◆ Add the flour, baking soda and salt and mix until moistened.
◆ Finally, fold in the bran flakes.
◆ Fill muffin cups about half full and bake at 400° for 15 to 20 minutes.

Nutrition (per serving): 121 calories; total fat 0 g; protein 4 g; carbohydrates 26 g; cholesterol 1 mg; fiber 0 g; vitamin A 216 IU; sodium 300 mg; iron 1 mg; vitamin C 0 mg.

Low-Fat Broccoli, Bacon and Cheddar Toss

Yield: 8 servings

4 cups raw broccoli flowerets
3 ounces lowfat Cheddar cheese, shredded
⅓ cup raisins
¼ cup chopped red onions
8 slices turkey bacon, crumbled
Dressing
½ cup nonfat mayonnaise dressing
2 tablespoons sugar
2 tablespoons lemon juice

◆ Combine all salad ingredients in a large bowl.
◆ Combine the mayonnaise, sugar and lemon juice in a small bowl for the dressing, whisking to mix well.
◆ Pour dressing over salad and toss gently to coat.
◆ Just before serving, sprinkle with bacon and toss.

Nutrition (per serving): 100 calories; total fat 2 g; protein 5 g; carbohydrates 14 g; cholesterol 7 mg; fiber 1 g; vitamin A 680 IU; sodium 258 mg; iron 1 mg; vitamin C 43 mg.

PARMESAN CHICKEN

Yield: 4 servings

¼ cup seasoned bread crumbs
¼ cup Parmesan cheese, freshly grated
½ teaspoon oregano
¼ teaspoon rosemary
¼ teaspoon basil
¼ teaspoon pepper
4 skinless chicken breasts
½ cup buttermilk

◆ Combine first 6 ingredients in shallow bowl or plate.

◆ Dip chicken in buttermilk and roll in the bread, cheese, herb mixture.

◆ Coat a baking pan with non-stick shortening spray.

◆ Place chicken (bone side down) in oven proof dish.

◆ Bake, covered, at 350° for 25 minutes, remove cover and bake another 20 minutes (or until juices run clear when pierced with a knife).

Note: Bake at 325°, if using glass dish.

Nutrition (per serving): 305 calories; total fat 5g; protein 58 g; carbohydrates 6 g; cholesterol 142 mg; fiber 0 g; vitamin A 111 IU; sodium 325 mg; iron 2 mg; vitamin C 3 mg.

MUSHROOM AND ARTICHOKE CHICKEN   *Yield: 4 servings*

¼ teaspoon pepper
1 teaspoon salt
1 tablespoon rosemary, fresh
   (or tarragon)
1 teaspoon paprika
2 skinless chicken breasts,
   whole (split in half to make
   4 servings)
2 teaspoons olive oil
1 (14 ounce) can artichoke
   hearts (water-packed),
   drained and quartered
¼ pound mushrooms, sliced
2 green onions, chopped
1 cup chicken broth
¼ cup dry sherry
2 tablespoons flour
2 tablespoons water

◆ Combine first four ingredients and dredge chicken in those seasonings.

◆ Heat olive oil in a skillet and brown chicken 3 to 5 minutes on each side.

◆ Arrange chicken in a 2-quart baking dish.

◆ Tuck artichoke in between.

◆ Meanwhile, add the mushrooms and onions to the skillet and sauté for 2 to 3 minutes. Add broth, sherry and bring to a boil.

◆ Combine flour and water. Add to stock and stir 2 to 3 minutes.

◆ Pour sauce over chicken and artichokes.

◆ Cover and bake at 375° for 40 minutes.

Nutrition (per serving): 224 calories; total fat 5 g; protein 31 g; carbohydrates 14 g; cholesterol 68 mg; fiber 1 g; vitamin A 563 IU; sodium 1079 mg; iron 2 mg; vitamin C 9 mg.

BAKED EGGS AND BACON FLORENTINE

Yield: 4 servings

4   slices Canadian bacon
8   fresh spinach leaves,
    washed and patted dry
½   tablespoon fresh thyme
    leaves, snipped
4   eggs
    Nutmeg to taste
    Salt and pepper to taste
2   teaspoons margarine,
    melted

◆ Preheat oven to **325°**.

◆ Lightly brown Canadian bacon on both sides. Cut into ¼-inch pieces.

◆ Remove stems from the spinach. Stack four leaves at a time and roll together tightly. Slice on the diagonal into ⅛-inch slivers. (You should have ½ cup).

◆ Spray each of the ramekins with non-stick spray.

◆ Divide spinach among 4 ramekins. Sprinkle each with a pinch of thyme and top with a piece of bacon.

◆ Break an egg on top of bacon in each ramekin. Sprinkle with nutmeg, salt and pepper.

◆ Spoon ½ teaspoon melted margarine over top of each egg.

◆ Bake on center rack of oven for 12 to 14 minutes (until egg is "set").

Nutrition (per serving): 165 calories; total fat 9 g; protein 15 g; carbohydrates 5 g; cholesterol 226 mg; fiber 1 g; Vitamin A 7919 IU; sodium 631 mg; iron 4 mg; Vitamin C 37 mg.

VEGETABLE RICE TOSS
Yield: 6 servings

½ cup cucumbers, peeled, seeded, and diced
½ cup carrots, diced
⅓ cup peas (frozen English)
¼ cup green onions, chopped
2 tablespoons pimientos, diced
1 cup long grain rice, cooked and cooled
1½ tablespoons cider vinegar
¼ teaspoon salt
Dash bottled hot pepper sauce
1½ tablespoons canola oil
Lettuce leaves

◆ Press cucumber between paper towels to remove excess moisture; set aside.

◆ Combine carrots and peas in a small saucepan; cover with water, and cook 3 minutes until just tender crisp. Drain and rinse with cold water.

◆ Combine vinegar, salt, hot sauce, and oil in a small bowl; beat with a wire whisk until blended.

◆ Pour vinegar mixture over rice and vegetable mixture, and toss gently.

◆ Serve on lettuce leaves.

Nutrition (per serving): 127 calories; total fat 4 g; protein 1 g; carbohydrates 23 g; cholesterol 0 g; fiber 0 g; vitamin A 2773 IU; sodium 105 mg; iron 1 mg; vitamin C 9 mg.

OLATHE SWEET CORN SALAD
Yield: 6 servings

6 tomatoes, fully ripe
2 cups corn, fresh, uncooked (four ears)
½ cup sour cream (regular or light); yogurt may be substituted
½ teaspoon salt
½ teaspoon dillweed, crushed
Ground pepper to taste
¼ cup green onion, sliced

◆ Cut a thin slice from the stem end of each tomato. Using a teaspoon, scoop out pulp and seeds. Turn tomatoes upside down to drain.

◆ Cut corn from cobs.

◆ Mix sour cream, salt, dillweed and pepper.

◆ Stir in corn and onions.

◆ Sprinkle inside of each tomato with salt and pepper and stuff with corn mixture.

◆ Serve on a chilled salad plate on top of a whole bib lettuce leaf.

Nutrition (per serving): 141 calories; total fat 5 g; protein 3 g; carbohydrates 21 g; cholesterol 8 mg; fiber 1 g; vitamin A 1041 IU; sodium 218 mg; iron 1 mg; vitamin C 39 mg.

PUMPKIN APPLE BUNDT CAKE

Yield: 12 servings

1 cup whole wheat flour
1 cup unbleached flour
1 tablespoon baking powder
1 teaspoon baking soda
½ teaspoon ground cinnamon
½ teaspoon ground nutmeg
¼ teaspoon ground ginger
¼ teaspoon ground cloves
1 cup brown sugar
4 egg whites
½ cup canola oil
1 cup canned pumpkin
2 cups unpeeled, chopped apples (core removed)

◆ In a large bowl, combine dry ingredients.

◆ Mix well and add remaining ingredients in order given. Mix thoroughly.

◆ Spray a Bundt pan with non-stick spray and pour batter into the pan.

◆ Bake at 350° for 50 to 55 minutes or until toothpick, when inserted, comes out clean.

◆ Cool in pan.

Nutrition (per serving): 221 calories; total fat 10 g; protein 4 g; carbohydrates 30 g; cholesterol 0 mg; fiber 1 g; vitamin A 4514 IU; sodium 179 mg; iron 1 mg; vitamin C 2 mg.

LOW-FAT CRÈME ANGLAISE

Yield: 12 servings

2 cups skim milk
¼ cup sugar
3 tablespoons cornstarch
¼ cup frozen egg substitute, thawed
1 teaspoon vanilla extract

◆ Whisk together skim milk, sugar, cornstarch and egg substitute in a small saucepan until smooth.

◆ Place over medium-low heat and cook until thickened, whisking constantly.

◆ Stir in vanilla extract and serve warm.

Note: Delicious under a slice of Chocolate Angel Food Cake (see index) or over fresh fruit!

Nutrition (per serving): 46 calories; total fat 1 g; protein 2 g; carbohydrates 8 g; cholesterol 1 mg; fiber 0 g; vitamin A 150 IU; sodium 31 mg; iron 0 mg; vitamin C 0 mg.

CHOCOLATE ANGEL FOOD CAKE

Yield: 15 servings

¾ cup cake flour, sifted
⅓ cup cocoa, sifted
1 teaspoon instant coffee granules
1½ cups sugar, divided
12 egg whites, room temperature
1 teaspoon cream of tartar
¼ teaspoon salt
1 teaspoon vanilla extract

◆ Combine flour, cocoa, instant coffee and ¾ cup of the sugar.

◆ Beat egg whites with cream of tartar and salt until whites hold soft peaks. Gradually beat in remaining ¾ cup of sugar and continue beating until whites hold stiff peaks. Add vanilla extract.

◆ Gently fold in flour mixture, being careful not to overmix. Pour batter into an ungreased 10-inch tube pan. Run a knife or spatula through batter to release any air bubbles.

◆ Bake at 325° until a toothpick, inserted into the center, comes out clean (about 45 minutes).

◆ Invert pan over a bottle and cool completely (about 1 hour). Run a knife around edge of pan to release cake.

Nutrition (per serving): 119 calories; total fat 0 g; protein 4 g; carbohydrates 26 g; cholesterol 0 mg; fiber 0 g; vitamin A 0 IU; sodium 112 mg; iron 1 mg; vitamin C 0 g.

Rio Grande

• ANASAZI RUINS, MESA VERDE •

WESTERN WONTONS

Yield: approximately 36

¾ pound ground beef
¼ cup green onion, chopped
2 tablespoons green pepper, chopped
⅓ (15 ounce) can vegetarian refried beans
¼ cup Cheddar cheese, shredded
1 tablespoon ketchup
1½ teaspoons chili powder
¼ teaspoon ground cumin
1 package wonton skins
  Cooking oil for frying
  Salsa or pico de gallo sauce

◆ For filling: In a large skillet, cook ground beef, onion, and green pepper until meat is brown and vegetables are tender. Drain off fat.

◆ Stir beans, cheese, ketchup, chili powder and cumin into meat mixture; mix well.

◆ Place a wonton skin with point toward you. Spoon a scant teaspoon of meat mixture onto center of skin. Fold bottom point of skin over filling. Seal sides with fingertip moistened in a cup of warm water. Repeat with remaining wonton skins and filling (you will probably not use all the skins in the package).

◆ Fry, a few at a time, in 2 to 3 inches of hot oil in pre-heated skillet, about 1 minute per side. Use a slotted spoon to remove wontons. Drain on paper towels.

◆ Serve warm with salsa or pico de gallo.

Hint: Can be frozen in a single layer on a cookie sheet and transferred to sealable plastic bag.

PICO DE GALLO

Yield: 3 to 4 cups

3 fresh tomatoes, diced
1 red onion, diced
¼ cup cilantro, chopped
1 Serrano pepper, seeded and chopped
  Juice of half of 1 lime

◆ Chop, mix, and let marinate for 1 hour. Serve with chips. Simple but good!

SALSA DE LEONARDO

1   (15 ounce) can black
    beans, drained and slightly
    rinsed
1½ cups fresh corn kernels,
    cooked
2   medium tomatoes, diced
    (¼-inch)
1   red pepper, diced (¼-inch)
1   green pepper, diced
    (¼-inch)
½   cup red onion, finely diced
2   fresh jalapeños, thinly
    sliced with seeds
⅓   cup fresh lime juice
⅓   cup extra virgin olive oil
⅓   cup fresh cilantro, chopped
1   teaspoon salt
½   teaspoon ground cumin
½   teaspoon ground red chili
    or pinch cayenne

◆ Combine all ingredients and
  refrigerate for 4 hours. Serve with
  chips.

HOLY GUACAMOLE

Yield: 2 to 2½ cups

4   medium avocados, halved,
    seeded and peeled
½   cup green Anaheim chile,
    roasted, seeded and
    chopped
½   medium tomato, chopped
    (about ½ cup)
2   teaspoons white onion,
    minced
2   teaspoons mayonnaise (or
    enough to make it to the
    consistency you like)
2   cloves garlic
½   teaspoon Worcestershire
    sauce
    White pepper and salt to
    taste

◆ In a medium bowl, mash the
  avocados with a fork until
  reasonably smooth.
◆ Mix in the remaining ingredients.
◆ Spoon the mixture into a serving
  bowl and serve with tortilla
  chips.

*Note: It is best if served immediately.
If made ahead, place plastic wrap on
the surface of the guacamole and
push out any air holes. You may
also prepare all the ingredients except
for the avocados and add them just
before serving.*

⊚ MEXICAN CORN SOUP

Yield: 6 servings

3½ cups frozen corn
1 cup chicken stock
¼ cup butter
2 cups milk
1 clove garlic, minced
1 tablespoon fresh oregano
   or 1 teaspoon dried
   Salt and pepper to taste
1 (4.5 ounce) can chopped
   green chiles
1 whole chicken breast,
   cooked, boned and
   chopped
1 cup tomatoes, diced
1 cup Monterey Jack cheese,
   grated
   Parsley for garnish

◆ Combine corn and chicken stock in a blender and purée. Combine butter and corn mixture and simmer slowly for 5 minutes, stirring.

◆ Add milk, garlic, oregano, salt and pepper and bring to a boil. Reduce heat, add chiles, simmer 5 minutes.

◆ Add chicken and tomatoes. Remove from heat. Add cheese; stir until melted. Garnish with parsley if desired.

Note: Do this soup ahead; it is great re-heated.

FOUR CORNERS TORTILLA SOUP

Yield: 6 to 8 servings

1 medium onion, chopped
2 garlic cloves, minced
2 tablespoons vegetable oil
1 (28 ounce) can whole
   tomatoes
1 (10.5 ounce) can
   condensed beef broth
1 (10.5 ounce) can
   condensed chicken broth
1 (10.5 ounce) can
   condensed tomato soup
1 cup water
½ cup picante sauce
2 teaspoons Worcestershire
   sauce
1 teaspoon ground cumin
1 teaspoon chili powder
4 corn tortillas, cut into
   ½-inch wedges
½ cup (2 ounces) Cheddar
   cheese, shredded

◆ Cook onion and garlic in oil in Dutch oven until onion is tender but not brown; drain well.

◆ Drain and coarsely chop tomatoes, reserving juice. Add tomatoes and juice to Dutch oven with remaining ingredients, except tortillas and cheese.

◆ Bring soup to a boil and reduce heat. Simmer uncovered 1 hour. Add tortillas; continue simmering 10 minutes.

◆ Ladle into soup bowls; sprinkle with cheese.

VOLCANO GREEN CHILI

Yield: approximately 3 quarts

1-1¼ pounds pork, diced
4½ cups tomatoes, diced
1 cup jalapeños, diced and seeded
½ onion, diced
1¼ cups chile strips, cut in half
⅓ cup chicken broth
⅓ cup beef broth
½ teaspoon salt
½ teaspoon garlic salt
¼ teaspoon red chiles (crushed, hot)
¼ teaspoon coriander
¼ teaspoon cumin

◆ Cook pork slowly in shortening until medium brown on outside (don't overcook).

◆ Place all other ingredients in large pot and heat to boil.

◆ Strain fat from pork. Add pork to other ingredients and simmer for 10 minutes.

This recipe is from the Redlands Dos Hombres restaurant.

DOS HOMBRES
FINE MEXICAN FOOD & COCKTAILS

WHITE CHICKEN CHILI

Yield: 9 (1 cup) servings

2 tablespoons oil
1 medium onion, chopped
2 cloves garlic, minced
1 pound boneless, skinless chicken breast, cut into small pieces
3 (14½ ounce) cans chicken broth
2 (15 ounce) cans northern white beans (drained)
8 ounces chopped green chiles
1 teaspoon oregano
½ teaspoon cumin
¼ teaspoon dried cilantro
Seasoned salt and pepper to taste
¼ cup Monterey Jack cheese for garnish

◆ Heat oil in large saucepan over medium heat until hot. Add onions, garlic and chicken. Cook until chicken is done.

◆ Stir in remaining ingredients, bring to a boil and simmer for 15 minutes, stirring often.

◆ Pour into bowls and garnish with cheese, either shredded or diced into chunks

This recipe is a favorite at Dos Hombres restaurant in Clifton.

PORK AND CHILE BURRITOS

Yield: 12 burritos

3 pounds boneless lean pork, cut into ½-inch cubes
1½ pounds onions, diced
½ pound green peppers, diced
½ bunch cilantro, chopped
2 tomatoes, chopped
1 teaspoon garlic powder
1 tablespoon salt
½ teaspoon ground cumin
¼ teaspoon ground cloves
¼ teaspoon black pepper
2 bay leaves
1 jalapeño chile, chopped and seeded
1 pound tomatillos
 Juice of ½ lemon
½ cup cornstarch, blended with 1 cup water
12 flour tortillas (12-inch)
 Monterey Jack and Cheddar cheeses, shredded

◆ Place meat in Dutch oven. Add 1 gallon water and bring to boil. Reduce heat and simmer, covered, until meat is half-cooked, about 35 minutes. Drain off water.

◆ Add onions, green peppers, cilantro, tomatoes, garlic powder, salt, cumin, cloves, pepper, bay leaves, and chile to meat and simmer.

◆ Remove husks from tomatillos and boil in saucepan in 1 quart water until tender, about 15 minutes. Drain off water. Mash tomatillos, add to meat mixture, and simmer, stirring constantly for 15 minutes. Add lemon juice.

◆ Blend cornstarch with 1 cup water, stir into meat mixture, and simmer 15 minutes longer, stirring constantly.

◆ Heat tortillas gently until softened (heat 1 at a time directly on burner of range, or wrap in foil and place in 350° oven for a few minutes).

◆ To make burritos, place a heaping ½ cup of meat mixture on tortilla. Fold sides in, then roll up from one end.

◆ Sprinkle burritos generously with cheese and place under broiler just until cheese melts.

STACKED ENCHILADAS

Yield: 12 to 14 servings

1 can mild enchilada sauce
½ jar Religious Experience Hot Sauce (choose own heat level) or any good quality hot sauce (1 cup)
1 large package flour tortillas
1 (7 ounce) can whole green chiles
2 pounds boned chicken, shredded
1½ pounds Monterey Jack cheese, shredded
   Green pepper circles and pimientos for garnish

◆ Mix the enchilada sauce and the hot sauce.

◆ Cut the flour tortillas into squares and "tile" the bottom of a 9 x 15-inch baking pan so it's completely covered with tortillas.

◆ Next, make a layer of split green chiles and spread with a layer of half the chicken. Pour half of the sauce evenly over this. Spread with an even layer of cheese. Repeat the above steps to form more layers until all ingredients are gone (you will have some left-over tortillas in the package).

◆ Make a design on top using green pepper circles and pimiento, if desired.

◆ Bake at 350° until cheese on top is nicely browned, 30 to 45 minutes. Let stand for 15 minutes outside the oven, then cut into squares to serve.

Note: Religious Experience hot sauce is a favorite of many West Slope salsa aficionados. It ranges from mild to "Wrath" which is a tasty and fiery blend.

MARINATED CHICKEN ENCHILADAS WITH GREEN CHILE AND MELON SALSA

Yield: 8 servings

1 cup beer
1 cup red or white wine
1 tablespoon Worcestershire sauce
½ cup olive oil
½ cup orange juice
½ teaspoon dried tarragon
¾ teaspoon dried thyme
¾ teaspoon salt
8 boneless chicken breasts
2 tablespoons olive oil (optional)
16 corn tortillas
3 cups Green Chile Sauce (see below)
1 cup Monterey Jack cheese, grated
1 cup Cheddar cheese, grated
2 cups Melon Salsa (see below)

GREEN CHILE SAUCE:
2 (1 pound, 13 ounce) cans green chile peppers or 7 cups, chopped
1 large onion, diced
8 cups water
2 tablespoons fresh oregano, chopped
1 tablespoon fresh garlic, minced
1 tablespoon chicken base or 2 cubes chicken bouillon
2 tablespoons salt
½ cup corn starch, mixed well with 1¼ cups water

◆ ENCHILADAS: Place beer, wine, Worcestershire sauce, ½ cup olive oil, orange juice, tarragon, thyme, and salt in a medium mixing bowl. Stir well.

◆ Add chicken and marinate for 2 hours in refrigerator.

◆ Remove chicken from marinade and grill until done. Cut into 1-inch strips, set aside.

◆ Preheat oven to 400°.

◆ Wrap tortillas in foil and heat in oven until warm (or you can heat in medium sauté pan in 2 tablespoons oil and then drain on a paper towel).

◆ On each oven-proof individual plate, place 1 tortilla, spread chicken strips on top. Spoon ½ cup green chile sauce on top, sprinkle ⅛ cup of each of the cheeses on top.

◆ Place another tortilla on top of the cheese and repeat another layer in the same order.

◆ Place the plates in the oven and heat until hot and bubbly (about 10 minutes).

◆ Serve with Melon Salsa and some additional green chile sauce on the side.

◆ SAUCE: Place green chiles, onions and water in a large saucepan over medium low heat and simmer.

◆ Add oregano, garlic, chicken base and salt. Simmer for 10 minutes.

◆ While stirring constantly, add

Continued on next page

Marinated Chicken Enchiladas (Continued)

MELON SALSA:

1 red bell pepper, seeded and diced
1 green pepper, seeded and diced
1 yellow pepper, seeded and diced
1 cup cantaloupe, diced
⅓ cup fresh cilantro, finely minced
⅓ cup fresh parsley, finely minced

cornstarch mixture and continue stirring over low heat about 10 more minutes until sauce has thickened.

◆ You may freeze this sauce in smaller amounts.

◆ SALSA: Mix ingredients. Cover bowl and refrigerate at least 1 hour before serving.

Note: A wonderful stacked dish. People love the wonderful fresh collage of flavors!!

CHICKEN ENCHILADAS

Yield: 12 enchiladas

1 (4.5 ounce) can chopped green chiles
1 (12 ounce) can evaporated milk
1 can cream of celery soup
1 can cream of chicken soup
1 onion, chopped
12 large flour tortillas
1 stick (½ cup) butter or margarine
1 chicken, roasted or boiled, boned and cut into bite size pieces
1 (8 ounce) package shredded cheese (colby, Jack or combined)· Chopped olives and tomatoes for garnish (optional)

◆ Sauté onion and chiles in butter or margarine. Add milk and soups. Simmer.

◆ Dip flour tortillas into sauce mixture then put a layer of chicken and a layer of cheese in the middle of the tortilla. Roll up and place in greased 9 x 13-inch pan. Repeat with remaining tortillas.

◆ Pour remaining sauce over the top of the rolled tortillas and top with cheese.

◆ Bake in 350° oven until hot and bubbly. Garnish with chopped olives and diced red tomatoes, if desired.

ENCHILADA MOLE SAUCE

Yield: approximately 12 servings

½ cup oil
3½ teaspoons unbleached white flour
2½ teaspoons chili powder
3 cups water or chicken stock
½ teaspoon ground cloves
½ teaspoon cinnamon
2 tablespoons cumin
1 (3 ounce) round Mexican chocolate, grated

◆ Heat oil in heavy saucepan. Mix flour and chili powder together. Add to oil and cook, stirring frequently until it starts to darken. Be careful not to burn it. Remove from heat. Add chicken stock or water and stir briskly to avoid lumps.

◆ In a small bowl, combine the spices with the chocolate, add to the sauce. Simmer for 2 to 3 hours over low heat, stirring occasionally. The sauce will thicken and become velvety.

◆ To make enchiladas, grease a 9 x 13-inch pan. Fry corn tortillas in hot oil a few seconds on each side to soften. Then dip each one in the sauce and fill with your favorite enchilada filling. Roll up and place in pan, seam side down. Top with remaining mole and grated cheese.

◆ Bake at 350° until bubbly, approximately 1 hour. Serve with sour cream, black olives and side of salsa.

This recipe is from Karen La Quey of Karen's Cafe in Norwood

SPANISH SOFT TACOS

Yield: 6 to 8 servings

1 whole chicken, cut up (approximately 3 to 4 pounds)
Salt and pepper to taste
12 ounces white corn
8 ounces creamed corn
2 ounces diced mild green chiles
½ cup slivered almonds
1 cup raisins (optional)
½ cup onion, grated
2 teaspoons chili powder
½ teaspoon ground cumin
1 teaspoon salt
½ teaspoon pepper
¼ teaspoon cayenne pepper
2 cups sour cream
2 teaspoons Worcestershire sauce
2 cups Monterey Jack cheese, shredded
12 flour tortillas
Sour cream

◆ Preheat oven to 350°.

◆ Sprinkle chicken pieces with salt and pepper. Place in a large glass baking dish. Cover with foil and bake for 30 minutes or until tender. Cool chicken.

◆ Skin, bone, and shred chicken. Combine chicken, white corn, creamed corn, green chiles, almonds, raisins, onion, chili powder, cumin, salt, pepper, cayenne pepper, sour cream, and Worcestershire sauce in a baking dish.

◆ Sprinkle with cheese and bake for 45 minutes.

◆ Spoon onto warm flour tortillas. Top each with a generous dollop of sour cream. Serve folded over or rolled up.

Note: Chicken may be prepared ahead of time. If only breast meat is desired, use 4 whole chicken breasts. This is a gourmet alternative to the basic chicken taco.

GARLIC TAMALES WITH BLACK BEAN CUMIN SAUCE

Yield: 12 to 14 tamales, 3 cups sauce

BLACK BEAN CUMIN SAUCE:

2 cups black beans, soaked overnight and cooked 4 to 5 hours in chicken stock to cover (or use canned)
1 Serrano pepper
2 tablespoons cumin
2 tablespoons lime juice
5 tomatillos, peeled
½ cup chicken stock
  salt and pepper to taste

TAMALE:

½ head garlic, roasted
½ cup shortening
2 cups fresh corn (canned or frozen if out of season)
½ cup masa harina (corn flour)
½ cup blue cornmeal
1 (2 ounce) bag corn husks, soaked
½ cup chicken stock
½ teaspoon ground cumin
¼ teaspoon cayenne

◆ SAUCE: Cook black beans with pepper, cumin, lime juice, tomatillos and enough chicken stock to cover beans until soft (4 to 5 hours). Add liquid as necessary to keep beans barely covered throughout cooking. Adjust seasonings.

◆ If using canned beans, simmer beans with the other ingredients for at least ½ hour for flavors to mingle.

◆ Blend in food processor until smooth, adding chicken stock to create a sauce the consistency of pudding.

◆ TAMALES: Break apart garlic, pierce and roast at 350° for 5 minutes or until soft and slightly brown. Squeeze from skin and blend in food processor.

◆ Add shortening and blend until fluffy.

◆ Add corn, one cup at a time.

◆ Add masa harina and cornmeal. Add ½ cup broth, salt and pepper and blend thoroughly.

◆ Spoon tamale mixture on to 6 to 8 softened husks. Fold each filled husk and tie with a strip or two torn from the husk.

◆ Steam tamales in a steamer basket about 30 minutes to an hour or until knife inserted comes out clean.

◆ Serve with Black Bean Cumin Sauce.

Note: Serrano peppers are usually found dried and are also know as chile seco. They are 1½ to 2 inches long, ½-inch wide, orange-red, thin-skinned, fruity flavored and hot.

COYOTE GREEN CORN TAMALES

Yield: 14 tamales

15 ears fresh corn (or 5 cups canned or frozen, if out of season)** (Reserve husks.)
1 cup yellow cornmeal
½ cup (1 stick) butter, room temperature
1½ teaspoons sugar
1½ teaspoons salt
2 tablespoons milk
28 strips canned green chiles
½ pound sharp Cheddar cheese, cut into ¼-inch cubes
Butter
Salt
**Bag of dried corn husks if using processed corn

◆ Carefully remove husks from corn, reserving tender inside husks (if using bagged husks, soak in warm water). Cut corn from cobs and measure 5 cups. Transfer to mill or grinder and grind, adding cornmeal gradually until well blended.

◆ Cream butter in medium bowl until light and fluffy. Stir in ground corn, sugar, salt and milk (mixture will be thick).

◆ Fold reserved husks in half to prevent curling. Overlap 2 husks in palm of hand. Spread about ¼ cup corn mixture over husks and top with 2 strips of chile and some of the cheese. Cover with 2 more tablespoons mixture and 2 more overlapping husks.

◆ Set tamale on 9-inch square of foil and fold up, turning ends. Repeat with remaining corn mixture and husks.

◆ Arrange tamales in top of steamer set over boiling water. Cover and steam 1 hour. Serve immediately with butter and salt.

Note: This is a great vegetarian main dish.

233

Tamale Pie

Yield: 12 servings

¼ cup vegetable oil, divided
1 (2 pound) can tomatoes (home-canned are the best. Any kind will do, stewed, etc.)
1 (1 pound) can creamed corn
1 medium onion, chopped
1 green pepper, seeded and chopped
1 pound ground venison (or elk or antelope)
1½ cups yellow corn meal
1 large can ripe olives
1 teaspoon salt
1 tablespoon chili powder

◆ Heat ½ of the oil (⅛ cup) in a skillet, add corn and tomatoes, letting it heat slowly.

◆ In another pan, heat the remaining oil; fry the onion and green pepper until tender. Add meat and cook slowly for 20 minutes.

◆ Stir cornmeal into corn/tomato mixture and allow to cook slowly for 15 minutes.

◆ Combine the 2 mixtures. Add olives, salt, and chili powder.

◆ Place in lightly greased 9 x 13-inch baking dish. Bake at 350° for approximately 45 minutes.

Chile Relleno Torta

Yield: 8 to 10 servings

½ pound Cheddar cheese, grated
½ pound Monterey Jack cheese, grated
5 eggs
⅓ cup flour
1⅔ cups half-and-half
1 (4 ounce) can chopped green chiles, drained
¼ cup picante sauce

◆ Preheat oven to 375°.

◆ Mix grated cheeses and spread evenly in buttered 10-inch pie plate.

◆ Beat eggs, add flour slowly, and then beat in half-and-half. If mixture is lumpy, strain it.

◆ Pour egg mixture over cheeses in pie plate. Carefully spoon chiles over the surface, then spoon picante sauce over all.

◆ Bake about 45 minutes or until center is set.

Note: Let set for 10 to 15 minutes after baking, so it is easier to cut.

JALAPEÑO RELISH

Yield: approximately 2 quarts

30 fresh red jalapeños, seeded (wear rubber gloves to do this)
1 shot tequila
3 shots (6 ounces) white vinegar
3 pinches salt
10 fresh cilantro leaves

◆ Wash and seed jalapeños.
◆ Chop all ingredients, but leave chunky.
◆ Put in clear jars, seal and refrigerate for 2 weeks before use (the relish will mellow).

Note: Use as a side dish or condiment with smoked meat or with Southwestern food.

ARROZ DURANGO

Yield: 4 servings

1 cup raw rice, rinsed and drained
3 tablespoons olive oil
1 cup onion, diced
1 clove garlic, minced
2 cups tomatoes, chopped
1 tablespoon diced green chiles
1 tablespoon pickled jalapeños (see previous recipe)
2 cups chicken broth

◆ Heat oil in a heavy skillet and sauté onion until clear.
◆ Add rice and garlic and sauté until lightly brown.
◆ Add tomatoes, green chiles, pickled jalapeños and broth. Cover skillet tightly and simmer over low heat for 30 minutes.

SOUTHWESTERN PASTA SALAD

Yield: 12 servings

1 pound medium to small shell macaroni, cooked al dente, thoroughly drained
⅔ cup cider vinegar
¼ cup vegetable oil
1 cup celery, minced (about 2 stalks)
½ cup green pepper, chopped (about ½ large pepper)
6 green onions, minced
1 (2 ounce) jar chopped pimiento, drained
3 generous dashes Worcestershire sauce
3 dashes hot pepper sauce
1 tablespoon green chile pepper, roasted and minced
1 teaspoon salt
½ teaspoon pepper, freshly ground
1 (15 ounce) can black-eyed peas, drained
1 (12 ounce) can corn, drained
½ cup pitted black olives, drained and chopped
1 (2 ounce) jar pimiento-stuffed green olives, drained and chopped
⅓ cup mayonnaise (approximately)

◆ Place macaroni in a large bowl. Pour vinegar over and let stand while preparing other ingredients.

◆ Add all other ingredients to macaroni and mix well. Cover and refrigerate 2 to 3 days. Taste for seasoning before serving (There should be a suggestion of chile and a tart tang from the vinegar).

Note: An unusual approach to the traditional macaroni salad. Make it 2 or 3 days ahead; but do taste before serving since it may need a dash more salt and an extra splash of vinegar.

Vegetables can be chopped in food processor. If chopping by hand, place green pepper (cut into strips), green onions, celery and chile pepper on a board and cut up all at once. This reduces your chopping time by 75 percent.

LAYERED MEXICAN SALAD

Yield: 6 to 8 servings

2 (16.75 ounce) cans kidney beans, drained
1 cup onions, chopped
4 teaspoons chopped green chiles
2 (16.75 ounce) can garbanzo beans, drained
4 large tomatoes, chopped or 1½ cups salsa
⅔ cup ripe olives, sliced
4 avocados, peeled and mashed
2 cups Cheddar cheese, shredded
6 cups lettuce, shredded
1⅓ cups sour cream
4 tablespoons taco sauce (or to taste)
2 cups nacho-flavored chips, coarsely crushed

◆ In a large glass bowl layer ingredients as they appear in the recipe.

◆ Chill until ready to serve.

Hint: This recipe can be cut in half.

BLACK BEAN SALSA SALAD

Yield: 4 to 6 servings

2 cups canned black beans, rinsed and drained
3 tablespoons olive oil
3-4 tablespoons fresh lime juice
½ cup corn (canned or fresh cooked)
1 large or 2 medium avocados, peeled, pitted and finely diced
½ green pepper, seeded and finely diced
1 red pepper, seeded and finely diced
½ red onion, finely diced
1 teaspoon ground cumin
½ cup fresh cilantro, finely chopped
Salt and pepper to taste

◆ Combine all ingredients in a mixing bowl, toss well. Correct seasoning, adding salt or lime juice to taste.

Note: This is wonderful as a side dish to chicken or fish. It may also be served with tortilla chips as an appetizer.

SILVERTON INDIAN FRY BREAD

Yield: 4 to 5 pieces

1 cup flour
½ cup powdered milk
1¼ teaspoons baking powder
¼ teaspoon salt

◆ Combine ingredients in a bowl, and then add enough warm water so dough will hold together (¼ cup at a time).

◆ Knead 50 times. Roll or pat thin on floured surface into 4 or 5 pieces.

◆ Deep fry at **375°** until golden brown.

◆ Serve hot with butter and honey.

Note: This bread can also be used as the tortilla part of a taco to make a Navajo Taco, a popular fast-food in the Four Corners area.

JALAPEÑO CORN BREAD

1 (8.5 ounce) can creamed corn
1 cup yellow cornmeal
1 cup sharp Cheddar cheese, grated
¾ cup milk
3 eggs, slightly beaten
¼ cup jalapeño peppers, chopped or 1 (3.5 ounce) can hot chopped green chiles
1 teaspoon salt
½ teaspoon baking soda
2 tablespoons butter

◆ Combine corn, cornmeal, half of the Cheddar cheese, milk, eggs, peppers, salt and baking soda in a bowl. Mix well.

◆ Put butter in 1½-quart casserole (preferably a glazed Mexican earthenware casserole) or 9-inch cast iron skillet. Place in pre-heated hot oven (**400°**) until butter is hot but not brown. Immediately pour in the batter. Sprinkle top with remaining cheese.

◆ Bake at **400°** for 40 to 45 minutes. If (after about 35 minutes) the top appears too brown, cover with foil. Serve hot.

BEAVER CREEK TROUT IN JALAPEÑO MARINADE

Yield: 4 servings

12 ounces trout fillets (Four 3-ounce fillets of firm red meat variety of trout)
3 jalapeño peppers (1½-inch to 2 inches), seeded and finely chopped**
4 tablespoons light brown sugar
1 tablespoon lime juice
1 tablespoon white wine
2 fat cloves of garlic, minced

◆ **Use rubber gloves (and even a mask) to seed and chop jalapeños.

◆ Combine ingredients for marinade and marinate the trout fillets in the mixture for at least 4 hours, turning occasionally.

◆ Grill 4 minutes on each side over hot coals. Baste with the marinade. (If the fillet is more than ¾-inch thick, add 30 seconds per side. Do not overcook.) Serve immediately.

SOUTHWEST SOLE

Yield: 6 servings

4 medium carrots, peeled and cut into fine julienne strips
½ jícama, peeled, cut into fine julienne strips
4 green onions, sliced
¼ cup butter or margarine
Salt and pepper to taste
6 sole, cod or orange roughy fillets
¾ cup salsa
¼-½ cup wine
1 avocado, peeled and cut into 6 wedges
3 sprigs of cilantro
Jalapeño chiles
Lime slices

◆ Sauté carrots, jícama and onions in butter until tender-crisp. Season to taste with salt and pepper.

◆ Place vegetables in individual ramekins and top with the fish. Pour salsa and wine over all, then place avocado wedge and cilantro sprig on side of each fish fillet.

◆ Bake at 450° about 10 to 12 minutes or until fish flakes easily when tested in center with fork. Garnish with chiles and lime slices.

CHICKEN BREAST WITH WARM SALSA

Yield: 4 servings

4 boneless chicken breasts, skin removed
1 tablespoon olive oil
¼ cup white wine
2 tablespoons lime juice
3 garlic cloves, minced
2 teaspoons reduced-sodium soy sauce
½ teaspoon ground pepper
1 tablespoon vegetable oil

♦ Combine olive oil, white wine, lime juice, garlic cloves, pepper and soy sauce in a medium size bowl. Mix thoroughly.

♦ Cover chicken breasts with marinade mixture and refrigerate overnight.

♦ Remove from refrigerator 15 minutes before cooking. Preheat a 3-quart sauté pan on medium heat. Add 1 tablespoon of oil. Heat oil, then add chicken breasts (discard marinade).

♦ Allow chicken breasts to cook for 5 or 6 minutes on each side or until lightly brown. Chicken will release easily with a flat-edged, flexible metal spatula. Do not overcook.

♦ Remove from pan and top with Warm Salsa. Garnish with fresh cilantro.

WARM SALSA:
1 tablespoon olive oil
⅓ cup onion, chopped
2 cloves of garlic
2 tomatoes, chopped
1 jalapeño pepper, seeds removed, finely chopped (use rubber gloves)
2 tomatillos, chopped
1 tablespoon cilantro, chopped
¼ teaspoon black pepper

WARM SALSA:
♦ Preheat a 1-quart sauté pan. Add olive oil and heat for 1 minute.

♦ Add chopped onion and garlic cloves, sauté for 2 to 3 minutes. Add chopped tomatoes, tomatillos and jalapeño peppers.

♦ Reduce heat to maintain a low simmer and cook for 15 minutes, stirring occasionally. Remove from heat. Add cilantro and black pepper.

MEXICAN CHICKEN ROLL-UPS

Yield: 8 servings

8 chicken breast halves, skinned and boned
1 (7 ounce) can diced green chiles
4 ounces Monterey Jack cheese, cut in 8 strips
½ cup fine dry bread crumbs
¼ cup Parmesan cheese, grated
1 tablespoon chili powder
½ teaspoon salt
¼ teaspoon ground cumin
¼ teaspoon black pepper
Butter, melted

◆ Pound chicken pieces to about ¼-inch thickness. Put about 2 tablespoons chiles and 1 Jack cheese strip in center of each chicken piece. Roll up and tuck ends under.

◆ Combine bread crumbs, Parmesan cheese, chili powder, salt, cumin and pepper.

◆ Dip each stuffed chicken in shallow bowl containing 6 tablespoons melted butter and then roll in crumb mixture.

◆ Place chicken rolls, seam side down, in an oblong baking dish (9 x 13-inch) and drizzle with a little melted butter. Cover and chill 4 hours or overnight.

◆ Bake uncovered at 400° for 20 minutes or until done. Serve with Tomato Sauce.

TOMATO SAUCE:
1 (16 ounce) can tomato sauce
½ teaspoon ground cumin
⅓ cup green onions, sliced
Salt and pepper to taste
Hot pepper sauce to taste

◆ TOMATO SAUCE: Combine tomato sauce, cumin, and green onions in small saucepan. Season to taste with salt, pepper, and hot pepper sauce. Heat well. Makes about 2 cups.

SALSA BEEF

Yield: 4 servings

1 ½   pounds boneless extra lean
      beef chuck, cubed
1   tablespoon olive oil
1   cup prepared chunky salsa
      (mild, medium or hot level
      of bravery)
2   tablespoons brown sugar,
      packed
1   tablespoon reduced-sodium
      soy sauce
1   clove garlic, crushed
3   tablespoons cilantro,
      coarsely chopped
2   tablespoons fresh lime juice

◆ Trim all fat from beef. In Dutch oven (or electric frying pan), heat oil over medium heat until hot. Add beef and brown, stirring occasionally.

◆ Stir salsa, sugar, soy sauce and garlic into beef. Bring to a boil; reduce heat to low. Cover tightly and simmer for 1 hour.

◆ Remove cover; continue cooking, uncovered, another 30 minutes or until beef is tender. Remove from heat. Stir in chopped cilantro and lime juice.

◆ Serve over white rice. Garnish with cilantro, if desired.

CRESTED BUTTE CHILI CHEESE SUPREME

Yield: 10 to 12 servings

2 tablespoons vegetable oil
1 medium green pepper, chopped
1 clove garlic, minced
1 (15.5 ounce) can kidney beans, drained
1 (16 ounce) can tomatoes, with juice, coarsely chopped
1 (15 ounce) can tomato sauce
1 tablespoon chili powder, or to taste
1 (15 ounce) carton ricotta cheese
2 cups (8 ounces) Monterey Jack cheese , shredded
1 (4 ounce) can chopped green chiles, drained
1 bunch green onions, finely chopped
3 eggs, beaten
1 (8 ounce) bag tortilla chips
2 cups (8 ounces) mild or medium Cheddar cheese, shredded

◆ Heat oil in skillet over medium high heat. Sauté green pepper and garlic until tender. Add kidney beans. Set aside.

◆ In saucepan, combine tomatoes, tomato sauce and chili powder. Bring to a boil, then reduce heat and simmer, uncovered, for 15 minutes. Add to kidney bean mixture.

◆ Combine ricotta and Monterey Jack cheeses, chiles, onions, and eggs.

◆ Spread ¼ of cheese mixture evenly in greased 9 x 13-inch glass baking dish. Arrange ¼ chips over cheese. Spread ¼ tomato mixture over chips.

◆ Repeat layer 3 more times.

◆ Cover with foil and bake at 325° for 30 to 40 minutes. Remove foil and top with Cheddar cheese. Bake 10 to 15 minutes more. Let stand 5 minutes before serving.

INDIVIDUAL ORANGE FLANS

Yield: 6 servings

½ cup sugar
2 teaspoons hot water
2 cups milk
3 eggs
½ cup sugar
1 teaspoon orange-flavored liqueur
½ teaspoon orange extract
Dash of salt
Grated orange rind

◆ Place ½ cup sugar in a heavy saucepan over medium heat. Shake pan and stir occasionally until sugar melts and turns a light golden brown. Remove from heat; add water, stirring well.

◆ Pour hot caramel mixture into six 6-ounce custard cups, tipping each cup quickly to coat bottom evenly. Let cool (mixture may harden and crack slightly as it cools).

◆ Place milk in top of a double boiler; bring water to a boil. Cook until milk is thoroughly heated (do not boil). Set aside.

◆ Beat eggs until frothy. Add ½ cup sugar and next 3 ingredients; beat well. Gradually stir about ½ cup hot milk into egg mixture; add to remaining milk, stirring constantly.

◆ Pour egg mixture evenly into the custard cups. Place cups in a 9 x 13-inch baking dish; add hot water to a depth of 1 inch into the dish.

◆ Bake at 350° for 45 to 50 minutes or until a knife inserted in center of custard comes out clean.

◆ Remove cups from water; cool. Chill flans 2 to 3 hours.

◆ To serve, loosen edges of custards with a spatula, and invert onto individual dessert plates. Sprinkle with grated orange rind.

Campfire Café

CAMPFIRE HINTS

◆ Transport your dry ingredients in a sealable plastic bag. At the campsite, add your liquids to the bag and close it firmly, then mix with your fingers from the outside. This saves time and cleanup!

◆ Use jumbo sealable plastic bags to separate socks and other clothing in your duffel bag. It also keeps things dry in damp weather.

◆ Transport fresh eggs by breaking them into a plastic jar with a narrow opening. They will pour out, one at a time.

◆ Put butter, oils, peanut butter, etc. into plastic squeeze bottles. This saves space and makes it easier to use the ingredient.

◆ Keep matches dry in a heavy sealable plastic bag.

◆ Give every camper a mini–maglite that has been put on a shoestring–like string with an o–ring. Tie it on your belt or put it around your neck to free your hands and prevent its loss.

◆ Transport bread in a shoe box.

◆ Take plenty of wipes for quick and easy cleanups.

◆ Place a film of soap on the outside of your cooking pans. The black deposit will clean off much easier.

◆ Pack out everything that you take in! Leave nothing to spoil the back country for those who come after you.

←——————————◆——————————→

COWBOY COFFEE

Yield: One quart strong coffee

½ cup coffee grounds to 1 quart water

◆ Fill coffee pot with cold water and put in appropriate amount of coffee grounds.

◆ Boil for several minutes over fire.

◆ Remove from heat and add a small amount of cold water to settle the grounds.

◆ Wait a few minutes for grounds to settle and then pour.

When keeping your coffee warm over the coals and it keeps boiling over, place a green willow twig over the top of the coffee pot.

APRICOT ICED TEA

Yield: 6 to 8 servings

5 cups water
8 tea bags, small
1 cup sugar
1 (12 ounce) can apricot nectar
   Juice of 4 lemons
2 ounces rum or apricot liqueur, optional

◆ Boil water in covered pot.

◆ Place tea bags in pot and remove from heat.

◆ Steep for about 5 minutes.

◆ Add sugar, apricot nectar, and lemon juice.

◆ Pour over ice or chill in stream.

◆ Add rum or apricot liqueur just prior to serving, if desired.

IRON MAN TRAIL MIX

Yield: 5 cups

1 cup raisins
1 cup peanuts
1 cup crunchy granola
1 cup nonprocessed cheese, cubed
1 cup diced jerky
   M&M-type candies to taste, optional

◆ Mix all ingredients together and place in ziplock bags.

This is a very high energy mix that no camper should be without!

MOUNTAIN MAN JERKY

Yield: about 24 strips of jerky

2 pounds lean meat (beef, venison, elk)
2 tablespoons seasoned salt
1 teaspoon onion salt
½ teaspoon pepper
½ teaspoon garlic powder
½ cup Worcestershire sauce
1 tablespoon sugar
½ bottle liquid smoke
Chili powder to taste

◆ Slice partially frozen meat into strips as thin as possible, and trim all fat as it will get rancid in time.

◆ Sprinkle with the seasonings, add Worcestershire, liquid smoke, and sugar.

◆ Cover and marinate overnight.

◆ Cover an oven rack with foil and evenly place the meat strips in a single layer on the foil.

◆ Leaving door ajar, bake at 150° for about 8 hours or until chewy and feels like old shoe leather.

◆ Store in an airtight container in the feezer.

Cut meat against the grain for tenderness.

MOUNTAIN MAN JERKY MILK GRAVY

Yield: 4 cups

3-4 cups jerky
2 tablespoons bacon drippings
2 tablespoons flour
1 cup milk

◆ Pound jerky into pieces and powder.

◆ Place into a heated heavy skillet with the bacon drippings.

◆ Mix well, stir in flour, and brown.

◆ Pour in milk slowly, stirring constantly until desired consistency is reached.

◆ Serve over hot biscuits, potatoes, or even rice.

Probably will not need any seasoning as jerky is usually seasoned well.

Variation: Substitute sausage for jerky.

LARIAT FRUIT LEATHER

Yield: Makes about 8 individual rolls

4   cups fruit pulp (peach, apple, pear, strawberry, apricot, cherry, or banana)
½   cup sugar, or to taste
1   teaspoon fresh lemon juice

◆ Wash, peel, stem, and seed fresh fruit. Cut into pieces.

◆ Purée in blender or processor, one cup at a time.

◆ Mix fruit, sugar, and lemon juice.

◆ Spread evenly on plastic wrap or on a greased 11 x 16-inch cookie sheet so that it is no more than ⅛ to ¼-inch thick.

◆ Bake in a slow oven at 150° until it looks like leather and is barely sticky. (Leave oven door slightly ajar to allow moisture to escape, during the drying process.)

◆ Peel the fruit leather from the pan, roll, and cut into individual serving rolls.

Nuts and spices may be added to the purée for more flavor.

TRAIL BARS

Yield: 12 large bars

1   cup light corn syrup
½   cup packed brown sugar
¼   teaspoon salt
1½   cups chunky peanut butter
1   teaspoon vanilla
1   cup powdered milk
1   cup granola cereal (crush large pieces)
1   cup whole bran cereal
1   cup raisins
6   ounces chocolate chips

◆ Line a 9 x 13-inch pan with waxed paper.

◆ In saucepan, combine syrup, sugar, and salt. Bring to a boil. Remove from heat.

◆ Add peanut butter and vanilla. Stir in remaining ingredients and add chocolate chips.

◆ Press all ingredients into pan.

◆ Let cool and cut into bars.

◆ Store in refrigerator.

DUTCH OVEN COOKING

Many of the following recipes can be cooked in a Dutch oven. If you haven't used a Dutch oven, you might like to try this wonderful method of cooking out in the wilderness. It makes a perfect oven while away from home. The true Dutch oven is cast iron and has a rimmed lid to hold coals and legs so it can be placed over your coals for baking. The oven may be placed in a hole over hot briquettes or firewood, and then more of the hot fuel placed on the lid. It is not necessary to dig a hole, you may place your fire on any safe surface. Be sure your fire is not too hot, ashes should be gray in color, use plenty of liquid or fat to prevent sticking and dryness, and use some kind of pothook. The idea is to create a uniform heat so your food will cook evenly. Dutch ovens may be stacked to conserve fuel and aluminum foil is handy as a base or to block the wind. An inverted lid of a Dutch oven makes a good frying pan. Most people use too much fuel. For a 12-inch oven try 8-12 briquettes under and 12-18 briquettes on top. If you bury your oven in coals you can leave for the day and come home to a cooked meal. Don't be afraid to experiment, that's the only way to learn.

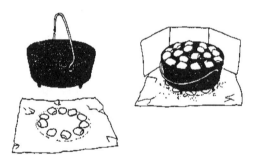

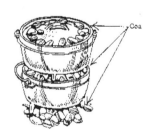

Coa

EGGS IN A TORTILLA

Yield: 8 to 10 servings

12   eggs
⅛   cup water
½   teaspoon salt
½   teaspoon ground pepper
2   tablespoons butter
2   ounces creamed cheese, cut into chunks
2   ounces Cheddar cheese, grated
½   cup tomato, diced
½   cup green pepper, diced
½   cup onion, diced, optional
1   cup ham or bacon cut into pieces
1   tablespoon fresh parsley, snipped, or 1 teaspoon parsley, dried
8-10   medium flour tortillas, warmed

◆ In large bowl, beat together eggs, water, salt and pepper.

◆ Melt butter in skillet, pour in egg mixture, and stir until it starts to thicken.

◆ Add cream cheese, grated cheese, and next 5 ingredients. Continue stirring until eggs are creamy.

◆ Place eggs into warm tortilla, wrap or fold up, and serve immediately.

Serve with salsa if desired.

MOUNTAIN BLUEBERRY PANCAKES

Yield: 8 pancakes

1   cup sifted flour
1½   teaspoons baking powder
1   tablespoon sugar
½   teaspoon salt
¼   teaspoon cinnamon
2   tablespoons melted butter
1   egg, separated
¾   cup milk
¾   cup drained blueberries

◆ Stir flour, baking powder, sugar, salt and cinnamon together.

◆ In a separate bowl, add butter to beaten egg yolk, and stir in milk.

◆ Add this mixture to dry ingredients, mixing just enough to moisten.

◆ Fold in stiffly beaten egg white.

◆ Add blueberries and mix very lightly.

◆ Pour batter on hot greased griddle, turning when batter bubbles.

◆ Serve with butter and syrup.

Place all dry ingredients in a sealable plastic bag to transport to camp.

BEER-CAN BISCUITS

Yield: 12 servings

1 (12-ounce) can of beer
2 cups all-purpose flour
1 tablespoon baking powder
½ teaspoon salt
⅓ cup lard or vegetable
shortening

◆ Empty the can of beer, reserve beer.

◆ Use a can opener to remove the top of the can. Set can aside.

◆ Heat oven to **450°** or preheat Dutch oven using some oil.

◆ In a bowl, combine flour, baking powder, and salt.

◆ Add lard and cut into dry ingredients with a pastry blender or two forks until mixture is the texture of coarse meal.

◆ Add ¾ cup of beer and stir with a fork until a ball of dough forms. Transfer dough to a floured board and knead it 10 to 12 times.

◆ Roll out to a thickness of ½-inch (no thinner).

◆ Use the beer can to cut out biscuits.

◆ Gather scraps, roll them out, and cut more biscuits.

◆ Transfer biscuits to an ungreased cookie sheet or your greased Dutch oven.

◆ Bake for 10 to 12 minutes, or until raised and lightly browned.

◆ Serve with ribs, fried chicken, or chili. Break biscuits in half, spread with cheese spread and serve as an appetizer.

Dough may also be used as a topping for a meat pie or casserole. Roll or pat out to fit baking dish and add during final 10 to 15 minutes of baking time.

PAUL'S HAM SALAD

Yield: 4 to 5 cups

3 cups diced or chunked ham
1½ cups onion, chopped
4-6 medium stalks celery
2 medium carrots
2 canned jalapeños (each about the size of a thumb)
3-4 dill pickles
Mayonnaise-type salad dressing
Salt and pepper to taste

◆ Using a handgrinder or food processor, grind the first 6 ingredients into a bowl.

◆ Add salad dressing until moist enough to spread.

◆ Salt and pepper to taste.

◆ Serve as salad, on your favorite rolls, or stuff pita bread or tortilla.

You might want to add jalapeños a little at a time until you find a comfortable "heat".

CURRIED CHICKEN SALAD

Yield: 8 servings

4 chicken breasts, boned and skinned
½ cup celery, diced (1 large rib)
4 green onions, sliced (using some of green tops)
1 cup plus 1 tablespoon of mayonnaise
¾-1 teaspoon curry powder
¼ teaspoon white pepper
¼ teaspoon seasoned salt
½ cup almonds, sliced (optional)

◆ Cook chicken until tender.

◆ Cool and refrigerate until firm.

◆ Cut chicken in cubes.

◆ Add green onions, celery, and other ingredients. Mix well.

◆ Serve on a bed of lettuce, stuff tomatoes, or use as a sandwich filling.

CORTEZ CHILE CON QUESO

Yield: 6 cups

¼ cup canned green chile peppers, chopped, plus juice from can
3 onions, chopped fine
3 raw tomatoes, peeled and chopped
6 tablespoons flour
½ cup milk
3 cups sharp Cheddar cheese
Salt
Bottled hot pepper sauce to taste
Worcestershire sauce

◆ Combine chile peppers, onions, tomatoes, and add flour.
◆ Simmer milk and add to mixture.
◆ Put into heavy pan and place in a larger pan or skillet (which has water in it), add cheese, and cook over fire until melted.
◆ Add salt, red pepper, and Worcestershire sauce to taste.
◆ Serve hot, with corn chips.

Can be frozen over and over, or reheated.

◎ SILVER DOLLAR SLAW

Yield: 4 servings

1 medium-sized head cabbage
½ teaspoon salt
1 tablespoon sugar (or to taste)
1¼ cups water
1 cup vinegar
2 cups celery, sliced
½ cup carrots, grated
½ cup green onions, sliced
1 large red or green pepper, sliced
1 teaspoon celery seed

◆ Shred cabbage, sprinkle with salt, and let stand 2 hours in refrigerator or cooler.
◆ Combine sugar, water, and vinegar in saucepan and boil 2 minutes; cool at room temperature.
◆ Pour off any liquid from cabbage and add celery, carrots, onions, bell pepper, and celery seed.
◆ Add vinegar solution and let chill 24 hours.

Will last about a week in refrigerator or cooler.

TIMBERLINE STEAK SANDWICH WITH CORN RELISH

Yield: 8 servings, sandwiches

3 teaspoons ground cumin
1 tablespoon chili powder
1 teaspoon salt, or to taste
2 teaspoons ground pepper, or to taste
½ teaspoon ground coriander
¼ teaspoon cayenne pepper
2 pounds top round steak, trimmed
8 crusty sourdough bread rolls
3 cups Spicy Corn Relish (see recipe)

◆ Sandwich: Combine first 6 ingredients in bowl.

◆ Generously rub both sides of steak with spice mixture. Cover and chill at least 1 hour and up to 8 hours.

◆ Grill steak to desired doneness, about 4 minutes per side for medium-rare. Cool 5 minutes. (Can be made 1 day ahead. Cover and chill).

◆ Cut steak across grain into thin slices.

◆ Cut rolls in half horizontally and cut out bread centers, leaving 2-inch thick shells.

◆ Mound sliced steak in each roll.

◆ Divide relish among sandwiches.

◆ Place top of roll over filling; press to compact. (Can be made 1 hour ahead. Wrap in foil; chill.)

Yield: 4 cups

SPICY CORN RELISH:

2 cups fresh corn kernels (from about 3 ears) or frozen, thawed
1 cup red onion, chopped
1 cup red and green bell pepper, chopped
1 cup cider vinegar
½ cup celery, finely chopped
1 (4-ounce) can diced mild green chiles, drained
⅓ cup golden brown sugar, packed
2 tablespoons dry mustard
2 teaspoons mustard seeds
2 teaspoons garlic, finely chopped

SPICY CORN RELISH:

◆ Combine all ingredients in heavy large saucepan.

◆ Bring to boil, stirring occasionally. Reduce heat, simmer until almost all liquid has evaporated, stirring occasionally, about 45 minutes.

◆ Cool completely. Cover and chill.

◆ Bring to room temperature before using.

Relish can be made 5 days ahead.

FRESH FRUIT IN GINGERED WHITE WINE

Yield: 10 servings

10 cups cut up assorted fresh fruit (your choice of apples, oranges, pineapple, peaches, apricots, strawberries, cherries)
2 tablespoons lemon juice
1½ cups water
¾ cup sugar
1 cup white wine
1 tablespoon fresh ginger root, peeled and finely chopped

◆ Place fruit in a large bowl.
◆ Add lemon juice and toss until blended.
◆ Combine water and sugar in heavy saucepan over medium-high heat.
◆ Bring mixture to boil, stirring until sugar dissolves.
◆ Add wine and cook 1 to 2 minutes.
◆ Remove from heat and stir in ginger.
◆ Cool completely and pour syrup over fruit.
◆ Cover and chill until cold.
◆ Transport to campsite in a cold cooler.

CRAB FETTUCINI

Yield: 8 servings

2 (12-ounce) bags spinach noodles
3 cloves garlic, minced
¾ pound butter (3 sticks)
½ cup dried parsley
1 (12 ounce) can condensed milk (or substitute half-and-half)
4 cans crab meat
12 ounces Parmesan cheese, grated

◆ Heat pasta water, and cook pasta.
◆ Mince garlic, sauté in butter.
◆ Add parsley, milk, and crab. Heat.
◆ Drain noodles, put into a bowl.
◆ Pour in sauce, stir, add cheese and serve.

Goes well with a cold bean salad.

Great on outdoor trips because only the butter must be refrigerated and is easy to carry.

RED MOUNTAIN STUFFED PORK CHOPS   *Yield: 4 to 6 servings*

5-6 pork chops (ask butcher to cut a pocket in chops)
¾ cup onion, chopped
⅓ cup celery, chopped
¼ cup butter
½ loaf bread, broken into bread crumbs
½ teaspoon salt
1 tablespoon fresh sage, or to taste
1 tablespoon fresh thyme
1 cup chicken stock
1 can cream of celery soup
½ can water
10 small mushrooms
Garlic (optional)

◆ Sauté onions and celery in butter until onions are clear.

◆ Put bread crumbs in a large bowl and sprinkle with salt, sage, and thyme.

◆ Mix in sautéed vegetables and chicken broth. Mix together and stuff into the pork chops.

◆ Place stuffed chops into a well greased 12-inch Dutch oven.

◆ Mix the soup, water, mushrooms, and garlic in a bowl and pour over pork; cover with lid.

◆ Put the Dutch oven on hot coals and place more coals on the lid.

◆ Bake 90 minutes, turning a quarter turn every 20 minutes. (Or bake in conventional oven at 350° for 20 to 30 minutes.)

BARBECUED CHICKEN AND RIBS

Yield: about 10 servings.

2 pounds beef short ribs
2 pounds country-style pork ribs
2 whole chickens, skinned and cut up
Salt and pepper to taste
2 tablespoons oil
2 onions, chopped
2 cups water
1 cup vinegar
4 cups ketchup
1 cup brown sugar, packed

◆ Trim any excess fat from beef and pork ribs. Season ribs and chicken to taste with salt and pepper.

◆ Heat oil in 12-inch Dutch oven placed on evenly distributed hot coals.

◆ Add onions and sauté until transparent but not browned.

◆ Stir in water, vinegar, ketchup, and brown sugar. Cook, stirring often, until mixture thickens, about 1 hour.

◆ Add ribs to sauce, stirring to coat well. Continue cooking, stirring often and replacing coals as needed, about 1 hour.

◆ Add chicken pieces, stir to coat well, and continue cooking until ribs and chicken are very tender, about 1 hour longer.

◆ Dutch oven may or may not be covered. Sauce is thicker if Dutch oven is not covered.

For conventional range cooking, use an 8-quart pot and cook on range top according to previous directions.

Foil is a useful camping accessory. It is a lightweight, convenient cooking utensil, serving dish, and clean-up aid. For the same reasons, it is useful for the back yard chef. These recipes can be prepared partially ahead and added to the fire when the coals and ashes are perfect. Always use heavy duty foil.

MOUNTAIN TROUT PREPARED IN FOIL

Fresh trout from the stream
Butter
Ground pepper
Seasoned salt
Garlic powder
Fresh lemon
Onion
Fresh parsley, chopped

♦ For each serving, prepare on heavy duty foil:
♦ One freshly cleaned trout.
♦ 1 or 2 pats of butter.
♦ Ground pepper to taste.
♦ Seasoned salt to taste.
♦ Garlic powder to taste.
♦ 2 to 3 slices lemon.
♦ 2 to 3 slices onion.
♦ 1 tablespoon parsley.
♦ Wrap in foil.
♦ Place on coals and cook a few minutes until done, about 10 to 15 minutes.

Trout doesn't get any better than this!

BREAD ON A STICK

Biscuit baking mix
Honey, jam, or your choice of filling

♦ Cut a green stick on your hike.
♦ Prepare biscuit baking mix according to package directions.
♦ Pat out until it is about ¼ to ⅜-inch thick, cut into 1½-inch wide strips.
♦ Wrap around the stick, slightly overlapping the dough. Pinch end closed over end of the stick.
♦ Holding over fire, rotate the stick until evenly cooked and golden in color.
♦ Allow to cool slightly and tap the stick to loosen bread, and remove from stick.
♦ Fill hollow with honey, jam, or other filling of your choice.

 CHICKEN FAJITAS

Yield 4 to 6 servings

1 pound chicken tenders, cut into long, thin slices
1-2 cups oil and vinegar salad dressing
2-3 green bell peppers, sliced into strips
1-2 large onions, sliced into rings
4-6 flour tortillas, warmed
Heavy duty aluminum foil

CONDIMENTS:
Guacamole
Cheddar cheese, shredded
Sour cream
Salsa
Tomatoes, chopped
Ripe olives

- Place the sliced chicken tenders in a large bowl and add enough oil and vinegar dressing to coat well.
- Marinate for 2 to 3 hours, stirring occasionally.
- Using two large sheets of heavy duty aluminum foil, spoon the chicken mixture onto aluminum foil (including oil and vinegar dressing).
- Place the sliced green bell peppers and onions on top of the chicken.
- Wrap the mixture into a secure foil package.
- Using a sharp knife, cut two to three 2-inch slits in the top of the aluminum foil.
- Place foil package on grill and cook over campfire or back yard charcoal or gas grill for 30-45 minutes.
- Place chicken, green bell peppers, and onions on a platter and serve with warmed flour tortillas and your choice of condiments.

CHICKEN ON A STICK

Yield: 4 to 8 servings

4-8 chicken breasts (1-2 per adult)
1 cup teriyaki
¼ cup brown sugar
2 cloves fresh garlic, minced
2 teaspoons fresh ginger
2 teaspoons sesame seeds

- Bone and skin chicken breasts.
- Cut into long strips and weave onto a wooden skewer in an S pattern.
- Combine remaining ingredients and marinate chicken sticks overnight.
- Cook on grill or campfire, basting several times.

CRESTED BUTTE BANANAS IN FOIL
Yield: one banana per person

PER PERSON:
1   banana
½   tablespoon coconut or
    granola
1   teaspoon butter
1   teaspoon brown sugar

◆ Cut heavy duty aluminum foil in 12-inch squares.

◆ Peel banana and discard peel.

◆ Cut down center of banana.

◆ Stuff with coconut or granola.

◆ Place 1 banana in center of foil, add butter and brown sugar. Wrap securely.

◆ Heat (about 5 minutes) over coals until sugar and butter form sauce and banana is heated.

◆ Open foil a little and serve in the foil.

Quick and delicious dessert cooked in coals or on the grill. Be careful when opening, as the syrup will be very hot.

BUTCH CASSIDY LAYERED TENDERLOIN IN FOIL
Yield: 8 to 10 servings

1   beef tenderloin, (about 4 to 5 pounds) sliced in 1½ to 2-inch medallions
2   onions
4-6   potatoes, parboiled and sliced
8-10   tablespoons parsley
8-10   tablespoons onion soup mix
3-4   ounces butter or margarine

◆ For each serving, prepare on heavy duty aluminum foil (in this order):

◆ 1 slice beef tenderloin.

◆ sliced onion to cover.

◆ parboiled potato slices.

◆ 1 tablespoon parsley, chopped.

◆ 1 tablespoon dried onion soup mixture.

◆ 1 teaspoon butter or margarine.

◆ Wrap in foil.

◆ Place on coals or grill and cook until desired doneness.

BEAVER CREEK BLUEBERRY BINGE

Yield: 12 servings

2 cups flour
¾ cup water
⅓ cup pecans, chopped
1½ teaspoons baking powder
½ cup vegetable oil
1½ cups sugar
1 teaspoon almond flavoring
4 eggs
2 teaspoons vanilla extract
1 (3½ ounce) package French vanilla pudding mix
1 teaspoon butter flavoring
1 teaspoon salt
1 cup sour cream
¼ cup poppy seeds
1½ cans blueberry pie filling

- ◆ Combine all cake ingredients except blueberries in a bowl. Beat for 2 minutes.
- ◆ Scrape batter into a greased and floured 12-inch Dutch oven. Bake for 30-40 minutes with 6 to 8 briquettes on the bottom and 10 to 12 on the top.
- ◆ Remove from heat when cake begins to pull away from the side of the oven and toothpick inserted into the middle comes out clean.
- ◆ Let cool with lid off for 5 to 10 minutes, then invert cake onto a rack.
- ◆ Invert again onto the Dutch oven lid so that cake is right side up. Allow to cool for an additional ½ hour.
- ◆ Split the cake in half horizontally. Set top half to the side.

BINGE ICING:
8 ounces cream cheese, softened
2 teaspoons vanilla extract
⅓ cup fresh lemon juice
14 ounces sweetened condensed milk

BINGE ICING:
- ◆ Combine all ingredients and whip with a whisk until smooth.
- ◆ Spread half of icing on bottom half of cake, then spread on half of blueberry topping.
- ◆ Replace top half of cake.
- ◆ Repeat step with icing and blueberries on top.
- ◆ Cut into wedges and serve.

The Cookie Jar

· RICH MINING LEGACY...REDSTONE CASTLE ·

GRANDMA PROCTOR'S FILLED COOKIES   *Yield: 36 3-inch cookies*

½ cup shortening
1 cup sugar
1 egg
3½ cups flour, sifted
3 teaspoons baking powder
½ cup milk

FILLING:
1 cup raisins, chopped
½ cup water
½ cup sugar
1 tablespoon flour

◆ Cream shortening and sugar until creamy.

◆ Add egg.

◆ Add flour and baking powder alternately with milk to creamed mixture.

◆ Chill. Roll and cut into 3-inch circles.

◆ Preheat oven to 350°.

◆ FILLING: Mix ingredients in a medium pan and cook over medium-low heat, about 10 minutes (burns easily, so watch carefully).

◆ Assemble: Put 3-inch circle on lightly greased cookie sheet, put about 1 teaspoon filling in center, and cover with another circle.

◆ Flute edges with a fork to seal, cut slit in top if you wish. Bake at 350° for 15 to 17 minutes.

Variation: Can use mincemeat or preserves for the filling.

From the **Plateau Valley Cook Book**

The original recipe only listed ingredients and directions to cut dough into circles and to cook filling carefully as it will burn. No time or temperature was given as this was made in a wood-burning stove. For those without a woodburning stove, we have added directions for use in a modern kitchen.

VIENNA CHOCOLATE BARS

Yield: 2 dozen

2 sticks (8 ounces total) butter
1½ cups sugar, divided
2 egg yolks
2½ cups flour
1 (10 ounce) jar raspberry preserves
1 cup semi-sweet chocolate chips
¼ teaspoon salt
4 egg whites
2 cups nuts, finely chopped

◆ Cream butter with egg yolks and ½ cup sugar.

◆ Add flour and knead with fingers.

◆ Pat batter (⅜-inch thick) on greased cookie sheet.

◆ Bake 15-20 minutes at **350°** until lightly browned.

◆ Remove from oven, spread with preserves, and top with chocolate chips.

◆ Beat egg whites with salt until stiff. Fold in remaining cup of sugar and nuts.

◆ Gently spread on top of jelly and chocolate. Bake for about 25 minutes at **350°**.

◆ Cut into 3-inch by 1-inch bars.

PECAN PIE SQUARES

Yield: 70 squares

DOUGH:
3 cups flour
¾ cup margarine or butter, softened
¼ cup plus 2 tablespoons sugar
½ teaspoon salt

PECAN FILLING:
4 eggs, slightly beaten
1½ cups light or dark corn syrup
1½ teaspoons vanilla extract
1½ cups sugar
3 tablespoons margarine or butter, melted
2½ cups pecans, chopped

◆ Heat oven to **350°**.

◆ Grease jelly roll pan (15½ x 10½ x 1-inch).

◆ Beat flour, sugar, margarine, and salt in large bowl on medium speed until crumbly (mixture will be dry).

◆ Press firmly in pan.

◆ Bake about 20 minutes or until light golden brown.

◆ PECAN FILLING: Mix all ingredients except pecans until well blended. Stir in pecans.

◆ Pour over baked layer; spread evenly.

◆ Bake about 25 minutes or until filling is set; cool.

◆ Cut into 1½ inch squares.

TURTLE COOKIES

Yield: 28

CRUST:
2 cups flour
1 cup brown sugar, lightly packed
½ cup shortening
2 cups pecans, chopped
CARAMEL:
1 cup butter
1½ cups brown sugar, lightly packed
3 tablespoons corn syrup
TOPPING:
1 (12 ounce) package semi-sweet chocolate chips

◆ CRUST: Combine flour, brown sugar, and shortening. Spread in 9 x 13-inch pan.
◆ Sprinkle chopped pecans over crust.
◆ CARAMEL: Mix butter, brown sugar, and corn syrup in a pan. Boil 1 minute, stirring constantly.
◆ Pour caramel over crust and pecans. Bake at **350°** for 22 minutes until surface bubbles.
◆ Sprinkle chocolate chips over all as soon as pan is out of the oven; spread as they melt.
◆ Cool. Cut into squares.

CHOCOLATE CHIP MERINGUE BARS

Yield: 16 bars

CRUST:
½ cup shortening or butter
½ cup sugar
½ cup brown sugar
2 egg yolks, beaten
1 teaspoon vanilla extract
¼ teaspoon salt
¼ teaspoon soda
1 tablespoon water
2 cups flour
1 cup pecans, chopped
1 (12 ounce) package chocolate chips
MERINGUE TOPPING:
2 egg whites
1 cup brown sugar

◆ CRUST: Cream shortening and sugars. Add next six ingredients and mix well.
◆ Pat into bottom of 8 x 12-inch greased pan.
◆ Press chocolate chips and nuts into dough.

◆ MERINGUE TOPPING: Beat egg whites until stiff; mix with brown sugar.
◆ Spread evenly over crust in the pan.
◆ Bake 25 to 30 minutes at **325°**.
◆ Cool 20 minutes and cut into squares.

SASSAFRAS OATMEAL DATE BARS

Yield: 28 bars

CRUST:

1½	cups flour
½	teaspoon baking soda
½	teaspoon salt
½	pound margarine, softened
1¼	cups light brown sugar
½	cup whole wheat flour
1¾-2	cups quick oats

FILLING:

1	pound dates, chopped
¼	cup honey (or ½ cup sugar)
¼	cup lemon juice
½	cup walnuts, chopped
1½	cups water

◆ CRUST: Sift white flour, baking soda, and salt; set aside.

◆ In medium bowl, beat margarine and brown sugar until light and fluffy.

◆ Add flour mixture, wheat flour, and oats; mix well by hand.

◆ Press half the mixture into greased 9 x 13-inch pan.

◆ FILLING: In a small saucepan combine dates, honey, and water. Cook over medium heat, stirring constantly, until mixture thickens (about 5 to 7 minutes). Remove from heat.

◆ Stir in lemon juice and add nuts. Cool.

◆ Spread cooled filling over the crust in the pan. Spread the remaining crust mixture over the filling to cover the filling completely.

◆ Bake 25 to 30 minutes at **375°**.

◆ While still warm, cover with tin foil. Cut when cool or as needed.

OLD FASHIONED SUGAR COOKIES

Yield: 2 to 3 dozen

1	cup butter
1	cup sugar
1	large egg
1	teaspoon almond extract
½	teaspoon vanilla extract
2⅓	cups flour
1	teaspoon cream of tartar
1	teaspoon baking soda

◆ Cream butter and sugar until fluffy.

◆ Add egg and flavorings to creamed mixture.

◆ Mix dry ingredients thoroughly and add to creamed mixture.

◆ Cool dough in refrigerator for at least ½ hour. Divide into 3 or 4 parts and roll out with rolling pin.

◆ Cut out shapes with cookie cutter and place on clean, ungreased cookie sheets.

◆ Bake in pre-heated 350° oven for 5 minutes.

◆ Remove immediately and cool on racks. May be frosted.

Historical Note: This recipe, dating from Colonial times, was obtained during the 1976 Bicentennial celebration. It won a Blue Ribbon at the Mesa County Fair.

GRANDMA'S OLD FASHIONED AMISH SUGAR COOKIES

Yield: 3 to 4 dozen

1 cup butter
1 cup vegetable oil
1 cup powdered sugar
1 cup sugar
1 teaspoon vanilla extract
2 eggs
4 cups flour
1 teaspoon baking soda
1 tablespoon cream of tartar (may use 2 teaspoons baking powder)
1 teaspoon salt

◆ Cream together first 4 ingredients.
◆ Add vanilla and eggs and beat until smooth and creamy.
◆ Sift together flour and remaining ingredients.
◆ Gradually mix the dry ingredients into the creamed mixture (will be a firm dough).
◆ Can be rolled out and cut into shapes or made into small balls, flattened with the bottom of a glass coated with powdered sugar.
◆ Bake in pre-heated 350° oven for about 12 minutes (do not brown).

APRICOT BOW TIES

Yield: 8 dozen

DOUGH:
1 pound margarine
1 pound creamed cottage cheese
4 cups flour, sifted

FILLING:
1 pound dried apricots
2 cups sugar
2 cups water

◆ Mix first 3 ingredients with a fork.
◆ Mix dough thoroughly and roll thin.
◆ Cut into 2-inch by 2-inch squares.
◆ Cook filling ingredients until thick. Cool.
◆ Put ½ to 1 teaspoon filling in center of each square and fold top and bottom together to form a bow tie appearance.
◆ Bake on a greased cookie sheet at 375° for approximately 12 minutes or until golden. Cool on wire racks.

Fun to make and delicious!

MOLASSES SUGAR COOKIES

Yield: 3 dozen

¾ cup vegetable shortening
1 cup sugar
¼ cup mild molasses
1 egg
2 teaspoons baking soda
2 cups flour, sifted
½ teaspoon ground cloves
½ teaspoon ground ginger
1 teaspoon cinnamon
½ teaspoon salt

- Melt shortening in saucepan.
- Remove from heat and let cool. Transfer to large mixer bowl.
- Add sugar, molasses, and egg and beat well.
- Sift together soda, flour, cloves, ginger, cinnamon, and salt and add to first mixture, beating until the dry ingredients are just mixed in with the wet ingredients.
- Chill for several hours.
- Form into 1-inch balls, roll in additional sugar and place on greased cookie sheet 2 inches apart.
- Bake at 350° for 10 minutes or until top is cracked and looks firm. Cool.

Note: Dough is heavy and needs a heavy mixer.

ORANGE SHORT COOKIES

Yield: 3 dozen

1 cup shortening
1 cup sugar
1 egg
1 tablespoon orange rind, grated
1 tablespoon orange juice
2¼ cups flour
1 teaspoon baking powder
Pinch of salt
1 cup pecans, chopped

◆ Cream shortening; gradually add sugar, beating at medium speed until light and fluffy.

◆ Add egg, orange rind, and orange juice; beat well.

◆ Combine flour, baking powder, and salt. Add to creamed mixture, beating until just blended.

◆ Shape dough into 15-inch long roll; wrap in waxed paper. Chill for 2 hours or until dough is firm.

◆ Unwrap dough and roll in chopped pecans, pressing them in if necessary.

◆ Cut into ¼-inch slices; place on lightly greased cookie sheets.

◆ Bake at **375°** for 15 to 17 minutes or until lightly browned.

◆ Cool on wire racks.

TRIPLE THREAT CHOCOLATE COOKIES

Yield: 12 to 18 large cookies

¼ cup butter, softened
1 cup sugar
2 eggs
1 (4 ounce) German chocolate bar
1 (1 ounce) square unsweetened chocolate
¾ cup flour
⅛ teaspoon salt
1 teaspoon vanilla extract
½ cup walnuts, chopped
1 cup semi-sweet chocolate chips

◆ Cream butter, sugar, and eggs.

◆ Melt German chocolate and chocolate square in microwave or in double boiler.

◆ Add flour and melted chocolate to creamed mixture.

◆ Add salt and vanilla.

◆ Add nuts and chocolate chips to mixture.

◆ Refrigerate at least 1 hour. May be rolled into 2 to 3-inch log and wrapped in waxed paper prior to refrigerating or freezing.

◆ To bake: slice log into ¾-inch slices and bake in preheated **350°** oven for 13 to 15 minutes. Cool on wire rack.

Serve to chocoholics! Very rich and yummy. Store in tin.

271

A WHOPPER OF A COOKIE

Yield: 1½ dozen

2 cups flour
1 teaspoon baking soda
¼ teaspoon salt
1 cup sugar
⅓ cup cocoa
¾ cup milk
⅓ cup vegetable oil
1 large egg
2 teaspoons vanilla extract, divided
½ cup butter or margarine, softened
¼ cup marshmallow cream
1 cup powdered sugar, sifted

◆ Combine first 5 ingredients in a large mixing bowl; stir well.

◆ Add milk and oil; beat at medium speed until blended.

◆ Add egg, beating well. Stir in 1 teaspoon vanilla.

◆ Drop by heaping teaspoons 2 inches apart onto greased cookie sheets.

◆ Bake at **350°** for 6 to 8 minutes. Cool on wire racks.

◆ Beat butter and marshmallow cream at medium speed until fluffy.

◆ Gradually add powdered sugar, beating well. Stir in remaining 1 teaspoon vanilla.

◆ Spread flat side of cookie with filling and top with another cookie, placing cookies flat side down.

Kids love these! Wrap individually for snacks or school lunches.

CRISP OAT COOKIES

Yield: 3 dozen

2 cups flour
2 teaspoons baking soda
1 teaspoon baking powder
¼ teaspoon salt
1 cup shortening
1 cup brown sugar, packed
¾ cup sugar
2 eggs
1 teaspoon vanilla extract
2 cups quick-cooking oats, uncooked
1¾ cups corn flakes cereal

◆ Combine flour, soda, baking powder, and salt; set aside.

◆ Cream shortening; gradually add sugars, beating well at medium speed.

◆ Add eggs and vanilla; beat well.

◆ Add flour mixture, mixing well.

◆ Stir in oats and corn flakes.

◆ Shape dough into 1½-inch balls. Place on lightly greased cookie sheets and flatten slightly.

◆ Bake at **325°** for 12 to 14 minutes. Cool slightly on cookie sheets.

ENSTROM'S TOFFEE CHIP COOKIES

Yield: 6 dozen

2¼ cups unbleached flour
1 teaspoon baking soda
½ teaspoon salt
½ pound (2 sticks) margarine
¾ cup sugar
¾ cup brown sugar, packed
1½ teaspoons vanilla extract (or almond extract)
2 eggs
1 cup oatmeal
9 ounces Enstrom's Toffee**(or other high quality toffee), broken up to about the size of chocolate chips

◆ Sift flour, baking soda, and salt together. Set aside.

◆ Beat margarine, sugars, vanilla, and eggs until fluffy.

◆ Add flour mixture and blend thoroughly; stir in oatmeal and toffee pieces.

◆ Chill dough about one hour.

◆ Preheat oven to **375°**.

◆ Drop by teaspoonful on un-greased cookie sheet 2 inches apart.

◆ Bake at **375°** for 10 to 12 minutes until golden.

**See ordering information on special address page in back of this book.

MOCHA CHIP COOKIES

Yield: 6½ dozen

½ cup shortening
½ cup butter or margarine, softened
½ cup sugar
½ cup powdered sugar
1 large egg
1½ teaspoons instant coffee granules
1 tablespoon hot water
2¼ cups flour
½ teaspoon baking soda
½ teaspoon salt
3 tablespoons cocoa
½ teaspoon cream of tartar
1 cup semi-sweet chocolate chips
⅔ cup pecans or walnuts, chopped
Sugar for coating

◆ Beat shortening and butter or margarine at medium speed until fluffy.

◆ Gradually add ½ cup sugar and powdered sugar, beating well. Add egg and beat well.

◆ Dissolve coffee granules in hot water and add to creamed mixture, beating well.

◆ Combine flour and next four ingredients; gradually add to creamed mixture, beating well. Stir in chocolate chips and nuts. Cover and chill for 1 hour.

◆ Shape into ½-inch balls; roll in additional sugar.

◆ Place on lightly greased cookie sheet. Press slightly to flatten.

◆ Bake at **350°** for 8 to 10 minutes or until lightly browned. Cool on wire racks.

WILD WEST OATMEAL COOKIES

Yield: 7 dozen

1   cup butter or margarine, softened
1   cup sugar, divided
¾   cup brown sugar, packed
2   large eggs
1   teaspoon vanilla extract
1½ cups flour
½   cup whole wheat flour
1   teaspoon baking soda
½   teaspoon salt
1½ cups quick-cooking oats, uncooked
1½ cups raisins
4   teaspoons ground cinnamon

◆ Beat butter in a large mixing bowl at medium speed until fluffy.

◆ Gradually add ¾ cup sugar and brown sugar, beating well.

◆ Add eggs, one at a time, beating well after each addition. Stir in vanilla.

◆ Combine flours, baking soda, and salt; gradually add to creamed mixture, beating well.

◆ Stir in oats and raisins.

◆ Combine remaining ¼ cup sugar and cinnamon in a small bowl; stir well. Shape dough into 1-inch balls; roll in cinnamon-sugar mixture. Place 2 inches apart on greased cookie sheets.

◆ Bake at **375°** for 7 to 9 minutes or until lightly browned. Cool on wire racks.

 # PEANUT BUTTER BUSTERS

Yield: 1½ dozen

1½ cups flour
½ teaspoon baking soda
¼ teaspoon salt
½ cup sugar
½ cup shortening
½ cup creamy peanut butter
¼ cup light corn syrup
1 tablespoon milk
⅓ cup plus 2 teaspoons creamy peanut butter

◆ Combine first 4 ingredients in a medium bowl; cut in shortening and ½ cup peanut butter until mixture is crumbly.

◆ Add syrup and milk, stirring until blended.

◆ Shape dough into a 9-inch roll; wrap in waxed paper and chill at least 8 hours.

◆ Unwrap roll and cut into ¼-inch slices.

◆ Place half of slices 2 inches apart on greased cookie sheet. Spread each slice with ½ teaspoon peanut butter. Cover with remaining dough slices and press edges with a fork to seal.

◆ Bake at **350°** for 14 to 16 minutes or until lightly browned. Cool on wire racks.

Worth the extra effort!

CHERRY BLOSSOMS

Yield: 24 bars

½ cup margarine
2 cups sugar
⅔ cup evaporated milk
1 cup miniature marshmallows
12 ounces cherry chips
1 teaspoon vanilla extract
¾ cup peanut butter
12 ounces chocolate chips
1 large pack salted peanuts, crushed (12-16 ounces)

◆ Melt and cool margarine. Add sugar, milk, and marshmallows and cook over low heat for 5 to 7 minutes.

◆ Remove from heat. Add cherry chips and mix well.

◆ Add vanilla extract and half of the peanut butter.

◆ Grease a 9 x 13-inch pan and spread cherry mixture on the bottom.

◆ Melt chocolate and remaining peanut butter. Stir in peanuts and pour over the cooled cherry mixture. Refrigerate. Cut into bars.

A colorful and tasty treat!

LADY BUG COOKIES

Yield: 3 dozen

1 ½ cups flour
½ cup light brown sugar, packed
½ cup butter or margarine, softened
2 eggs
¼ teaspoon salt
½ teaspoon vanilla extract
¼ teaspoon baking soda
½ square (½ ounce) unsweetened chocolate, melted
8-10 maraschino cherries, chopped

Early in day or up to 1 week before serving:

◆ Into large bowl, measure flour and next 6 ingredients.

◆ With mixer at low speed, beat ingredients until just mixed; increase speed to medium; beat 3 minutes, occasionally scraping bowl with rubber spatula.

◆ Spoon 3 tablespoons dough into a small bowl and stir in chocolate.

◆ Wrap both chocolate and light-colored dough with waxed paper, foil or plastic wrap and refrigerate for about 1 hour for easier handling.

◆ Preheat oven to **350°**. With floured hands, roll light-colored dough into 1-inch balls; shape each ball in a lightly floured teaspoon; slip onto greased cookie sheets, about 1 inch apart.

◆ With knife, draw a deep line lengthwise down the center of each cookie. Press 2 cherry pieces on each side of line.

◆ Shape chocolate dough into pea-size balls; flatten each on tip of a cookie to resemble head of ladybug.

◆ Bake 12 to 15 minutes until light brown. Cool.

Variation: Tint light-colored dough with red food coloring and use raisins instead of cherries for dots. Kids love these "lucky" and wonderful cookies.

MINCEMEAT FILLED COOKIES

Yield: 18 filled cookies

½ cup brown sugar
½ cup butter
1 teaspoon vanilla extract
2 eggs
2½ cups unbleached flour, sifted
2 teaspoons baking powder
½ teaspoon salt
1 jar mincemeat

◆ Cream sugar and butter. Beat in vanilla, eggs, flour, baking powder, and salt.

◆ Chill dough for 4 hours.

◆ Roll out dough a portion at a time and cut with a 2½-inch round cutter.

◆ Place 1 round on cookie sheet; place 2 teaspoons of mincemeat in center, cover with a second round of dough, and seal edges.

◆ Cut a ½-inch cross through the top of the cookie to allow excess steam to escape.

◆ Bake at **350°** about 15 minutes or until golden but not brown.

Note: Store in single layers in tin. These are particularly good warm. May be heated in microwave for 8 seconds before serving.

DOUBLE-DIPPED PEANUT BUTTER BALLS

Yield: about 48 balls

1 pound confectioners' sugar (2⅔ cups)
½ pound (2 sticks) margarine, melted
2 cups creamy peanut butter
11 double squares of graham crackers, crushed
1 (12 ounce) package milk chocolate chips
3 tablespoons white corn syrup

◆ Combine melted margarine, peanut butter and sugar in food processor or mixer.

◆ Add graham crackers and mix well.

◆ Make 1-inch balls and place on waxed paper. Refrigerate.

◆ Melt chocolate and corn syrup in double boiler. Add water, if needed, to thin to a dipping consistency.

◆ Use a toothpick or spoon and dip each ball into chocolate mixture. Let harden on wax paper and dip once more.

◆ Store in refrigerator.

Fun for kids to help make and eat!

277

MOM'S FAVORITE FUDGE

Yield: Not nearly enough!

4 cups sugar
1 cup milk
¼ pound butter (1 stick)
3 tablespoons white corn syrup
2 (7 ounce) milk chocolate bars, broken into small pieces
8 ounces semi-sweet chocolate chips
1 ounce dark unsweetened chocolate
10 large or 60 small marshmallows
1 teaspoon vanilla extract
1 cup walnuts (optional)

◆ Cook sugar, milk, butter, and corn syrup in a large saucepan. Cook until the mixture reaches the soft-ball stage (when a drop of the mixture is dropped in a cup of cold water and forms a soft ball).

◆ Pour hot mixture over the two broken chocolate bars, chocolate chips, unsweetened chocolate and marshmallows.

◆ Mix until smooth. Add vanilla extract. Add nuts, if desired.

◆ Pour into buttered pie plate or 9 x 9-inch baking dish.

Hint: Butter rim and sides of the cooking pan so the mixture will not crystalize on the sides of the pan.

Variation: May pour some in one dish without nuts and the rest in a dish with nuts or coconut.

CHOCOLATE COVERED COCONUT DROPS

Yield: about 48 balls

1 (14 ounce) can sweetened condensed milk
¼ pound butter (1 stick), melted
1½ pounds confectioners' sugar
16 ounces flaked coconut
16 ounces milk chocolate chips
3 tablespoons white corn syrup

◆ Mix milk, butter, sugar, and coconut in a large bowl.

◆ Let stand in refrigerator for 30 minutes. Roll into 1½-inch balls and place on cookie sheet covered with waxed paper and refrigerate for 2 hours or more.

◆ Melt chocolate in a double boiler. Add corn syrup; add hot water, if needed, to thin to a dipping consistency.

◆ Dip balls in chocolate and place back on waxed paper and cool. Store in refrigerator.

A great addition to those holiday and gift platters!

CRACKLE CARAMEL CORN

Yield: 6 quarts

6 quarts corn, popped
8 ounces margarine (2 sticks)
2 cups brown sugar
½ cup light corn syrup
1 teaspoon salt
½ teaspoon baking soda
1 teaspoon vanilla extract
  Non-stick vegetable
  shortening spray

◆ Heat oven to 250°.

◆ Coat bottom and sides of a large roasting pan with spray. Place popped corn in pan.

◆ In heavy saucepan over medium heat, melt margarine. Stir in sugar, syrup, and salt and bring to a boil, stirring constantly.

◆ When it reaches the boiling point, stop stirring and let boil for about 5 minutes.

◆ Remove from heat and stir in baking soda and vanilla extract.

◆ Pour over popped corn and mix until well coated.

◆ Bake uncovered for 1 hour, stirring every 15 minutes.

◆ Remove from oven and cool completely. Break apart and store in tin.

Note: This is easy to do ahead and enjoy. Add nuts and other ingredients if you want to experiment.

CRUNCHY MICROWAVE CHOCOLATE FUDGE   *Yield: 30 squares*

1   pound confectioners' sugar (2⅔ cups)
½   cup cocoa
¼   teaspoon salt
¼   cup milk
1   tablespoon vanilla extract
½   cup butter
1   cup chocolate candies with colorful sugar shells

◆ Line 8 x 8-inch pan with waxed paper, extending the paper 1 inch above rim.

◆ In 1½-quart casserole or large bowl, stir sugar, cocoa, salt, milk, and vanilla together until partially blended (mixture is too stiff to thoroughly blend in all dry ingredients).

◆ Cut butter in 4 pieces and place in center of the mixture.

◆ Microwave on high for 2 minutes, or until the milk feels warm on the bottom of the dish.

◆ Remove from microwave and stir vigorously until smooth. If all butter has not melted in cooking, it will as mixture is stirred.

◆ Blend candies into chocolate mixture.

◆ Pour mixture into prepared dish. Chill 1 hour in the refrigerator or 20 to 30 minutes in the freezer.

◆ Lift out of pan and cut into squares.

Note: You may leave out the candies, add nuts or just eat pure and smooth!

Grand Finale

• BLACK CANYON OF THE GUNNISON RIVER •

PERFECT PASTRY

Yield: 2 single 8 to 10–inch pie crusts

3 cups unbleached flour
1 teaspoon salt
2 teaspoons sugar
1 cup (2 sticks) cold, unsalted butter, or other fat (lard or vegetable shortening) cut into small pieces (if using a food processor, freeze the butter)
½ cup or more ice water

◆ Combine the flour, salt and sugar in a bowl and mix well.

◆ Mix the butter or other fat into the flour mixture until it resembles coarse bread crumbs.

◆ Sprinkle ½ cup ice water onto the mixture and mix until it holds together. If too crumbly, add more water, 1 tablespoon at a time.

◆ Turn half of the mixture onto a sheet of waxed paper, roll into a ball and flatten to a disc shape about 5 to 6 inches in diameter. Wrap and refrigerate for at least 15 minutes.

◆ Roll out

NEVER FAIL PIE CRUST

Yield: 5 single 9–inch pie crusts

4 cups flour
1¾ cups vegetable shortening
1 tablespoon sugar
2 teaspoons salt
1 tablespoon vinegar
1 egg
1 cup water (approximately)

◆ Mix flour, shortening, sugar and salt.

◆ In a separate bowl, beat remaining ingredients.

◆ Combine all ingredients and stir until moistened.

◆ Mold into 5 equal balls and chill at least 1 hour.

◆ Roll out on a floured board, handling as little as possible.

◆ Bake as directed in pie recipe.

GREAT GRANDMA'S FRESH PEACH PIE

Yield: 6 servings

⅛ pound butter, softened
1 scant cup sugar
5 tablespoons flour
Cinnamon to taste
3½ medium peaches
Pie crust

♦ Mix first 4 ingredients into a crumb mixture.

♦ Place ½ of the crumb mixture onto the bottom of the pie crust.

♦ Peel peaches and cut in half.

♦ Place peaches, cut side down in a circle on the crumb mixture with a half peach in the center.

♦ Top with remaining mixture.

♦ Bake at 425° for 10 minutes then 350° for 30 minutes, or until bubbly and crust is golden.

Additional flour or instant tapioca will thicken the mixture if the peaches are very juicy. Do not add too much or it will change the lovely flavor. Do not use overripe peaches (too juicy)!

This is a soupy pie, but worth it!

PALISADE GROWERS PEACH PIE FILLING

Yield: 2 (8 to 9–inch) pies

4 pounds fresh peaches (about 16 medium) peeled and sliced

MIXTURE:
1 cup sugar
⅓ cup quick cooking tapioca
4 teaspoons fruit fresh
½ teaspoon salt
½ teaspoon ground cinnamon

PIE CRUST:
2 tablespoons butter or margarine
Pie crust of your choice

♦ Add peaches to mixture and turn gently to coat.

♦ Line a 9–inch pie pan with foil.

♦ Pour ½ of the peaches into the pan. Dot with 1 tablespoon butter. Cover with foil. Freeze. Repeat with second pie filling.

♦ When making the pie, place frozen peach mixture in pastry lined 9–inch pie plate and top with crust. (Option: Brush with egg white and sprinkle with sugar.)

♦ Bake pie 1 hour and 15 minutes or until crust is golden and peaches begin to bubble.

Hint: You may want to cover edges with foil.

APPLE PIE WITH WARM CINNAMON CIDER SAUCE

Yield: 6 to 8 servings

1 pie crust
¾ cup granulated sugar, or to taste
¼ teaspoon salt
1-1½ teaspoons ground cinnamon
⅛ teaspoon ground cloves
8 peeled, cored and thinly sliced crisp apples (about 3 cups)
1 tablespoon lemon juice, freshly squeezed
1 teaspoon lemon zest, grated or minced
4 tablespoons (½ stick unsalted butter, cut into small pieces
1 egg white, lightly beaten
1 egg yolk lightly beaten with 2 tablespoons heavy (whipping) cream for glazing
Granulated sugar for sprinkling

◆ Prepare the pastry by rolling out half of it. Line a 9–inch pie pan, and partially bake. Reserve the remaining pastry for the top crust. Cool the pie shell about 15 minutes before filling.

◆ In a large bowl, combine the sugar, salt, cinnamon and cloves and mix well.

◆ Add the apples and toss to thoroughly coat the slices with the dry ingredients. Sprinkle with the lemon juice and zest and toss to blend.

◆ Turn the apples into the cooled shell, mounding them slightly in the center. Dot with butter.

◆ Roll out the remaining pastry to a circle about ¹⁄₁₆–inch thick. Using another pie pan as a guide, cut a disk slightly larger than the top of the pie, including the rim. Moisten the edges of the pie shell with beaten egg white and cover the pie with the top crust.

◆ Press the edges of the top and bottom crusts together; pinch off any excess dough and smooth the edges with your fingers.

◆ Cut air vent holes and brush the pastry with the egg glaze.

◆ Decorate the top if desired with cutouts made from pastry scraps and brush them with the egg glaze and sprinkle with sugar.

◆ Bake at **425°** for 10 minutes. Reduce the heat to **350°** and cook until the crust is golden brown, about 40 minutes longer.

Continued on next page

Apple Pie with Warm Cinnamon Cider Sauce (Continued)

WARM CINNAMON CIDER SAUCE:
- 2 tablespoons unsalted butter
- 1 tablespoon all–purpose flour, preferably unbleached
- 2 cups apple cider
- 2½ teaspoons ground cinnamon

- ◆ Transfer to a wire rack and cool.
- ◆ Serve slightly warm with Warm Cinnamon Cider Sauce.

- ◆ To make the Cinnamon Cider Sauce, melt the butter in a saucepan over low heat.
- ◆ Whisk in the flour and cook, stirring constantly, for about 3 minutes.
- ◆ Slowly whisk in the cider and stir until smooth.
- ◆ Add the cinnamon and cook, stirring constantly, for about 2 minutes.
- ◆ Serve warm over apple pie.

WILD BERRY COBBLER

Yield: 6 to 8 servings

- 2 quarts marionberries (may use boysenberries or blackberries) fresh or frozen and thawed
- 2 cups sugar
- 5 tablespoons cornstarch
- 1 teaspoon vanilla extract
- 1 cup butter
- 1½ cups brown sugar
- ½ teaspoon salt
- 2 cups uncooked oatmeal
- 1½ cups flour
- 1 teaspoon baking powder

- ◆ Combine first four ingredients and cook until thick. Set aside.
- ◆ Cut butter into dry ingredients. Pat half of crumb mixture into 9 x 13–inch baking pan.
- ◆ Pour berry filling onto crust. Top berries with remaining crumb mixture.
- ◆ Bake at **375°** for 45 minutes or until golden.

Serve with ice cream or frozen whipped topping.

PAPER BAG APPLE PIE

Yield: 6 to 8 servings

1 unbaked 9–inch pie pastry
3-4 large baking apples (or more)
½ cup sugar
2 tablespoons flour
½ teaspoon cinnamon
2 tablespoons lemon juice

TOPPING:

½ cup sugar
½ cup flour
½ cup butter or margarine

◆ Prepare pie pastry.

◆ Peel and core apples and cut into quarters, rinse in water and place in a large bowl.

◆ Combine ½ cup sugar, 2 tablespoons flour and cinnamon in a cup.

◆ Sprinkle mixture over the apples and coat well.

◆ Spoon mixture into the pastry shell and drizzle with lemon juice.

◆ Combine topping and sprinkle mixture over the pie ingredients.

◆ Slip the pie into a paper bag. (Do NOT use a recycled paper bag!)

◆ Fold open end twice and fasten with paper clips.

◆ Place on a cookie sheet and bake at **425°** for one hour. Be sure bag does not come into contact with heat source in oven.

◆ The apples will be tender and juicy and the top will be bubbly and golden.

◆ Slit the bag open, remove the pie and allow to cool on a wire rack.

STRAWBERRY SUPER PIE

Yield: 8–10 servings

CRUST:

- ¾ cup (1½ sticks) unsalted butter, melted
- 1½ cups all-purpose flour
- 1 tablespoon confectioners' sugar
- ¾ cup chopped pecans

TOPPING:

- 2 pounds strawberries, divided
- ½ cup water
- 1 cup sugar
- 3 tablespoons cornstarch

FILLING:

- 1¼ cups whipping cream
- ¼ pound cream cheese, softened
- ¾ teaspoon vanilla extract
- ½ cup confectioners' sugar

◆ Preheat oven to **375°**.

◆ CRUST: Mix melted butter with flour, confectioners' sugar, and pecans. Press into a buttered 10-inch pie plate.

◆ Bake for 25 minutes or until light brown. Allow to cool completely.

◆ TOPPING: Mash enough strawberries to make 1 cup. Cut the tops off the rest of the strawberries and set aside.

◆ Place mashed berries in a saucepan and add water.

◆ Mix sugar and cornstarch into crushed berry mixture and bring to a boil on top of stove, stirring. Boil about 1 minute or until clear and thickened. Set aside to cool.

◆ FILLING: Whip cream until stiff.

◆ In another bowl, beat cream cheese with vanilla and confectioners' sugar. Carefully fold whipped cream into cream cheese mixture.

◆ Spread in cooled crust and refrigerate.

◆ When crushed berry mixture is cool, pie can be assembled.

◆ Stand whole (or halved, if you prefer) strawberries on top of the cream filling, cut side down. When entire filling is covered with whole berries, carefully spoon cooled crushed berry mixture over all. Cream filling should not be seen between the whole berries. Once the crevices have been filled, do not overload the pie with the crushed berry mixture, as it will just drip over the sides.

Any leftover crushed berry mixture is delectable on toast or English muffins.

FUDGE PIE

Yield: 6 to 8 servings

2 eggs
1 cup sugar
½ cup flour
½ stick butter
2 squares chocolate (semi–sweet)
1 teaspoon vanilla extract
⅛ teaspoon salt

◆ Beat eggs, sugar and flour together.
◆ Melt butter and chocolate together; add vanilla and salt.
◆ Combine mixtures and mix well.
◆ Pour into a 9–inch pie pan (sprayed with non–stick vegetable spray).
◆ Cook at 350° for 30 minutes or until you touch the middle and it springs back.

Serve this excellent pie while still warm with peppermint ice cream or vanilla ice cream with ground peppermint candy on top.

CHOCOLATE ANGEL PIE

Yield: 6 to 8 servings

2 egg whites
⅛ teaspoon cream of tartar
⅛ teaspoon salt
½ cup sugar
½ cup chopped walnuts
½ teaspoon vanilla extract

◆ Beat egg whites with cream of tartar and salt until foamy. Add sugar slowly and beat until stiff peaks form. Fold in nuts and vanilla.
◆ Spread in a greased 8–inch or 9–inch pie pan. Build up the sides ½–inch above the pan.
◆ Bake at 300° for 50 minutes. Cool.

FILLING:

4 ounces German sweet chocolate
3 tablespoons water
1 cup heavy cream, whipped
1 teaspoon vanilla extract
Additional chocolate bar for shaved topping

◆ FILLING: Melt the chocolate and water over low heat stirring constantly. Cool until it is slightly thick.
◆ Add vanilla and fold in whipped cream.
◆ Pile into cooled crust.
◆ Top with shaved chocolate.
◆ Chill at least 2 hours before serving.

You can make this pie in the morning for dinner that evening.

IRRESISTIBLE ALMOND CARAMEL PIE

Yield: 8 servings

CRUST:
1   9–inch pie crust (may use pre–made pie crust if desired)
1   teaspoon flour

FILLING:
¼   cup margarine or butter, softened
2   teaspoons flour
8-9   ounces almond paste, cut up and crumbled into small pieces
2   eggs
1   cup caramel ice cream topping, divided
3   tablespoons flour
½   cup sliced almonds

TOPPING:
1-2   cups frozen whipped topping
      Remaining caramel topping

◆ Heat oven to 400°. Prepare pie crust using a 9–inch pie pan. Sprinkle with 1 teaspoon flour.

◆ FILLING: In a medium bowl combine butter, 2 teaspoons flour, almond paste and eggs. Mix at medium speed until well blended. (Mixture will be slightly lumpy.)

◆ Spoon mixture into pie crust. Spread evenly.

◆ Bake at 400° for about 16 to 18 minutes or until light brown.

◆ Reserve ⅓ cup caramel topping. Blend in a small bowl the remaining caramel topping and 3 tablespoons flour. Stir in almonds. Carefully spoon mixture over baked filling in pie pan.

◆ Return to the oven and bake 8 to 10 minutes longer, until golden brown. Cool 30 minutes.

◆ Refrigerate 2 to 3 hours or overnight.

◆ TOPPING: Before serving, dollop frozen whipped topping around the outside perimeter of the pie. Cut servings and drizzle with a small amount of the remaining caramel topping.

 LEMON MERINGUE PIE

Yield: 6 servings

1 cup sugar
1¼ cups water
1 tablespoon butter
¼ cup cornstarch
3 tablespoons cold water
6 tablespoons fresh lemon
juice
1 teaspoon lemon peel,
grated
3 egg yolks
2 tablespoons milk
1 8-inch pie crust, baked

MERINGUE:
3 egg whites
6 tablespoons sugar
1 teaspoon fresh lemon juice

◆ In a medium saucepan combine sugar, 1¼ cups water and butter. Cook over medium heat until sugar dissolves.

◆ Blend cornstarch with 3 tablespoons cold water and add to the saucepan. Cook slowly until clear, about 8 minutes.

◆ Add lemon juice and peel. Cook 2 minutes.

◆ Beat egg yolks with 2 tablespoons of milk and slowly add to mixture. Bring mixture to boiling. Cool.

◆ Pour into cooled baked pastry shell.

◆ MERINGUE: Beat egg whites until stiff but not dry. Add sugar gradually. Add lemon juice last.

◆ Spread over cooled filling, sealing to edge of pastry.

◆ Brown in a **350°** oven for 13 to 15 minutes.

Use a glass bowl to beat meringue for this great pie.

ALMOND TOFFEE TART

Yield: 10 to 12 servings

1½ cups whipping cream
1½ cups sugar
½ teaspoon orange peel, grated
½ teaspoon salt
2 cups almonds, sliced
½ teaspoon almond extract
   Press–in pastry

◆ In a 2 to 3 quart pan, combine whipping cream, sugar, orange peel and salt. Bring to a boil over high heat, stirring occasionally. Reduce heat to medium and cook sauce for 5 minutes, stirring often.

◆ Remove from heat and stir in almonds and extract.

◆ Pour nut mixture into press–in pastry.

◆ Bake in a **375°** oven until lightly browned, about 35 minutes for a 12–inch tart, 40 minutes for an 11–inch tart.

◆ Set tart on a wire rack and let stand until just warm to touch.

◆ For easier serving, remove pan rim and slide a long, slender spatula between crust and pan bottom to free pastry from pan. Leave tart on pan for support.

◆ Cool to room temperature.

◆ Cut in slender wedges to serve.

PRESS–IN PASTRY:
2 cups flour
3 tablespoons sugar
¾ cup butter
2 egg yolks

◆ PRESS–IN PASTRY: With your fingers rub the flour and sugar with the butter. Cut into chunks until mixture is evenly mixed (or whirl in a food processor).

◆ With a fork, stir in egg yolks until dough holds together in a ball.

◆ Press dough evenly over the bottom and sides of an 11–inch or 12–inch fluted tart pan with removable bottom.

◆ Bake in a **325°** oven for 10 minutes. Color will be pale. Use hot or cold.

2 cups of walnuts or filberts may be substituted for the almonds. Omit almond extract if either of these are used.

 # TWEED CAKE

Yield: 8 to 10 servings

CAKE:
½ cup butter
½ cup sugar
2 cups cake flour
3 teaspoons baking powder
Salt
1 cup milk
1 teaspoon vanilla extract
3 squares unsweetened baking chocolate
2 egg whites
½ cup sugar

FROSTING:
¾ cup butter, softened
3 egg yolks
2¼ cups confectioners' sugar
3 tablespoons cocoa

TOPPING:
½ cup semi–sweet chocolate chips
2 tablespoons water

◆ Preheat oven to **350°**.

◆ To make the cake, butter and flour 2 8–inch round cake pans. Cream butter and sugar.

◆ Sift dry ingredients in another bowl. Add to the creamed mixture. Add milk and vanilla.

◆ Grate chocolate and blend into the batter so that it looks like tweed (do not over–blend).

◆ Beat egg whites in a clean, dry bowl until frothy. Add 1 table-spoon sugar at a time. Beat until stiff peaks form. Fold whites into tweed batter. Pour into prepared pans.

◆ Bake for 20 to 25 minutes. Allow to cool.

◆ FROSTING: Cream butter, choco-late, egg yolks and powdered sugar together.

◆ Frost tops of both cooled cake layers and stack. Frost sides.

◆ TOPPING: Melt chocolate chips. Add water and blend. Pour over the frosted cake allowing it to drip freely down the sides.

Variation: Melt vanilla chips and drizzle on top of the cake.

TALBOTT'S PACKING SHED CAKE

Yield: 18 to 24 servings

2 large eggs
1 cup vegetable oil
2 cups sugar
1 teaspoon vanilla extract
2 cups sifted flour
2 teaspoons cinnamon
1 teaspoon soda
½ teaspoon salt
4 cups apples, thinly sliced
½-1 cup nuts, chopped
FROSTING:
2 small packages cream cheese
3 tablespoons butter
1½ cups confectioners' sugar

◆ Beat together eggs and oil until foamy. Add dry ingredients and vanilla. Batter will be very thick.

◆ Use your hands to mix in apples and nuts.

◆ Place batter in greased 9 x 13–inch pan.

◆ Bake at **350°** for 45 minutes to 1 hour.

◆ FROSTING: When cake has cooled, mix cream cheese, butter and confectioners' sugar for frosting. (Add more confectioners' sugar if needed.) Spread on cake.

Freezes well without the frosting.

This recipe contributed by Talbott's Orchard.

BESSIE'S CHOCOLATE CAKE

Yield: 10 to 12 servings

½ cup butter
1½ cups sugar
2 eggs, unbeaten
1 cup buttermilk
2 cups flour
2 (1 ounce) squares unsweetened chocolate
1 teaspoon vanilla extract
1 tablespoon vinegar
1 teaspoon baking soda
FROSTING:
1 pound box confectioners' sugar
½ cup butter
6 tablespoons whipping cream
2 ounces unsweetened chocolate
2 teaspoons vanilla extract

◆ Cream the butter and sugar well.

◆ Add eggs, 1 at a time, beating after each.

◆ Sift flour 2 times and add to the creamed ingredients with buttermilk and melted chocolate.

◆ Add the baking soda to the vinegar and dissolve completely. Add to the batter and fold in.

◆ Add the vanilla last and pour into 2 8 (or 9) inch greased and floured cake pans.

◆ Bake in a **350°** oven for 25 to 30 minutes.

◆ FROSTING: Melt chocolate and combine with the butter, sugar, cream and vanilla.

◆ Frost cake and serve.

ENSTROM'S OATMEAL CHOCOLATE TOFFEE CAKE

Yield: 10 to 12 servings

1¾ cups boiling water
1   cup oatmeal
1   cup brown sugar, lightly packed
1   cup sugar
½   cup butter
2   eggs
½   teaspoon salt
1¾ cups flour
1   teaspoon baking soda
1   teaspoon vanilla extract
1   tablespoon cocoa
2   cups Enstrom's Almond Toffee, (or other fine quality chocolate–covered toffee) finely chopped
¾   cup nuts

◆ Pour boiling water over oatmeal. Let stand at room temperature for 10 minutes.
◆ Add sugars and butter and stir until melted.
◆ Add eggs, mix well.
◆ Sift together flour, soda, salt and cocoa, add to sugar mixture, beat well. Add vanilla.
◆ Add ½ of the toffee crumbs. Pour batter into greased and floured 9 x 13–inch pan. Sprinkle with the remaining toffee and nuts.
◆ Bake at 350° for 45 minutes.

This superb recipe was contributed by Enstrom's Almond Toffee.

CHOCOLATE SHEET CAKE

Yield: 15 to 20 servings

2   cups sugar
2   cups flour
1   teaspoon soda
½   cup buttermilk
2   eggs
1   teaspoon vanilla extract
1   (4 ounces) stick margarine
1   cup water
4   tablespoons cocoa
½   cup cooking oil (or ½ cup applesauce)

FROSTING:
1   (4 ounces) stick margarine
4   tablespoons cocoa
6   tablespoons milk
1   pound confectioners' sugar
½   cup nuts (optional)

◆ Combine sugar, flour, soda, buttermilk, eggs and vanilla in a large bowl and beat.
◆ Combine (4 ounces) margarine, water, 4 tablespoons cocoa and cooking oil in a saucepan and bring to a boil. Cook 1 minute.
◆ Combine the ingredients in the saucepan with those in the bowl. Cool for 5 minutes.
◆ Bake in greased sheet cake pan at 350° for 30 minutes.
◆ FROSTING: Boil margarine, cocoa and milk for 1 minute. Add 1 pound confectioners' sugar and ½ cup nuts (if desired). Frost while cake is warm.

MILK CHOCOLATE POUND CAKE

Yield: 8 to 10 servings

1 cup butter or margarine, softened
1½ cups sugar
4 eggs
6 (1.55 ounce) milk chocolate candy bars, melted
2½ cups all–purpose flour
¼ teaspoon baking soda
Pinch of salt
1 cup buttermilk
1 cup chopped pecans
1 (5½ ounce) can chocolate syrup
2 teaspoons vanilla extract

◆ Cream butter, gradually add sugar, beating well at medium speed.

◆ Add eggs, one at a time, beating after each addition.

◆ Add melted candy bars.

◆ Combine flour, soda and salt. Add to chocolate mixture alternately with buttermilk, beginning and ending with flour mixture.

◆ Mix just until blended after each addition.

◆ Add pecans, chocolate syrup and vanilla, blending well and pour into a well–greased 9 x 5 x 3–inch loaf pan.

◆ Bake at **350°** for 1 hour or until toothpick inserted in the center comes out clean.

Optional: Sprinkle confectioners' sugar over top of the cake.

THREE CITRUS CAKE

Yield: 8 to 10 servings

3½ cups all–purpose flour
2¼ cups sugar
4 teaspoons baking powder
1 teaspoon salt
¾ cup vegetable shortening
1½ cups milk
4 eggs
2 teaspoons vanilla extract
2 teaspoons each, lemon, orange and lime rind
Yellow, red and green food coloring (few drops of each)
Lemon filling (or lemon pudding) and orange cream frosting

◆ Grease and flour 3 9–inch layer cake pans, tapping out excess flour.

◆ Sift flour, sugar, baking powder and salt into bowl of electric mixer or food processor. Add shortening, milk, eggs and vanilla. Beat at low speed until blended.

◆ Divide batter among 3 bowls. Add lemon rind and yellow food coloring to first bowl. Add lime rind and green food coloring to second bowl. Add orange rind and red food coloring to third bowl. Stir just to blend.

◆ Pour each bowl of batter into one of the baking pans.

◆ Bake in **350°** oven for 30 minutes or until tops spring back when touched. Cool slightly. Loosen cakes with a knife. Remove from the pans. Cool.

◆ Put layers together with lemon filling (or use instant lemon pudding). Frost side and top with most of the orange cream frosting.

◆ Pipe frosting for decorative border.

◆ Arrange orange sections in a swirling pattern on top. Insert a pecan between orange sections and place a lime slice in the middle. Refrigerate until serving time.

◆ LEMON FILLING: Makes enough to fill 3 layer cake. Combine ½ cup sugar, ¼ cup cornstarch and ¼ teaspoon salt in a large saucepan. Beat in 2 egg yolks and ¾ cup water with a wire whip until

LEMON FILLING:
½ cup sugar
¼ cup cornstarch
¼ teaspoon salt
2 egg yolks
¾ cup water
⅓ cup lemon juice
2 tablespoons butter or margarine

Continued on next page

Three Citrus Cake (Continued)

smooth. Cook, stirring constantly until mixture thickens. Remove from heat. Stir in ⅓ cup lemon juice and 2 tablespoons butter (or margarine). Cover and cool completely.

ORANGE CREAM FROSTING:
½ cup butter or margarine
1 pound sifted (ten times) confectioners' sugar
Dash of salt
2 tablespoons orange juice
2 tablespoons corn syrup
2 teaspoons vanilla extract
Red and yellow food coloring

◆ ORANGE CREAM FROSTING: Beat ½ cup (1 stick) butter or margarine until soft. Beat in 1 pound sifted (ten times) confectioners' sugar and a dash of salt. Beat in 2 tablespoons orange juice, 2 tablespoons corn syrup and 2 teaspoons vanilla until spreadable. Tint with red and yellow food coloring until desired color is obtained.

◆ Garnish: Orange sections, pecans and lime slices.

Very rich, elegant cake. Serve small slices.

Freezing the cake will make it much easier to frost! (After it is baked.)

RASPBERRY UPSIDE DOWN CAKE

Yield: 10 to 12 servings

3 cups raspberries
1 cup sugar
1 package red gelatin (raspberry)
1 package yellow cake mix

◆ Grease a 13 x 9 x 2–inch pan and place raspberries in the bottom of the pan.

◆ Sprinkle sugar and gelatin on top of the raspberries. Mix the cake according to package directions and pour on top of the raspberry layer.

◆ Bake at 350° for 35 to 40 minutes or until the cake is done when tested with a tester.

◆ Cool on a wire rack and cut and serve with fresh raspberries or raspberry sauce (see index for White Chocolate Mousse with Raspberry Jewel Sauce) on top.

May use any fresh fruit in season and complementary gelatin.

APPLE CAKE WITH HOT CARAMEL RUM SAUCE

Yield: 12 servings

CAKE:
1½ cups sweet (no salt) butter
1½ cups sugar
3 eggs
2¼ cups flour
1½ teaspoons cinnamon
½ teaspoon nutmeg
1½ teaspoons baking soda
1 tablespoon vanilla extract
4 medium apples, cored and chopped

SAUCE:
1 cup sugar
1 cup brown sugar
1 cup cream
1 cup butter
¼ cup rum

◆ Preheat oven to **350°**.

◆ Beat butter and sugar until light.

◆ Add eggs, one at a time and beat well.

◆ Add flour, cinnamon, nutmeg and soda and beat well.

◆ Add vanilla, chopped apples and stir to combine. Pour into a greased and floured 10–inch Bundt pan.

◆ Bake 1 hour or until done. Serve with warm sauce (ice cream optional).

◆ SAUCE: Combine sugars and cream and boil 6 minutes. Add rum and boil 2 minutes. Add butter and beat into sauce. Serve warm.

Serve sauce in a preheated pitcher on the side so people may use as much (or little) as they wish. Leftover sauce may be stored in the refrigerator and reheated in the microwave.

PLUM CAKE

Yield: 12 to 16 servings

1 cup (2 sticks) unsalted butter
¼ cup granulated sugar
¾ cup dark brown sugar, firmly packed
2 large eggs
1 teaspoon vanilla extract
2½ cups all–purpose flour (high altitude: add 2 tablespoons)
2 teaspoons baking powder (high altitude: subtract ½ teaspoon)
1 teaspoon baking soda
½ teaspoon salt
2 teaspoons ground cinnamon
1 (16 ounce) can purple plums packed in syrup, well drained, the syrup reserved and the plums chopped
Confectioners' sugar

♦ Preheat oven to **400°**.
♦ In a large mixing bowl, beat the butter until creamy and light, then gradually add the sugars, beating until creamy and smooth.
♦ Beat in the eggs, then the vanilla.
♦ Sift the flour, baking powder, baking soda, salt and cinnamon together.
♦ Stir the dry ingredients into the butter mixture, alternating with ½ cup reserved syrup, beginning and ending with dry ingredients.
♦ Stir in the plums.
♦ Pour the batter into a buttered 9 x 13–inch pan.
♦ Bake for 25 to 30 minutes or until a toothpick inserted in the center of the cake comes out clean.
♦ Turn the cake out onto a rack and allow it to cool, then dust with confectioners' sugar.

RAISIN SPICE CAKE

Yield: 10 to 12 servings

2 cups raisins
1 cup brown sugar
1 cup sugar
1 cup butter or margarine
4 eggs
½ cup milk
1½ cups flour
1 teaspoon baking soda
1 teaspoon salt
1 teaspoon cinnamon
1 teaspoon allspice
1 teaspoon ground cloves

♦ Put raisins in a saucepan covered with water, heat to boiling and boil 15 minutes. Drain.
♦ Use a mixer to blend sugar, butter, eggs and milk.
♦ Add remaining ingredients all at once and mix thoroughly.
♦ Pour mixture into a greased and floured 13 x 9 x 2–inch cake pan.
♦ Bake at **350°** for 45 minutes.
♦ Frost with butter frosting (see index).

Makes a rich and moist cake.

PINEAPPLE MERINGUE CAKE

Yield: 12 servings

1 cup sifted cake flour
2 teaspoons baking powder
⅛ teaspoon salt
4 large eggs, separated
1½ cups sugar
2 teaspoons vanilla extract
½ cup shortening
5 tablespoons milk
¾ cup finely chopped pecans or walnuts

FILLING:
1 (13½ ounce) can crushed pineapple, drained thoroughly
1 cup whipping cream
1½ teaspoons confectioners' sugar
¼ teaspoon vanilla extract

♦ Grease well and flour 2 8–inch cake pans.

♦ Beat egg whites to soft peaks and gradually beat in 1 cup sugar, continuing to beat until stiff. Fold in 1 teaspoon vanilla and set aside.

♦ Cream shortening thoroughly with remaining ½ cup sugar. Beat in egg yolks.

♦ To 1 cup sifted cake flour add 2 teaspoons baking powder and ⅛ teaspoon salt. Sift. Add this mixture alternately with the milk to the shortening mixture. Stir in the remaining teaspoon of vanilla.

♦ Divide the batter evenly between cake pans.

♦ Top each with half of the meringue and sprinkle with nuts. (Do not spread meringue quite to the edge.)

♦ Bake at **350°** for about 40 to 45 minutes, until cake tests done and meringue is light golden brown.

♦ Remove from the oven and cool in pans.

♦ Loosen edges of cake and meringue with a small spatula and turn out.

♦ Place 1 cake layer meringue side down on a serving plate and spread with pineapple cream filling. Top with the second cake layer, meringue side up.

♦ FILLING: Drain pineapple thoroughly. Beat cream with confectioners' sugar and vanilla until stiff. Fold in well– drained crushed pineapple.

Continued on next page

Pineapple Meringue Cake (Continued)

◆ Refrigerate overnight before serving.

It might be well to line the cake pans with wax paper.

Bake in spring form pans to make it easier to remove the meringue–topped cakes.

THREE–LAYER CARROT CAKE

Yield: 10 to 12 servings

3 eggs
1 cup brown sugar
½ cup white sugar
1¼ cups vegetable oil
1 teaspoon vanilla extract
2 cups white flour
½ cup wheat flour
1 teaspoon cinnamon
½ teaspoon nutmeg
½ teaspoon ginger
2 teaspoons baking soda
1 teaspoon salt
3 cups carrots, shredded
1 cup walnuts, chopped
1 cup raisins
  Fine bread crumbs

FILLING:
2 (8 ounce) packages cream cheese
5 cups confectioners' sugar
1 teaspoon grated orange rind

◆ Preheat oven to 350°.

◆ Grease 3 8–inch cake pans with vegetable shortening. Line pans with wax paper and sprinkle fine bread crumbs on wax paper.

◆ Mix eggs, sugars and vanilla until creamy. Add oil and blend until smooth. (Use a mixer or food processor.)

◆ Mix dry ingredients in a separate bowl. Add to creamed mixture. Stir until just blended together, not too much. Fold in carrots, walnuts and raisins.

◆ Divide cake batter equally among the 3 pans.

◆ Bake at 350° for about 25 minutes or until cake springs back when touched or a toothpick comes out clean.

◆ Cool for 5 minutes.

◆ Remove from the pans and cool an additional 30 minutes before removing the wax paper.

◆ FILLING: While the cake is cooling, mix cream cheese and confectioners' sugar until smooth. Fold in orange rind.

◆ Assemble cake by liberally spreading filling between layers and on top.

◆ Sprinkle cake with cinnamon sugar if desired.

LEMON LOAF POUND CAKE

Yield: 8 servings

¼ cup butter or margarine, softened
¼ cup shortening
1 cup sugar
2 eggs
¼ teaspoon baking soda
1½ teaspoons lemon juice
½ cup milk
1½ cups all–purpose flour
⅛ teaspoon salt
1½ teaspoons lemon extract

◆ Cream butter and shortening. Gradually add sugar, beating well at medium speed.

◆ Add eggs, one at a time, beating after each addition.

◆ Combine soda, lemon juice and milk. Let stand 1 minute or until soda dissolves.

◆ Combine flour and salt, add to creamed mixture alternately with milk mixture beginning and ending with flour mixture. Mix just until blended after each addition.

◆ Stir in lemon extract.

◆ Pour batter into a greased and floured 8½ x 4½ x 3–inch loaf pan.

◆ Bake at **350°** for 55 to 60 minutes or until toothpick inserted in center comes out clean.

◆ Cool in pan 10 to 15 minutes. Remove from pan and let cool completely on a wire rack.

Serve with Raspberry Jewel Sauce. (See index for White Chocolate Mousse with Raspberry Jewel Sauce.)

FANTASTIC FROSTED FATTENING BROWNIES   *Yield: 42 servings*

1   cup margarine (2 sticks)
½   cup cocoa
2   cups sugar
1 ½   cups all–purpose flour
     Pinch of salt
4   eggs
½   cup nuts (optional)
1   teaspoon vanilla extract

FROSTING:
¼   cup margarine (½ stick)
⅓   cup cocoa
⅓   cup milk
1   teaspoon vanilla extract
1   pound confectioners' sugar
4 ½   cups miniature
     marshmallows

◆ Place 1 cup margarine and ½ cup of cocoa in a saucepan and heat over low heat until the margarine melts. Mix well.

◆ Place 2 cups sugar, the flour, salt and eggs in a mixing bowl. Stir in the chocolate mixture and add the nuts (if used) and vanilla, mix well.

◆ Pour into a greased jelly roll pan.

◆ Bake in a 350° oven for 20 minutes.

◆ FROSTING: While the brownies are baking, make the frosting.

◆ Place margarine, cocoa and milk in a saucepan. Heat over low heat stirring until smooth.

◆ Add the vanilla and confectioners' sugar. Beat until smooth.

◆ To assemble: When the brownies have finished baking, remove from the oven and turn off the oven. Distribute the miniature marshmallows over the top of the brownies and place back in the oven for 2 minutes.

◆ Remove and pour warm frosting over the marshmallows and spread.

WHITE CHOCOLATE MOUSSE WITH RASPBERRY JEWEL SAUCE

Yield: 6 to 8 servings

1	(¼ ounce) envelope unflavored gelatin (scant 1 tablespoon)
½	cup white crème de cacao
4	eggs, separated, room temperature
2	whole eggs, room temperature
½	cup sugar
1¼	cups milk
½	cup butter
8	ounces white chocolate, coarsely chopped Raspberry Jewel Sauce
¼	teaspoon salt
1½	cups whipping cream, whipped
6–8	fresh raspberries, if desired

RASPBERRY JEWEL SAUCE:
1	pint fresh or frozen raspberries
	Sugar to taste (about ½ cup if raspberries are fresh)
1	tablespoon raspberry liqueur (optional)

◆ In a small bowl, stir gelatin into crème de cacao, let stand 5 minutes to soften.

◆ In a medium saucepan, combine 4 egg yolks, 2 whole eggs, sugar, milk and butter. Cook over medium heat, stirring constantly, until mixture coats the back of a metal spoon. Remove from heat.

◆ Add gelatin mixture, stir 1 minute or until dissolved.

◆ Strain through a fine sieve into a large bowl.

◆ Add chocolate pieces, let stand 5 minutes. Stir until chocolate is melted and mixture is smooth.

◆ Refrigerate, stirring occasionally, until mixture begins to mound when spooned on top of itself.

◆ Prepare Raspberry Jewel Sauce: Combine raspberries, sugar and liqueur; set aside.

◆ In a small mixer bowl, beat 4 egg whites and salt until stiff but not dry.

◆ Stir ⅓ of the egg whites into chocolate mixture to lighten. Fold in remaining egg whites, then whipped cream.

◆ Spoon ½ of the mousse into 6 to 8 stemmed wine or sherbet glasses. Leave top uneven so sauce can form a decorative design.

◆ Drizzle each serving with about 2 tablespoons Raspberry Jewel Sauce.

◆ Spoon remaining mousse into

Continued on next page

White Chocolate Mousse with Raspberry Jewel Sauce (Continued)

glasses, drizzle with more sauce or serve the sauce with the mousse.

- ◆ Garnish each serving with a fresh raspberry if desired.
- ◆ Cover and refrigerate 4 hours or until set.

FUDGE CUP

Yield: 30 to 36 servings

CRUST:

1¾	cups flour
⅓	cup cocoa
¼	cup sugar
1	teaspoon salt
¾	cup butter
⅓	cup coffee

FILLING:

¼	cup cream
2	tablespoons butter
2	cups good quality semi-sweet chocolate chips
⅔	cup sugar
2	eggs
1	teaspoon vanilla extract

- ◆ CRUST: Process all ingredients in a food processor, add coffee until it is a pliable dough.
- ◆ Roll in hands and flatten (to approximately a 1-inch ball flattened between waxed paper) to fit in mini muffin tins that have been generously greased with vegetable shortening.
- ◆ Make decorative edges, if desired.
- ◆ FILLING: Combine cream, butter and chocolate chips and melt carefully in a double boiler. Stir until satin smooth.
- ◆ Add sugar, eggs and vanilla. Pour into pastry lined mini muffin tins.
- ◆ Bake at 350° for approximately 20 minutes until it is dry to touch.
- ◆ Garnish with whipped cream

Options: Add ⅔ cup nuts and/or 3–4 tablespoons liqueur (Amaretto, peach, etc.)

This recipe is from Slice of Life Bakery.

ABSOLUTELY ALL CHOCOLATE ROLL – YULE LOG

Yield: 8 to 10 servings

CAKE:

- 5 medium eggs
- ½ cup sugar
- ½ teaspoon vanilla extract
- 3 tablespoons cocoa
- ¾ cup flour
- 2 tablespoons melted butter

FILLING:

- ⅔ cup cream
- 2 tablespoons butter
- 10 ounces dark sweet chocolate, broken into pieces
- 2 ounces coffee liqueur

◆ Preheat oven to moderate **350°** for 15 minutes.

◆ Butter a baking sheet 10 x 14 inches, line with waxed paper and butter the waxed paper.

◆ Separate 5 medium eggs at room temperature.

◆ Beat the egg yolks with ½ cup sugar and ½ teaspoon vanilla extract (using an electric mixer for 5 to 10 minutes) until eggs are thick and very pale in color.

◆ Combine 3 tablespoons cocoa and ¾ cup flour and sift together. Beat the egg whites until stiff and fold gently into the cocoa–flour mixture along with 2 tablespoons melted butter.

◆ Spread the batter on the prepared baking sheet approximately ½–inch deep.

◆ Bake in the oven for 8 to 10 minutes. Remove from oven and roll cake immediately, lengthwise, leaving cake on waxed paper.

◆ FILLING: Bring ⅔ cup cream and 2 tablespoons butter to a rapid boil. Remove from heat.

◆ Add (10 ounces) dark sweet chocolate, which has been cut into pieces, and stir until chocolate is melted and mixture is smooth.

◆ Refrigerate until chilled but still workable.

◆ Beat vigorously using an electric mixer. Add (2 ounces) coffee liqueur and continue to beat until

Continued on next page

Absolutely All Chocolate Roll – Yule Log (Continued)

TOPPING:
3 ounces dark sweet chocolate
1 ounce of coffee liqueur
1 cup heavy cream

filling is thick.

◆ Refrigerate until proper consistency (of a custard) for spreading.

◆ TOPPING: Melt (3 ounces) of dark sweet chocolate with (1 ounce) of coffee liqueur.

◆ Whip 1 cup heavy cream and fold cream into chocolate mixture thoroughly but gently, using a whisk.

◆ Procedure to fill: Unroll cake, removing waxed paper.

◆ Spread with filling and roll again. Place on a long serving board.

◆ Swirl the topping over the top and sides of the roll and sprinkle generously with shaved chocolate.

◎ CHOCOLATE MOUSSE

Yield: 8 servings

8 ounces semi–sweet chocolate bits
5 tablespoons water
1 tablespoon instant coffee
5 eggs, separated
2 tablespoons light rum
Whipping cream
Peppermint, crushed

◆ In the top of a double boiler, melt chocolate bits, water and instant coffee until melted and smooth.

◆ Separate the 5 eggs. Beat the yolks into the melted chocolate mixture.

◆ Beat in the light rum and allow to cool slightly.

◆ In a separate bowl, beat the 5 egg whites to soft peaks. Fold them gently into the chocolate mixture.

◆ Pour mixture into individual cups or bowls with lids or covers and refrigerate for 24 hours.

◆ Serve with a dollop of whipped cream garnished with peppermint candy.

MOCHA VELVET TORTE

Yield: 8 *servings*

1 tablespoon instant coffee granules
1 cup boiling water
1½ cups sugar
2½ cups semi–sweet chocolate morsels
1½ cups melted butter
6 eggs
1 teaspoon vanilla extract

CREAM:
1 cup whipping cream
2 (4 ounce) packages of bittersweet chocolate
1½ tablespoons butter

◆ Grease the bottom of a 9–inch spring form pan and line with wax paper. Grease wax paper.

◆ Dissolve the coffee in boiling water.

◆ Add sugar and stir until dissolved.

◆ Add chocolate morsels and stir until melted.

◆ Add butter and eggs, one at a time, mixing well.

◆ Add vanilla.

◆ Pour into pan and bake at **225°** for 2½ hours. Cool completely on a wire rack.

◆ Release sides of the pan. Invert torte onto an 8–inch cardboard round.

◆ Place on a rack over a shallow pan and pour the cream over the top.

◆ Chill 8 hours.

◆ CREAM: Combine cream and ⅔ of the chocolate over medium heat and melt, stirring constantly.

◆ Add the remaining chocolate and stir until melted and the mixture is smooth.

◆ Add ⅓ of the butter, beating well until melted. Repeat with remaining butter.

◆ Let mixture cool until it is slightly thickened and of pouring consistency.

This recipe should be made the day before to have proper chilling time in the refrigerator.

LEMON GLAZED CHEESECAKE

Yield: 8 to 10 servings

2 cups graham cracker crumbs
6 tablespoons butter, melted
2 tablespoons sugar
3 (8 ounce) packages cream cheese, softened
¾ cup sugar
3 eggs
¼ cup lemon juice
2 teaspoons lemon rind, grated
2 teaspoons vanilla extract
2 cups sour cream
3 tablespoons sugar
1 teaspoon vanilla extract

LEMON GLAZE:
½ cup sugar
1½ tablespoons cornstarch
¼ teaspoon salt
¾ cup water
⅓ cup lemon juice
1 egg yolk
1–2 drops yellow food coloring (optional)
1 tablespoon butter
1 teaspoon lemon rind, grated

◆ Preheat oven to 350°.
◆ Combine the first 3 ingredients and mix thoroughly (you may have to add more butter to mix crumbs).
◆ Press crust evenly onto the bottom and sides of a buttered 9 x 3–inch spring form pan.
◆ Bake 5 minutes. Cool.
◆ Beat cream cheese until soft.
◆ Add sugar, blending thoroughly.
◆ Add eggs one at a time, beating well after each addition.
◆ Mix in lemon juice, rind and vanilla. Blend well and turn into a spring form pan.
◆ Bake 35 minutes.
◆ While cake is baking, blend sour cream, sugar and vanilla.
◆ Remove the cake from the oven. Gently spread the sour cream mixture over the top.
◆ Return to the oven and bake 12 minutes. Cool on rack for 30 minutes.
◆ Spread with Lemon Glaze and chill several hours or overnight before removing sides of pan.
◆ Garnish with curled lemon strips or slices of lemon.
◆ LEMON GLAZE: In a heavy 1–quart saucepan, mix sugar, cornstarch and salt.
◆ Combine water, lemon juice and egg yolk and add to sugar mixture. Cook over low heat stirring constantly, until the mixture comes to a slow boil and is thickened.
◆ Add butter and lemon rind. Allow to cool slightly, but spread on cheesecake before glaze sets.

This is a beautiful cheesecake!

LEMON NAPOLEONS WITH RASPBERRY SAUCE

Yield: 8 servings

FILLING:

¾ cup plus 4 teaspoons fresh lemon juice

¾ cup plus 4 teaspoons sugar

4 large eggs

4 large egg yolks

2 teaspoons grated lemon rind

1 cup (2 sticks) unsalted butter, cut into pieces

SAUCE:

1 (12 ounce) package frozen unsweetened raspberries, thawed or 3 cups fresh raspberries

6 tablespoons sugar

2 tablespoons raspberry liqueur

PASTRY:

2 (17¼ ounce) packages frozen puff pastry sheets (4 sheets), thawed

1 egg beaten with 1 teaspoon water (glaze)

◆ FILLING: Whisk first 5 ingredients in a large, heavy saucepan. Stir constantly over medium–low heat until mixture thickens and leaves a path on the back of the spoon when finger is drawn across, about 7 minutes. Do not boil.

◆ Add the butter and whisk until smooth.

◆ Cover and refrigerate overnight. (Can be prepared 2 days ahead.)

◆ SAUCE: Purée raspberries, sugar and liqueur in processor.

◆ Strain through a sieve to remove seeds.

◆ Cover and refrigerate until well chilled. (Can be prepared 2 days ahead.)

◆ PASTRY: Preheat oven to 425°.

◆ Roll out 1 pastry sheet on a lightly floured surface to an 11–inch square.

◆ Cut 6 rounds using a 4–inch diameter cookie cutter. Pierce rounds all over with a fork.

◆ Transfer to a cookie sheet.

◆ Roll out remaining pastry sheets and cut out rounds, forming 24 rounds total.

◆ Brush with egg glaze.

◆ Bake until they begin to puff, about 6 minutes.

◆ Press down on each one with a metal spatula to flatten. Continue baking until golden, about 8 minutes. Cool. (Can be prepared 8 hours ahead. Cover and let stand at room temperature.)

Continued on next page

Lemon Napoleons with Raspberry Sauce (Continued)

GARNISH:
8 whole strawberries with stems
Confectioners' sugar
2 cups assorted berries (such as raspberries, blueberries and halved, hulled strawberries)
8 fresh mint sprigs

◆ GARNISH: Starting just below the strawberry stem, make several lengthwise cuts through each whole berry. Fan berries.
◆ Place 1 pastry round on each of 8 plates.
◆ Spoon 3 tablespoons filling over each.
◆ Top with another pastry round.
◆ Spoon 3 tablespoons filling over each.
◆ Top with remaining pastry rounds.
◆ Sift confectioners' sugar over.
◆ Top with fanned strawberries.
◆ Spoon the sauce around each dessert.
◆ Garnish with berries and mint.

Elegant and easy.

◎ LEMON MOUSSE

Yield: 4 to 6 servings

1½ cups sugar
5 ounces butter
4 eggs
4 lemons, juiced
2 tablespoons lemon rind, grated and finely chopped
4 cups heavy cream
Fresh fruit of your choice

◆ Place sugar, butter, eggs, lemon juice and finely chopped lemon rind in a bowl over a double boiler and cook 45 minutes until thick.
◆ Strain and cool for 2 hours.
◆ Whip cream and fold into cool lemon mixture.
◆ Layer in parfait glasses with fresh fruit of your choice.

⊚ LEMON ICE CREAM

Yield: 4 to 6 servings

2 cups half and half or heavy cream
1 cup sugar
1–2 tablespoons lemon rind, freshly grated
⅓ cup lemon juice, fresh squeezed

◆ In a large bowl, stir all ingredients together.

◆ Place in an ice cream freezer and stir or use an electric freezer.

◆ Let "cure" for about ½ hour before serving or put into the freezer for later use.

Wonderful with Raspberry Jewel Sauce (see index for White Chocolate Mousse with Raspberry Jewel Sauce).

⊚ FRESH PEAR ICE

Yield: 6 to 8 servings

2 cups sugar
4 cups water
4 cups puréed fresh ripe pears
½ cup lemon juice

◆ Make a syrup of sugar and water over low heat.

◆ Peel and slice the pears, put in a food processor and add to the syrup immediately to keep them from turning dark. Cool, add the lemon juice and freeze in ice cream freezer or in a pan in the freezer.

◆ Before serving, scoop in food processor and turn on and off until smooth.

◆ Spoon in glasses or glass bowls.

◆ Garnish with mint leaves.

Excellent as a sorbet between courses.

SPRING BERRY TRIFLE   *Yield: 8 to 10 servings*

12 ounce pound cake, cut into
    1–inch cubes
 1 cup creme sherry
 4 cups strawberries, rinsed
    and hulled
 2 tablespoons confectioners'
    sugar
 1 cup plain nonfat yogurt
¼ cup snipped fresh mint
    (leave a few whole for
    garnish)
 1 cup raspberries (reserve a
    few for garnish)
 1 cup blueberries (reserve a
    few for garnish)
½ cup heavy whipping cream
    (optional)

◆ Line the bottom of a wide glass
  bowl with cake cubes. Drizzle
  with ½ cup sherry and let rest for
  30 minutes.

◆ Cut all strawberries into quarters.

◆ In a blender, purée 2 cups of the
  strawberries with 1 tablespoon of
  the confectioners' sugar. Pour
  over the cake.

◆ In a blender, purée another cup
  of strawberries with remaining
  tablespoon of sugar. Add the
  yogurt, remaining sherry and
  mint leaves. Set aside.

◆ Sprinkle raspberries, blueberries
  and remaining strawberries
  evenly over the cake.

◆ Pour the yogurt mixture over all.

◆ Cover and chill in the refrigerator
  for 4 to 6 hours.

◆ Before serving, whip cream to
  soft peaks and spoon over trifle.

◆ Garnish with reserved raspberries, blueberries and whole mint
  leaves.

This is a very light and elegant dish.

SMOOTH AS SATIN CHEESECAKE

Yield: 12 to 16 servings

CRUST:

1 section graham crackers, crumbled (about 20 graham crackers)
⅓ cup butter, melted
1 teaspoon cinnamon, ground
½ teaspoon nutmeg
3 tablespoons sugar
½ cup chopped nuts

FILLING:

2 (8 ounce) packages of cream cheese
2 eggs
¾ cup plus 2 tablespoons sugar
2 teaspoons vanilla extract
1 tablespoon lemon juice

TOPPING:

2 cups sour cream
4 tablespoons sugar
2 teaspoons vanilla extract
1 teaspoon lemon juice

♦ Combine crust ingredients and press into a 10–inch pan.

♦ FILLING: Cream cream cheese, add other filling ingredients and beat until ABSOLUTELY smooth. Pour into crust.

♦ Bake at 350° for 20 minutes.

♦ Remove from the oven and let cool for 10 minutes.

♦ TOPPING: Combine topping ingredients and spoon over filling.

♦ Bake at 350° for 5 minutes.

♦ Cool, and then refrigerate 4 to 5 hours before serving.

Excellent cheese cake. Be sure the filling is very smooth. May use food processor for blending.

Variation: Almond extract may be used in place of lemon flavoring. Add fruit purée of your choice as a side dish.

COOKIES AND CREAM CHEESECAKE

Yield: 8 servings

CRUST:
- 2 cups (24) crushed creme–filled chocolate cookies
- 6 tablespoons margarine, softened

FILLING:
- 1 envelope unflavored gelatin
- ¼ cup cold water
- 1 (8 ounce) package cream cheese, softened
- ½ cup sugar
- ¾ cup milk
- 1 cup whipping cream, whipped
- 1¼ cups (10) chopped creme–filled chocolate cookies

◆ To make the crust, combine crumbs and margarine.

◆ Press onto the bottom and 1½ inches up the sides of a 9–inch spring form pan.

◆ FILLING: Soften gelatin in water. Stir over low heat until dissolved.

◆ Combine cream cheese and sugar, mixing at medium speed until well blended.

◆ Gradually add gelatin and milk, mixing until blended.

◆ Chill mixture until thickened but not set.

◆ Fold in whipped cream.

◆ Reserve 1½ cups cream cheese mixture. Pour remaining cream cheese mixture over crust.

◆ Top with chopped cookies and reserved cream cheese mixture. Arrange ½ of the cookies in the center (3 halves).

◆ Chill until firm (3 to 4 hours).

Use sliced nuts or additional cookies for extra garnish, if desired.

◎ DIANA TORTE

Yield: 8 to 12 servings

28   shortbread cookies
1   quart chocolate ice cream
8   tablespoons fudge sauce
1   quart coffee ice cream
1½   cups Enstrom's Almond Toffee, chopped (or other fine quality chocolate–covered toffee)

◆ Spray an 8–inch spring form pan with vegetable spray.

◆ Process shortbread cookies into fine crumbs and place ½ of the cookies in the bottom of the spring form pan and press down.

◆ Soften chocolate ice cream and place on top of the cookie crust. Drizzle 4 tablespoons of fudge sauce over the chocolate ice cream. Layer remaining cookie crumbs.

◆ Soften the coffee ice cream and make the next layer.

◆ Drizzle 4 tablespoons fudge sauce over the coffee ice cream.

◆ Place crushed toffee over the top of the fudge.

◆ Place in the freezer.

◆ When ready to serve, take torte out of the freezer approximately 25 to 30 minutes before serving.

GREEK CUSTARD STRUDEL (GALOTABOURIKO)

Yield: 36 servings

6 cups milk
1 cup of butter
¾ cup cream of rice
¼ cup sugar
6 eggs
¾ cup sugar
1 cup of butter, melted
½ pound phyllo pastry

SYRUP:
3 cups water
3 cups sugar
   Juice of 1 orange

◆ Bring milk, cream of rice and 1 cup of butter to a boil. Stir until thickened.

◆ Add ¼ cup sugar and stir.

◆ Beat together eggs and ¾ cup sugar.

◆ Add slowly to thickened cream of rice mixture, stirring.

◆ Remove from heat.

◆ Brush a 17¾ x 11½–inch pan with melted butter and place one sheet of phyllo over the bottom of the pan. Brush with butter. Repeat until you have 6 sheets stacked and buttered on the bottom of the pan.

◆ Pour milk mixture into the pan over the layers.

◆ Cover with 6 layers of phyllo brushing each sheet well with butter.

◆ Score the top layer in 2–inch strips lengthwise.

◆ Bake at **350°** for 1 hour.

◆ Pour cooled syrup over immediately after removing from the oven.

◆ SYRUP: Squeeze the orange juice into the syrup and add the remaining orange into the syrup to boil.

◆ Boil syrup for 25 minutes and cool.

This recipe is a traditional Greek dessert provided by Connie Jouflas. The recipe was taught to her by her mother who brought it over from Greece.

See Special Section Guide for phyllo hints.

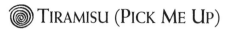 TIRAMISU (PICK ME UP)

Yield: 10 to 12 servings

1 (17 ounce) container of
  Mascarpone cheese
1 cup heavy cream
1 cup sugar
4 eggs, separated
1 cup espresso
1 small glass of Vin Santo
  (Italian dessert wine)
1 box of Italian ladyfinger
  biscuits (or 1 recipe of
  Ladyfingers, see below)
  Freshly grated chocolate

◆ Beat egg yolks with sugar in double boiler until smooth.

◆ In a separate bowl, beat egg whites until stiff.

◆ In another bowl, whip cream.

◆ Put Mascarpone in a large mixing bowl.

◆ Add the egg yolks and whipped cream to the Mascarpone.

◆ Mix gently until well incorporated.

◆ Carefully fold in egg whites and set aside.

◆ Mix the coffee and Vin Santo in a shallow bowl.

◆ Layer ⅓ of the Mascarpone cream in an oblong serving dish, (or divide among parfait glasses). Dip the biscuits into the coffee and Vin Santo and place side by side on top of the cream mixture.

◆ Spread another layer of the cream mixture and repeat with a layer of dipped biscuits.

◆ Finish with a layer of the cream mixture and dust with freshly grated chocolate.

◆ Place in the refrigerator to set and cool for at least 2 hours.

LADYFINGERS:
4 large eggs, separated
½ cup sugar
1 teaspoon vanilla extract
¾ cup flour
⅛ teaspoon salt
¼ cup confectioners' sugar

◆ LADYFINGERS: Beat yolks, sugar and vanilla in a medium bowl until pale yellow. Sift flour and salt over yolk mixture. Fold to combine.

◆ Whip egg whites to stiff peaks, gradually adding 2 tablespoons confectioners' sugar after whites foam. Stir ¼ cup whites into yolk mixture. Fold in remaining whites.

Continued on next page

Tiramisu (Pick Me Up)
(Continued)

◆ Preheat oven to **350°**.

◆ Spoon batter into a pastry bag fitted with a ½–inch plain tube.

◆ Pipe 30, 3 x 1–inch strips of batter, about 1 inch apart, onto a cookie sheet lined with greased parchment. Sift remaining confectioners' sugar over the strips of batter.

◆ Bake until golden, about 10 to 12 minutes.

◆ Cool on baking sheet for 5 minutes, then transfer them to a wire rack and cool completely. Yield: 30 ladyfingers

Hints:Can be stored in an airtight container up to 2 days.

Ladyfingers are simple to make if you use a good stiff batter that you pipe and bake immediately.

SOUTHERN BREAD PUDDING
Yield: 10 servings

4   cups skim or lowfat milk
1   loaf French bread (stale is best), cubed
2   teaspoons vanilla extract
2   cups sugar
3   eggs, beaten
3   tablespoons margarine or butter

BOURBON SAUCE:
1   stick margarine
1   cup sugar
1   egg, beaten
     Bourbon to taste

◆ Soak the bread cubes in milk in a large bowl.

◆ Melt the butter in a shallow baking dish.

◆ Add eggs, sugar and vanilla and mix well.

◆ Pour into the baking dish with the butter.

◆ Bake at **350°** for 1 hour.

◆ Serve with Bourbon Sauce ladled over the top.

◆ BOURBON SAUCE: Melt margarine, sugar and egg together. Add bourbon to taste (¼ cup) just before serving.

The Goodness of IN THE FRIENDSHIP INN

Good Pastures
RESTAURANT

RICE PUDDING

Yield: 4 to 6 servings

4	whole eggs
1	egg yolk
1	cup rice, boiled tender (well rinsed and strained)
1	cup sugar
2¼	cups heavy whipping cream
2¼	cups milk
1½	teaspoons cinnamon
1½	teaspoons nutmeg
2	teaspoons vanilla extract
	Raisins, to taste

◆ Blend eggs, egg yolk, sugar, heavy cream, milk and vanilla.

◆ Add cinnamon and nutmeg; mix well.

◆ Add raisins and rice and pour into a casserole dish.

◆ Bake at 250° until firm, ~~20 to 30~~ 60 minutes.

This recipe was contributed by Good Pastures Restaurant.

PEARS MELBA

Yield: 10 servings

3	cups water
2	cups white wine
¾	cup sugar
2	tablespoons fresh lemon juice
	Peel from one lemon
5	Bartlett pears, peeled, halved and cored

SAUCE:

1	(12 ounce) bag frozen unsweetened raspberries
½	cup sugar (optional)
2	tablespoons Chambord liqueur
1	tablespoon lemon juice
	Vanilla ice cream

◆ Bring first 5 ingredients to a boil, stirring to dissolve sugar. Boil until clear, about 1 minute.

◆ Add prepared pears to the syrup. Reduce heat and simmer 5 minutes.

◆ Transfer pears and sugar to a bowl and chill overnight, covered.

◆ SAUCE: Purée first 4 ingredients in a processor. Strain and cover.

◆ Chill until ready to serve.

◆ To assemble: Drain pears. Cut each half in 4 slices. Place a scoop of ice cream in the center of the plates. Fan the pear slices around ice cream (or set ice cream to one side and fan pears alongside). Spoon sauce over and serve.

BANANAS FOSTER

Yield: 8 servings

2¼ cups brown sugar
1 tablespoon cinnamon
1 cup butter
4 ounces banana liqueur
8 ripe bananas, peeled and sliced lengthwise
4 ounces white rum
Ice cream of your choice

◆ Melt the brown sugar, cinnamon and butter in a flat cooking pan.
◆ Add the banana liqueur and the sliced bananas.
◆ Baste the bananas with the hot liquid until well saturated with the liquid.
◆ Add the rum and allow to flame.
◆ Continue basting until the flame burns out.
◆ Serve immediately over ice cream in individual dishes.

CRANBERRY MOUSSE WITH RASPBERRY SAUCE

Yield: 10 to 15 servings

3 cups fresh cranberries
1 cup sugar
1 quart cranberry juice cocktail, divided
3 envelopes unflavored gelatin
⅓ cup light rum
2 cups cream, whipped

RASPBERRY SAUCE:
1 (10 ounce) package frozen raspberries, thawed
1 (10 ounce) jar raspberry preserves
¼ cup light rum

◆ In a saucepan combine cranberries, sugar and 1 cup cranberry juice. Heat to boiling and then simmer 5 minutes.
◆ Stir gelatin into 1 cup cranberry juice until soft, then stir gelatin mix into hot cranberry mixture.
◆ Add remaining cranberry juice and rum.
◆ Refrigerate until slightly thickened.
◆ Fold whipping cream into thickened gelatin. Mix.
◆ Pour mixture into a 2–quart mold
◆ SAUCE: Combine preserves and rum with thawed raspberries. Refrigerate.
◆ Serve each portion of mousse with Raspberry Sauce.

CHOCOLATE MOUSSE FROSTING

Yield: 2½ to 3 cups

4 ounces unsweetened chocolate, broken into pieces
4 ounces sweet chocolate, broken into pieces
2 teaspoons freeze–dried coffee
¾ cup sugar
½ cup water
8 egg whites
¼ teaspoon cream of tartar
Pinch of salt
7 egg yolks
2 teaspoons vanilla extract

◆ Finely chop chocolate and add coffee.
◆ Dissolve ½ cup sugar in water and bring to a rolling boil.
◆ Add to chocolate and beat until smooth.
◆ Beat egg whites with cream of tartar and salt until firm.
◆ Add remaining sugar and continue beating until stiff peaks form.
◆ Add egg yolks and vanilla to the chocolate mixture.
◆ Fold egg white mixture into cooled chocolate mixture.

This frosting will turn a plain cake into a celebration!

BUTTER CREAM FROSTING

Yield: 2⅓ cups

¼ cup plus 2 tablespoons butter, softened
4 cups confectioners' sugar, sifted
2-4 tablespoons whipping cream
1 teaspoon vanilla extract

◆ Cream butter and gradually add sugar, beating until light and fluffy.
◆ Add whipping cream, 1 tablespoon at a time, beating until spreading consistency.
◆ Stir in vanilla.

A rich and basic frosting that is good on just about anything!

From the Pantry

ROSE TREE JAM

Yield: Approximately 7 to 8 ½ pints of jam

2 cups apricots, finely chopped
1 cup raspberries, fresh (or use 1 cup frozen–thawed)
1 cup pineapple, crushed
6 cups sugar
1 pouch fruit pectin

◆ Stir sugar into fruit using a large, deep kettle.

◆ Bring to a boil over medium heat stirring constantly.

◆ When fruit comes to a full boil, stir in 1 pouch fruit pectin.

◆ Bring to boil again and continue boiling exactly 1 minute, stirring constantly.

◆ Remove from heat and skim away foam, if needed.

◆ Pour into sterilized ½ pint jars, leaving ½–inch headspace.

◆ To sterilize jars, wash jars in warm, soapy water and rinse thoroughly.

◆ Place jars, upside down, in boiling water bath for 10 to 15 minutes.

◆ In a separate saucepan, boil lids and rings 10 minutes.

◆ After jars are filled with jam, wipe rims with a clean damp cloth.

◆ Place sterilized hot lids on jars, then tightly screw on bands.

◆ Place jars upside down for 5 minutes, then place upright. Jars should seal as they cool (approximately 2 hours).

Variation: Jam can be sealed in jars by using hot paraffin wax.

Hint: Canning jars can be washed in the dishwasher just before needed. Take jars from dishwasher one at a time so the rest keep hot while canning.

Makes an excellent jam for that all time favorite, Peanut Butter and Jelly Sandwich! Excellent gift giving idea for the holidays or for that special hostess.

PALISADE PEACH JAM

Yield: 7 ½ pint jars

2 pounds ripe peaches, peeled and pitted (about 1 ½ quarts prepared peaches)
½ cup water
6 cups sugar

◆ Peel and pit peaches and chop in small pieces or crush with masher.

◆ Place fruit in a heavy enameled or stainless steel large saucepan, with water and cook gently for 10 minutes.

◆ Add sugar and stir until the sugar dissolves.

◆ Slowly bring fruit to a boil.

◆ Boil until mixture is thick, stirring often to keep from sticking (about 15 to 40 minutes).

◆ Pour the hot jam into hot sterilized ½ pint jars, leaving ½–inch headspace.

◆ Process in boiling water bath for 10 minutes.

Hint: Put clean jars in **200°** *oven for 10 minutes to get hot, then fill them one at a time.*

1 ½ quarts of chopped or crushed fruit equals 14 or 15 peaches.

CHILE JELLY

Yield: 6 to 7 ½ pints of jelly

6 cups sugar
1 ½ cups apple cider vinegar
½ cup hot red and green chili peppers (approximately 2 each)
½ cup red and green sweet bell peppers
1 (6 ounce) pouch of fruit pectin

◆ Chop or process in a food processor, chile peppers and sweet bell peppers.

◆ Mix sugar with peppers and apple cider vinegar in a large kettle and bring to a boil over high heat, stirring constantly.

◆ Remove from heat and let set for 3 minutes.

◆ Stir in fruit pectin.

◆ Pour into hot sterilized ½ pint jars, allowing ½–inch headspace.

◆ To sterilize jars, wash jars in warm, soapy water and rinse thoroughly.

◆ Place jars, upside down, in boiling water bath for 10 to 15 minutes.

◆ In a separate saucepan, boil lids and bands 10 minutes.

◆ After jars are filled, wipe rims with a damp clean cloth.

◆ Place pre–sterilized hot lids on jars, then tightly screw on bands.

◆ Place jars upside down for 5 minutes, then place upright. Jars should seal as they cool (approximately 2 hours or overnight).

Want a different appetizer? Try this on top of cream cheese and your favorite cracker! Makes a great homemade gift for that special friend at Christmas.

ORCHARD MESA SPICED PEACHES

Yield: 4 pints

12 firm ripe peaches
1 (25.4 ounce) bottle dry white wine
1 cup white wine vinegar
4 small cinnamon sticks
6 whole cloves
10 peppercorns
1 lemon, halved & squeezed into kettle
2 cups sugar

◆ Blanch firm ripe peaches in boiling water. Peel and pit peaches and cut in half.

◆ Place peaches and all other ingredients in a large non-aluminum kettle, preferably stainless steel. Over moderate heat, bring to simmer and cook approximately 10 minutes or until peaches are tender. Riper peaches will cook faster.

◆ Remove lemon.

◆ Put peaches and juice in sterilized pint jars, wipe rims with a clean damp cloth and screw on hot sterilized lids. Process according to hot water bath method.

Hint: When filling pint jars, pack peaches tightly as they will shrink when cooked in hot water bath.

Great holiday side dish.

BREAD AND BUTTER PICKLES

Yield: 8 pints

6	quarts sliced medium cucumbers (approximately 12 cucumbers)
6	medium onions, sliced
1	cup salt
1½	quarts vinegar (5 or 6% acidity)
6	cups sugar
¼	cup mustard seed
2	teaspoons celery seed
¼	teaspoon cayenne
¼	teaspoon turmeric

◆ Combine cucumbers, onions and salt. Let stand 3 hours.

◆ Drain and rinse.

◆ In a large kettle, combine vinegar, sugar, mustard seed, celery seed, cayenne pepper and turmeric. Bring to a boiling point over medium heat.

◆ Add cucumbers and onions. Return to boiling.

◆ Remove from heat.

◆ Fill hot sterilized jars leaving ½–inch headspace, wipe rims with a clean damp cloth and screw on hot sterilized lids.

◆ Process according to hot water bath method for 5 minutes.

PICKLED BEETS

24	small beets
1	cup water
1	pint vinegar
1¼	cups sugar
2	tablespoons salt
6	whole cloves
1	cinnamon stick (3–inch)
3	medium onions, sliced

◆ Wash beets, leaving roots and stems.

◆ Put beets in a large kettle and cover with water. Cook until tender. Drain.

◆ Remove skins and slice.

◆ Combine water, vinegar, salt and sugar in a large kettle. Put spices in a cheesecloth bag and add to vinegar mixture. Heat to boiling point.

◆ Add beets and onions and simmer for 5 minutes. Remove spice bag.

◆ Fill sterilized pint jars leaving ½–inch headspace. Process according to hot water bath method for approximately 30 minutes.

Adds a nice addition to your homemade goodies given to your friends during the holiday season.

GRAND VALLEY GREEN TOMATO PICKLES

Yield: 9 pints

20 cups sliced green tomatoes (approximately 15 pounds)
2½ cups onions, thinly sliced
¼ cup canning or pickle salt
3 cups brown sugar
4 cups vinegar (5% acidity)
1 tablespoon mustard seed
1 tablespoon allspice
1 tablespoon celery seed
1 tablespoon whole cloves

◆ Wash and slice tomatoes and onions.

◆ Put sliced tomatoes and onions in a bowl and sprinkle with salt. Cover with a lid and let sit 4 to 6 hours. Drain.

◆ Heat brown sugar and vinegar in a large saucepan until clear.

◆ Put spices in a cheese cloth bag and add to hot sugar and vinegar mixture, along with tomatoes and onions.

◆ If necessary, add enough water to cover.

◆ Bring to boil, turn heat down and simmer 30 minutes, stirring occasionally, until tomatoes are clear and tender. Remove spice bag.

◆ Fill sterilized pint jars and cover with liquid, leaving ½–inch head space. Remove any air bubbles and wipe the rims with a clean damp cloth. Screw on hot sterilized lids.

◆ Process pints in hot water bath method for 5 minutes (just long enough to seal).

◆————————◆————————▶

JALAPEÑO PICKLES

Yield: 6 pints

36-40	pickling cucumbers (approximately 3 inches in length)
8	cups of water
4	cups vinegar
½	cup canning salt (non–iodized)
6-7	heads of dill
2	garlic cloves per jar
½	jalapeño or 8 slices per jar

◆ Wash and scrub cucumbers. Cut ¼–inch slice from blossom end of each cucumber.

◆ Mix water, vinegar and salt in Dutch oven. Heat to boiling.

◆ Place dill heads, garlic and jalapeño slices in each of the six hot pre–sterilized jars. Pack cucumbers in jars, leaving ½–inch headspace.

◆ Cover with boiling brine, maintaining ½–inch headspace.

◆ Wipe rims of jars with clean damp cloth.

◆ Place pre–sterilized hot lids on jars, then tightly screw on bands.

◆ Stand the tightly sealed jars into the rack of the canner. Submerge into boiling water.

◆ Make sure that water in the canner covers the top of the jars. Process for 10 minutes.

◉ NOT YOUR AVERAGE MUSTARD

Yield: ¼ cup

½	cup yellow or brown mustard powder
2-3	tablespoons orange–flavored liqueur
3	tablespoons white–wine vinegar
¼	cup dark brown sugar (or to taste)
½	teaspoon salt

◆ Mix all ingredients in small bowl.

◆ Cover and refrigerate to allow flavors to blend, about 24 hours.

Hint: This mustard needs 24 hours for the flavor to develop properly.

Can be refrigerated at least 3 months in a sealed container.

APPLE PIE FILLING

Yield: 6 quarts or 12 pints

4½ cups sugar
1 cup cornstarch
2 teaspoons cinnamon, ground
¼ teaspoon nutmeg, ground
1 teaspoon salt
3 tablespoons lemon juice
10 cups water
5½-6 pounds tart apples (pared, cored, sliced)

◆ In a large saucepan blend first 5 ingredients.

◆ Stir in 10 cups of water.

◆ Stir over medium heat until mixture thickens and is bubbly.

◆ Add lemon juice.

◆ Pack apples into hot sterilized jars. Pour juice over the apples, leaving 1–inch headspace.

◆ Wipe rims of jars with clean damp cloth.

◆ Place sterilized hot lids on jars, then tightly screw on bands.

◆ Process using boiling water bath method for 15 minutes for pint jars and 20 minutes for quarts.

◎ CRÈME FRAÎCHE

Yield: 4 cups

4 cups heavy cream
1 tablespoon buttermilk
Powered sugar (optional)

◆ Combine cream and buttermilk in a large glass jar and cover. Store in a warm place away from drafts for 24 to 36 hours before refrigerating.

◆ Crème keeps two to three weeks in a tightly sealed jar in the refrigerator. Add sugar to taste for dessert toppings.

Variation: The addition of brown sugar or Grenadine to the basic Crème Fraîche makes a sweet, colorful topping for fruit salads.

Unlike commercial sour cream, crème fraîche will not curdle in a hot sauce. Add the optional powdered sugar to make a delicious topping for fruits, cobblers, pies.

FRESH PEACH SAUCE

Yield: 4 to 5 servings.

4 peaches, peeled, sliced in small chunks
¾ cup water (use up to 1 cup if peaches are not very juicy)
1 heaping teaspoon cornstarch
3 tablespoons sugar
⅛ teaspoon cinnamon
½ teaspoon margarine

◆ Cook peaches and water until peaches are slightly soft but not quite done.

◆ Mix cornstarch and sugar; blend into peach sauce.

◆ Cook until peaches are done. More cornstarch may be added if thicker sauce is desired.

◆ Stir in cinnamon and margarine.

Keeps well in an air tight container in refrigerator.

Wonderful served over waffles, pancakes or ice cream.

DARK CHOCOLATE FUDGE SAUCE

Yield: Approximately 2 cups sauce

¾ cup European–style cocoa
¾ cup granulated sugar
½ cup brown sugar, packed
Dash salt
¾ cup whipping cream
½ cup butter, softened
1 teaspoon vanilla extract

◆ In a medium saucepan, combine cocoa, sugar and salt. Blend in cream and butter.

◆ Cook over medium heat, stirring constantly, until mixture comes to a boil.

◆ Let stand 5 minutes. Stir in vanilla.

◆ Pour into air tight container and refrigerate until ready to use.

Prepare this chocolate fantasy in decorator jars and delight your friends at Christmas or give as a hostess gift.

Makes a wonderful hot fudge sundae!

SAUCE BÉARNAISE

Yield: 4 cups

4 tablespoons tarragon vinegar
4 tablespoons white wine
4 teaspoons shallots, chopped
4 teaspoons tarragon leaves, chopped
6 egg yolks, or equivalent egg substitute
4 tablespoons lemon juice
½ teaspoon salt
¼ teaspoon white pepper
½ pound butter (2 sticks), melted

◆ Mix first 4 ingredients in a small saucepan. Cook over medium heat to reduce liquid.

◆ Blend egg yolks, lemon juice, salt and white pepper.

◆ Blend melted butter into egg mixture a little at a time.

◆ Add herb mixture and blend 4 seconds.

This keeps well and can be made ahead and even frozen in an airtight container.

A wonderful accompaniment to roast beef or chicken.

GREAT BARBECUE SAUCE

Yield: 2 cups, 6 to 8 servings

¼ cup oil
¾ cup onion, chopped
¾ cup ketchup
¾ cup water
⅓ cup lime or lemon juice
3 tablespoons sugar
3 tablespoons Worcestershire sauce
3 tablespoons Dijon mustard
2 teaspoons salt
½ teaspoon pepper

◆ Heat a quart–sized saucepan and add oil. Sauté onions over medium heat until tender.

◆ Combine remaining ingredients and add to onions. Cover and simmer 45 minutes, stirring occasionally.

◆ Use the sauce to baste chicken or hamburgers when cooking on an outdoor grill.

This recipe can be made ahead and reheated when ready to use. It can also be doubled but be sure to use a larger pan.

YOUR FAVORITE TOMATO SAUCE

Yield: 4 cups

6 tablespoons olive oil
1 medium onion, thinly sliced
3 cloves garlic, crushed
3 cups ripe tomatoes, peeled, seeded and finely cut (or one 33 ounce can Italian plum tomatoes)
2 tablespoons fresh basil, minced (or 1½ teaspoons dried basil, thyme or tarragon)
1 teaspoon salt (or to taste)
1 teaspoon pepper, freshly ground
1 teaspoon sugar
½ cup tomato paste

◆ Sauté the onion and garlic in the oil.

◆ Add the tomatoes and crush with a wooden spoon.

◆ Add the basil, salt, pepper and sugar and simmer for 30 minutes.

◆ Add the tomato paste, stir well, and simmer for an additional 10 to 15 minutes.

◆ Correct the seasonings to taste.

Special Guides

QUICK AND EASY WINE SUGGESTIONS

Wines have been made and enjoyed by man for thousands of years. Our high desert region of Western Colorado has a flourishing but fairly young wine industry that has been growing in size and reputation. Out of the nine wineries in the state at this time, eight are in Western Colorado and of those, five are in the Grand Valley. The Colorado Mountain Wine Festival has become an annual fall celebration, anticipated by many. Visitors and residents alike enjoy the fruits of the harvest as the Aspen trees turn to gold in the crisp spectacular Western Colorado fall air.

Below is a Quick and Easy list to match wines with foods. If you are serving a light meal, select a wine from the top of the list; if serving a heavier meal, select a wine from further down the list. A more complete list of the categories and characteristics of wines follow.

Selected White Wines	Selected Red Wines
(lightest to weightiest)	(lightest to weightiest)
Soave	Beaujolais
Riesling	Valpolicella
Muscadet	Burgundy
Champagne	Pinot Noir
Chenin Blanc	Barbera
Pouilly-Fumé	Chianti Classico
French Chablis	Merlot
Sauvignon Blanc	Zinfandel
White Bordeaux	Cabernet
Pouilly-Fuissé	Syrah
Gewürztraminer	Barbaresco
Chardonnay	Barolo
White Rhône	

When Serving 2 Wines with a Meal:

Common sense should prevail and remember to go from simple to more complex:

> White before red; dry before sweet
> Light before full; young before old

WINE CATEGORIES, CHARACTERISTICS & FOODS

FOODS THAT GO WELL:

Very dry, light wines
Examples: Riesling, Chardonnay, Muscadet, Pinot, Pinot Blanc, Soave.
Characteristics: These wines are characterized by their fresh, tart and subtle flavors.

Lightly flavored dishes
Many seafoods
Light pasta dishes
Vegetables
Some soups

Dry, full-flavored whites
Examples: Chablis, Chardonnay, Graves, Macon, Pouilly-Fuissé, Pouilly-Fumé, Sauvignon Blanc, Alsatian Gewürztraminer, Semillon, and white Burgundy.
Characteristics: Also dry, these wines often have more fruit and body, with accompanying complexity. They will complement a wide range of foods.

Rich fish dishes
Poultry
Game
Light meats
Quiche
Chinese

Slightly sweet, fruity whites
Examples: Chenin Blanc, German wines, Johannisberg Riesling, Vouvray.
Characteristics: Fresh fruit flavors mark these wines, the best of which also have good acidity. Despite their reputation as "sipping" wines, they can accompany a number of foods.

Somewhat rich dishes
Spicy dishes

Sweet, full-bodied whites
Examples: German Spatlese, Late Harvest Riesling or Gewürztraminer, Muscat and Sauternes.
Characteristics: These wines are sweet, with lots of flavor, but not so heavy as many full-blown dessert wines.

Fruit and cheese
Some rich dishes

Fruity, light reds
Examples: Bardolino, Beaujolais, Gamay, Chianti, Italian Merlot, light Pinot Noir or red Burgundy, and light Zinfandel.
Characteristics: It is the style, not necessarily the grape, that makes this category — an emphasis on very fresh, berrylike flavors, light tannin and good acidity.

Can serve chilled
Sausage
Ham
Meatballs
Somewhat spicy dishes

Wine Categories, Characteristics & Foods

FOODS THAT GO WELL:

Medium-bodied reds

Examples: Bordeaux, red Burgundy, Pinot Noir and Merlot.

Characteristics: The differences between the wines in this category and the next is often not the grape but style. The wines in this group are made from any of the classic red wine grapes (Cabernet Sauvignon, Pinot Noir, etc.) but have less tannin, less body, often less alcohol than their "heftier" cousins. They often have nice complexity and richness of fruit, usually some oak aging. They are excellent wines for short-term drinking.

Poultry
Soufflés
Red meats
Casseroles

Full-bodied tannic reds

Examples: Barbera, Barolo, Cabernet Sauvignon, Merlot, Côtes du Rhône, Petite Sirah and Zinfandel.

Characteristics: These are the big red wines, deep and dark in color, dense in flavor and tannin, requiring aging in wood cask and bottle to develop their marvelous bouquets and smooth complexities. They are the quintessential food wines — not for sipping.

Game
Roasts
Barbecued meats
Full-flavored cheeses
Spicy casseroles

Rosé and "Blush" wines

Examples: Rosé of Cabernet or Grenache or Merlot, Pinot Noir Blanc and White Zinfandel.

Characteristics: These wines, though quite varied in appearance and style, share the common characteristic of being lightly colored wines made from red grapes. They vary from light to dry to rather dark-colored and quite sweet, but in any case are fresh, fruity, and simple. Usually served chilled, they are ideal picnic wines and accompany smoked or spicy meats like ham, salami, etc., better than just about anything else. Not wines for every occasion, they nevertheless have their place.

Ham
Salami
Smoked meats
Spicy meats

Wine Categories, Characteristics & Foods

FOODS THAT GO WELL:

Sparkling

Examples: Champagne, California "Champagne," Italian Spumante.

Characteristics: These vary dramatically in taste and quality, but all have bubbles, and all get served on fancy or festive occasions. It is not true that champagne goes with everything. But at the beginning or end of a meal, or with zesty flavored appetizers or not-too-heavy desserts, it does very well.

Full-bodied, sweet dessert wines

Examples: Sauternes, Dessert Madeira, Cream Sherry, Spatlese and Auslese Rhine wines. Champagne but select one that is extra dry rather than a bone-dry brut, as the latter may taste slightly sharp in conjunction with a rich dessert.

Soufflés
Cakes
Fresh fruit (not highly citric)

Port

Perfect after dessert

Walnuts, other nuts

SPECIAL ADDRESSES

Colorado Wineries

Carlson Vineyards
461 35 Road
Palisade, Colorado 81526
(303) 464-5554

Colorado Cellars Winery
3553 E Road
Palisade, Colorado 81526
(303) 464-7921   (800) 264-7696

Grande River Vineyards
787 37.3 Road
PO Box 129
Palisade, Colorado 81526
(303) 464-5867   (800) 264-7696

Minturn Cellars
107 Williams Street
Minturn, Colorado 81645
(303) 827-4065

Pikes Peak Vineyards
3901 Janitell Road
Colorado Springs, Colorado 80906
(719) 576-0075

Rocky Hill Winery
Montrose, Colorado 81401

Terror Creek Winery
1750 4175 Drive
Paonia, Colorado 81428
(303) 527-3484

Vail Valley Vintners
363 Troyer Road
Palisade, Colorado 81526
(303) 464-0559

COOKING & FOOD HINTS

PHYLLO TIPS:
◆ If frozen, defrost in refrigerator 24 hours
◆ Then, leave dough at room temperature two hours
◆ Cover sheets waiting to be used with plastic wrap to keep from drying out
◆ Instead of brushing the phyllo leaves with butter, spray with olive oil (for non–dessert recipes) or spray with imitation butter spray for dessert recipes

WHIP CREAM:
◆ May be whipped in advance!
◆ Whip cream to stiff peaks, then place in a cheesecloth strainer, suspended over a bowl (to drain excess liquid so the whipped cream does not collapse)
◆ Will last a few hours in the refrigerator

NO FAT WHIPPED CREAM:
◆ Pour ⅓ cup skim milk into a small stainless–steel or copper bowl
◆ Set it in the freezer until ice crystals just begin to form (about 15 to 20 minutes)
◆ Using a hand mixer, thicken the mixture by beating in ⅓ cup instant nonfat dry milk
◆ Continue to beat on high until soft peaks form (about two minutes)
◆ If you prefer a sweetened "cream", pour in 1 tablespoon honey and beat
◆ Yield: 1¾ cups
◆ Note: This "cream" will begin to separate after about 20 minutes, so whip this version just before serving

EGGPLANT:
◆ Really soaks up fat when sautéed
◆ Better: cut eggplant in half and wrap in wax paper
◆ Microwave first half on high about three minutes
◆ Repeat with other half
◆ The texture is perfect for stuffing or grilling

MICROWAVE TIPS:
◆ If you double a microwave recipe, **increase** the cooking time by half
◆ If you cut a microwave recipe in half, **reduce** the cooking time by one third

COOKING & FOOD HINTS

BETTER SOUP, ETC.:
◆ Freeze dried tomatoes in a plastic bag for an hour or so, then crush the tomatoes easily (in the bag) with a rolling pin
◆ Pulverize dried tomatoes and add to soups, sauces, and stews (even some salad dressings) for a richer flavor and color
◆ Mashed potatoes, or instant potato flakes, are an easy and nutritious way to thicken soups

FUNNY–LOOKING CAKE:
◆ If your cake is dry, peaks in the center, has a sticky outer crust, or has a heavy texture, *probably* the ingredients were not measured accurately!
◆ **Always** measure dry ingredients in a measuring cup with a flat rim so the contents can be leveled off with the flat side of a knife
◆ Never "tap down" flour or white sugar when leveling

FLAIR:
◆ Cut red or yellow (or a combination) bell peppers lengthwise into ⅛-inch strips (carrot strips would work, too)
◆ Boil tops from green onion (very briefly) to soften; rinse with cold water; cut in half lengthwise
◆ Gather pepper slices into a bundle and tie with the green onion tops
◆ This little extra effort not only adds some drama to your dinner presentation, but is nutritious as well

HERBS:
◆ To dry herbs, hang them upside down by the bunch for about three weeks
◆ When dry, put the bunch in a paper bag with the top twisted shut around the stems
◆ Hit the bag to shake the herbs from their stems
◆ What does not fall off the stems should be discarded
◆ Remember, for every tablespoon of fresh herbs, use one teaspoon of dried herbs

WEIGHTS, MEASURES & SERVINGS IN A CAN

APPROXIMATE NET WEIGHT

OR FLUID MEASURE	APPROXIMATE CUPS & SERVINGS
8 ounces	1 cup, 2 servings
10½ – 12 ounces	1 ¼ cups, 3 servings
12 ounces (vacuum)	1½ cups, 3 – 4 servings
14 – 16 ounces	1¾ cups, 3 – 4 servings
16 – 17 ounces	2 cups, 4 servings
1 pound 4 ounces	2½ cups, 5 servings
1 pint 2 fluid ounces	2½ cups, 5 servings
1 pound 13 ounces	3½ cups, 7 servings
3 pounds 3 ounces	5¾ cups, 10–12 servings
1 quart 14 ounces	5⅓ cups, 10–12 servings

COMMON KITCHEN PANS TO USE AS CASSEROLES

WHEN THE RECIPE CALLS FOR:

4 cup baking dish:
    9–inch pie plate
    8 x 1½–inch layer cake pan
    7⅜ x 3⅝ x 2¼–inch loaf pan
6 cup baking dish:
    8 or 9 x 1½–inch layer cake pan
    10–inch pie plate
    8½ x 3⅝ x 2⅝–inch loaf pan
8 cup baking dish:
    8 x 8 x 2–inch square pan
    11 x 7 x 1½–inch baking pan
    9 x 5 x 3–inch loaf pan
10 cup baking dish:
    9 x 9 x 2–inch square pan
    11¾ x 7½ x 1¾–inch baking pan
12 cup baking dish:
    13½ x 8½ x 2–inch glass baking pan
15 cup baking dish:
    13 x 9 x 2–inch metal baking pan
19 cup baking dish:
    14 x 10 1/2 x 2½–inch roasting pan

EMERGENCY SUBSTITUTES

If the recipe calls for:	Substitute:
1 teaspoon baking powder	¼ teaspoon baking soda plus ½ teaspoon cream of tartar
1 cup barbecue sauce	1 cup ketchup plus 2 teaspoons Worcestershire
brown sugar	3 parts white sugar to 1 part molasses
1 cup (2 sticks) butter	1 cup margarine OR ⅞ cup vegetable oil or vegetable shortening
1 cup buttermilk	1 cup plain yogurt OR 1 tablespoon vinegar (or lemon juice) plus enough milk to equal 1 cup (let stand 5 minutes) OR 1¾ teaspoon cream of tartar plus 1 cup milk
1 ounce chocolate (semisweet)	½ ounce unsweetened chocolate plus 1 tablespoon sugar
1 ounce chocolate (unsweetened)	3 tablespoon unsweetened cocoa plus 1 tablespoon butter or margarine
1 tablespoon cornstarch (as thickener)	2 tablespoon flour OR 2 teaspoons arrowroot

EMERGENCY SUBSTITUTIONS

1 cup corn syrup	1¼ cup white **OR** packed brown sugar plus ¼ cup liquid
1 cup cream (light/20%)	3 tablespoon butter plus enough whole milk to equal 1 cup
1 cup cream (sour)	1 cup plain yogurt **OR** ¾ cup sour milk, buttermilk, or plain yogurt plus ⅓ cup butter **OR** 1 tablespoon lemon juice plus enough evaporated milk to equal 1 cup
1 cup cream (whipping)	¾ cup whole milk plus ¼ to ⅓ cup butter
1 cup flour (sifted, all-purpose)	1 cup minus 2 tablespoons unsifted all-purpose flour
1 cup flour (sifted, cake flour)	1 cup minus 2 tablespoons sifted all-purpose flour
1 cup flour (sifted, self-rising)	1 cup sifted all-purpose flour plus 1½ teaspoons baking powder and ⅛ teaspoon salt
1 clove garlic	⅛ teaspoon garlic powder
1 tablespoon ginger root, fresh	⅛ teaspoon ground ginger
1 cup half and half	1½ tablespoons butter plus enough whole milk to equal 1 cup
1 tablespoon herbs, fresh	1 teaspoon, dried
1 cup honey	1¼ cup sugar plus ¼ cup liquid
1 teaspoon Italian herb seasoning	½ teaspoon dried oregano plus ¼ teaspoon each, dried basil and thyme
1 tablespoon lemon juice	1 tablespoon white vinegar
1 cup milk, skimmed	⅓ cup nonfat dry milk powder plus water to equal 1 cup
1 cup milk, whole	½ cup evaporated milk plus ½ cup water
1 teaspoon mustard, prepared	1 teaspoon powdered mustard **plus 1 teaspoon water**
2½ teaspoons pumpkin pie spice	1½ teaspoons ground cinnamon plus ½ teaspoon each ground nutmeg and ginger plus a dash of cloves
1 tablespoon sherry, dry	1 tablespoon dry vermouth
sweetened condensed milk	1 cup plus 1 tablespoon powdered milk plus ½ cup warm water plus ⅓ cup sugar. (Mix powdered milk and warm water, then dissolve sugar in that first mixture.)
3 cups tomato juice	1½ cups tomato sauce plus 1½ cups water **OR** 1 (6 ounce) can tomato paste plus 3 cans water, a dash of both salt and sugar
1 teaspoon vinegar	2 teaspoons lemon juice
1 cup yogurt	1 cup buttermilk

Note: Substitutions are based on how ingredients interact in the recipe.

WHEN WE SAY...WE MEAN....

Item   Amount, Raw & Prepared

FRUITS, VEGETABLES, & HERBS

Apple (1 medium)	1 cup, chopped
Avocado (1 medium)	1 cup, mashed
Cabbage (1 large)	10 cups, chopped
Carrots (2 medium)	1 cup, diced
Celery (3 stalks)	1 cup, diced
Eggplant (1 medium)	4 cups, cubed
Garlic (1 medium clove)	¼ teaspoon, chopped
Green Pepper (1 medium)	¾ cup, diced
Leek (1 medium)	⅔ cup, sliced thin
Lemon (1 medium)	2 to 3 tablespoons juice
Mushrooms (3 to 4 ounces)	1 cup, sliced
Onion (1 medium)	1 cup, diced
Orange (1 medium)	½ cup juice
Parsley (1–4 ounce bunch)	3½ cups, chopped
Potato (1 medium)	2 cups, diced – 1¼ cups, mashed
Shallots (1 medium)	1 tablespoon, minced
Spinach (10 ounces fresh)	12 cups, loose packed ; 1 cup cooked
Tomato (1 medium)	¾ cups diced
Tomato (28 ounces canned)	3 cups with juice; 1½ cups, drained
Winter Squash (1 medium)	4 cups, cubed
Zucchini (1 medium)	2 cups, diced

NUTS (Whole)

Almonds (8 ounces)	1 cup
Cashews (6 ounces)	1 cup
Peanuts (1 pound, unshelled)	2 to 2½ cups
Walnuts (6 ounces)	1 cup

OTHER

Cheese (1 pound hard)	4 cups, grated
Chicken (3½ pounds)	2 cups, cooked & diced
Crackers (15 graham)	1 cup fine crumbs
Crackers (22 soda)	1 cup fine crumbs
Meat (1 pound)	2 cups, diced
Raisins (5 ounces)	1 cup
Rice (1 cup, raw)	3 cups, cooked
Spaghetti (1 pound, uncooked)	7 cups, cooked

CONTRIBUTORS

Our sincere appreciation to the members of the Grand Junction Junior Service League and their friends and relatives who graciously contributed their recipes which were then triple–tested for quality and edited for clarity. In some cases, similar recipes were combined to create a slightly different recipe from the one submitted. Additional thanks to those who tested and tasted the recipes to assure the quality of the recipes we have included.

ALDRICH,NANCY
ARCIERI, SABBIE
AUST, BUZZIE
BACA, SUSAN
BANNON, DEBBIE
BARRY, DIANNE K.
BEHRHORST, CAROLYN
BIBER, SHAROL
BISH, CONNIE
BOWMAN, BARB
BRAFFETT, DEB
BRAGDON, LYNN
BRANNON, JODY
BRINEGAR, PAT
BROWN, JUDY
BUESCHER, MARY BETH
BURMEISTER, DIXIE
BUTHERUS, JULIE
CHAMBERLAIN, PATTI
CHRIST, NINA
CLARK–SORENSEN, CARRIE
CLARKE, ALICIA M.
CLASSEN, MARY
COATNEY, DON
COLBY, DEBE
COLETTI, STEVE
COLLINS, GAIL
COLORADO NATIONAL
    MONUMENT ASSOCIATION
COMERFORD, JANET
CONNER, DALE
CONNOLLY, ANNE
COPELAND, JANICE
COPELAND, VIRGINIA
CORNELL, JUDY
CRAWFORD, CINDY
CURTIS, SYBIL
CYPHERS, CAROLYN
DANBURY, MIA
DAVIS, KAREN
DEVITT, LORI
DILLON, JEAN
DORAN, MARY
DOSS, PATTY
DOTY, DALE
duPONT, CLARE
FARINA, BEVE
FEILD, RUTH ANN
FISHER, PEGGY
FLATT, ERIC
FOX, PAM
FRANCIS, BUD
FRANK, REBECCA
FULTON, BETTY
GARCIA, NATASHA
GERSON, GAYLE
GIESKE, JEANINE
GILMOR, CHRIS
GILMOR, TOM
GOLTER, SUZY
GORMLEY, SUE KALISZEWSKI
GOTTSCHLICH, MARGE
GREER, CONNIE
GRISIER, LENEE
GUNN, PEGGY
HAJEK, ELLEN

HALLER, MARILYN
HARDY, PRUE
HARTZELL, NANCY
HAY, MARY
HECKEL, CLAUDIA
HEFLEY, NITA
HILL, MARILYN
HOLLINGSWORTH, CATHY
HOLLINGSWORTH, JANET
HOLLINGSWORTH, PHYLLIS
HOOKER, STANLEY B.
HOWARD, LORI
HOWARD, MO
HUBER, DARSIE
JACKSON, MARI BETH
JACOB, JANET
JACOB, RUTH
JANSON, MARY ANN
JONES, ANYA
JONES, DOUG
JONES, MARILYN
JONES, PAUL
JONES–HIRATA,
    NOELLE
JOUFLAS, CONNIE
KELLER, DEBBIE
KILLIAN, KATHLEEN
KLEMENTS, SHERRY
KOLER, JO
KOLLER, ROSEMARY
KRAULAND, POLLY
KUGELER, JUDI
LACROIX, LINDA
LARSON, JUDY
LEEVER, RUTH
LEPISTO, EILEEN
LETEY, MARGARET
LOESCH, PAMELA
MADSEN, KAREN
MAHONEY, BRIAN
MARTIN, ALICE
MARTIN, STEPHANIE
MATHIS, CINDY
MCCLELLAND, KAREN
MCFATE, MIKE (M.E.)
MCGOVERN, LISA
MCLENNAN, STACEY B.
MCNEILL, ALICE
MEUWLY, JERRY
MEYER, JANELLE
MILIUS, ELIZABETH
MILIUS, PATTI
MILYARD, TONI
MITISEK, CHRISTIE
MOHLER, NANCY
MONTAGRIFF, MARY
MOORE, ELISABETH
MORGAN, GAIL
MORRIS, JUDY
MOSS, JUDY
MUTTER, LAURA
MYERS, REBECCA
NEAL, CINDY
NELSON, HANNEKE
NELSON, JOHN
NELSON, SCOTT

NELSON, SUSAN
NEUHOFF, FRANCIE
NEWMAN, AMALIE
NUERNBERG, AMY
OKLEN, CAROL
OSBORNE, DIANA
OSBORNE, MELBA
OWEN, CAROL
PEASE, NINA
PEASE, DENISE
PEASE, MARK
PENN, CARYN
PETERSBURG, NANCY
PHILLIPS, BRUCE
PHILLIPS, MELANIE
POLZINE, LEONARD
POLZINE, SYNTHIA
PRINSTER, ELISE
RALSTON, CINDY
RASMUSSEN, KAREN
REAMS, SALLY
REEVES, EARLINE
ROBERTS, KAREN
ROCKINGHAM, JOAN
ROCKINGHAM, MARG
ROSKOWSKI, KATHRYN
SAMMONS, BOB
SCHULTZ, RUTH
SCHUMANN, DEE
SCOTT, CHARLENE
SCOTT, CHERI
SHENKEL, RITA
SHEPHERD, CAMILLE
SHEPHERD, CONNOR
SHOFFNER, BOB
SHRUM, IDA
SIMONS, CYD
SIMONS, JAMEE
SIMONS, MARILYN
SIMS, RICHARD
SMITH, LEE
SMITH, SHARON
SNOWDEN, MARILYN
SODERBERG, VICKI
SPAROVIC, HELEN
SWIM, MONICA
TABER, EVELYN
TASLER, DONNA
TAYLOR, MYRTA
TERRILL, NANCY
THOMAS, JUDITH
THOMPSON, GAYLENE
TOMPKINS, CAROL
TOWNER, LORI
TOZER, COLLEEN
VANHOLE, SHERYL
VERDIECK, MARY
VOUGHT, HELEN
WALTON, HEATHER
WATKINSON, HELEN
WEAVER, GERALD
WEST, PERCY
WILBERT, JOSIE
WILBERT, RENA
WILLIAMS, SUZANNE
ZENTNER, LESLIE

SPECIAL ADDRESSES FOR YOUR INFORMATION

Cover Artist

Shirley Dickinson
611 North Third Street
Grand Junction, Colorado 81501

Pen and Ink Illustrations

Gail Collins
c/o JSL
PO Box 3221
Grand Junction, Colorado 81502

Restaurant Contributors

Blue Moon Bar & Grill
120 N. 7th Steet
Grand Junction, Colorado 81501
242-4506

Carol's Oriental Foods
2814 North Avenue
Grand Junction, Colorado 81501
245-3286

Crystal Cafe and Bake Shop
314 Main Street
Grand Junction, Colorado 81501
242-8843

Dos Hombres - Clifton
569 32 Road
Grand Junction, Colorado 81504
434-5078

Dos Hombres - Redlands
421 Brach Drive
Grand Junction, Colorado 81503
242-8861

G. B. Gladstone's
2531 North 12th Street
Grand Junction, Colorado 81501
241-6000

Good Pastures
733 Horizon Drive
Grand Junction, Colorado 81506
243-3058

Karen's Cafe
1610 Grand Avenue
Norwood, Colorado 81423
327-4840

River City
748 North Avenue
Grand Junction, Colorado 81501
245-8040

Rockslide Restaurant and Brewery
Corners 4th Street and Main
Grand Junction, Colorado 81501

Slice of Life Bakery
103 West 3rd Street
Palisade, Colorado 81526
464-0577

Sweetwater's
335 Main Street
Grand Junction, Colorado 81501
243-3900

Seventh Street Cafe
832 South 7th Street
Grand Junction, Colorado 81501
242-7225

Other Community Cookbooks Listed in West of the Rockies

Colorado Cookbook
University of Colorado
Campus Box 184
Boulder, Colorado 80309
To benefit the University of Colo-
rado Libraries, Boulder

Colorado Cache and Creme de Colorado
The Junior League of Denver, Inc.
C and C Publications
6300 East Yale Avenue
Denver Colorado 80222
To benefit the Junior League of
Denver's community projects.

*Delitefully HealthMark and Viva la
Mediterranean*
HealthMark Centers, Inc.
5889 Greenwood Plaza Blvd., Suite
200
Englewood, Colorado 80111
To benefit the Swedish Hospital.

Plateau Valley Cook Book
American Legion Auxiliary
Mrs. Charlotte Black
Box 203
Mesa, Colorado 81543
To benefit their programs.

Simply Colorado
Colorado Dietetic Association
2450 South Downing Street
Denver, Colorado 80210
To benefit the purposes and pro-
grams of the Colorado Dietetic
Association.

Steamboat Entertains
The Steamboat Springs Winter
Sports Club
2155 Resort Drive, Suite 207
Steamboat Springs, Colorado 80487
To benefit and support the ski
training programs for the U.S.
Olympic hopefuls.

Colorado Food Producers Listed in West of the Rockies

Enstrom Candies
200 South Seventh Street
PO Box 1088
Grand Junction, Colorado 81502
1-800-36708766
FAX (303) 245-7727
Wonderful almond toffee and hand-
dipped candies

Religious Experience Sauces
R and E Foods
820 Struthers Avenue
Grand Junction, Colorado 81501
Hot sauces that are mild to HOT
but super.

A

ALMOND
Almond Toffee Tart 291
Chicken Almond Spread 21
Irresistible Almond Caramel Pie 289
Amaretto 37
APPETIZERS
Artichoke Dip with Pesto 30
Artichoke Heart Dip 28
Cheese and Artichoke Appetizer 34
Chicken Almond Spread 21
Cocktail Meatballs 27
Cortez Chile con Queso 254
Crab Puffs with Sweet and Sour Sauce 19
Crabby Cheese Crescents 25
Creamy Salsa Dip 22
Holy Guacamole 223
Hot Cheese Balls 23
Hot Gouda Cheese 21
Iron Man Trail Mix 247
Josefinas 27
Lariat Fruit Leather 249
Lemon Cream (A dip for crudités) 35
Lime Garlic Shrimp with Mango Mint Salsa 26
Mountain Man Jerky 248
Mushroom Spread 22
Onion Pissaladière 32
Oriental Chicken Wontons 20
Pesto Sauce 30
Pico de Gallo 222
Roasted Peppers and Artichokes 31
Rumaki Pâté 23
Salsa de Leonardo 223
Sausage Strudel 28
Sausalito Crab Dip 25
Seafood Stars 24
Sesame Shrimp Toast 24
Sheep Dip 29
Shrimp Mold 26
Shrimp New Orleans 25
Smoked Salmon Cheesecake 114
Spanakopita 33
Stuffed Mushrooms 18
Sugar and Nut Glazed Brie 18
The "Best Ever" Deviled Eggs 35
Trout Pâté 29
Versatile Cheese Spread 35
Warmed Cranberry Brie 19
Western Wontons 222
APPLE
Apple Cake with Hot Caramel Rum Sauce 298
Apple Pie Filling 331
Apple Pie with Warm Cinnamon Cider Sauce 284

Apple–Stuffed Veal Rolls 139
Paper Bag Apple Pie 286
Pork Chops Normandy 213
Pumpkin Apple Bundt Cake 219
Spiced Apple Muffins 87
Talbott's Packing Shed Cake 293
Waldorf Salad 62
Yams and Apples 178
APRICOT
Apricot Bow Ties 269
Apricot Iced Tea 247
Grilled Venison with Apricot and Green Peppercorn 173
Rose Tree Jam 324
ARTICHOKE
Artichoke Dip with Pesto 30
Artichoke Heart Dip 28
Braised Carrots with Mushrooms and Artichokes 186
Cheese and Artichoke Appetizer 34
Chicken and Artichokes Italian 152
Curried Chicken Artichoke Salad 65
Green Grocer Lasagna 193
Mushroom and Artichoke Chicken 216
Roasted Peppers and Artichokes 31
Sheep Dip 29
Shrimp and Artichoke Casserole 121
Spinach Artichoke Casserole 189
Tomatoes Stuffed with Artichoke Hearts 65
Vegetable Melange 183
ASPARAGUS
Asparagus and Broccoli Quiche 108
Asparagus Gruyère Quiche 100
Ditch Bank Asparagus Toss 67
Green Grocer Lasagna 193
Scrambled Eggs with Asparagus 104
Whole Wheat Pasta with Vegetables 196
AVOCADO
Avocado Dressing 73
Garden Benedict 106
Holy Guacamole 223
Layered Mexican Salad 237
Orange-Avocado-Onion Salad 70

B

BACON
Baked Eggs and Bacon Florentine 217
Low-Fat Broccoli, Bacon and Cheddar Toss 214
Potato Bacon Casserole 180
BANANAS
Bananas Foster 321
Black-Bottom Banana Bread 90
Crested Butte Bananas in Foil 261
St. John's Banana Banana Bread 91
BARBECUE
Barbecued Chicken and Ribs 258

INDEX

Barbecue Sauce 133
Great Barbecue Sauce 333
Barley Stew, Veal and, 59
Bean Bake, Calico 182
Béchamel Sauce 200
BEEF
Anniversary Meatloaf 132
Beef Tenderloin 128
Boliche Asado de Colorado 137
Boneless Barbecue Beef Ribs 133
Bracciole 135
Butch Cassidy Layered Tenderloin in Foil 261
Calico Bean Bake 182
Cocktail Meatballs 27
Company Brisket 130
Fall River Rib Roast 136
Italian Meatloaf 132
Mountain Man Jerky 248
Mountain Man Jerky Milk Gravy 248
Mountain Man Mustard Sauce 133
Peppered Beef 131
Red Mountain Shells 195
Salsa Beef 242
South of the Border Stew 60
Spinach Stuffed Shells 201
Steak Ore House 129
Steak Rolls with Mushrooms 134
Steak Salad 71
Timberline Steak Sandwich with Corn Relish 255
Very Easy Fried Rice 199
Western Wontons 222
BEETS
Best Beets 184
Pickled Beets 328
BEVERAGES
Amaretto 37
Apricot Iced Tea 247
Cowboy Coffee 247
Cranberry Juice Punch 36
Elam BLT Peach Margarita 39
Gold Diggers' Painkillers 38
Hot Buttered Rum Mix 36
Irish Creme Liqueur 38
Lands End Nog 36
Mesa Margaritas 40
Peach Smash 39
Powderhorn Warm–up 38
Pumpkin Punch Bowl with Hot Mulled Cider 37
Skip and Go 39
Vail Hot Spiced Wine 37
BISCUITS
Beer-can Biscuits 252
Biscuit dough 158
Double-Decker High Altitude Cheese Biscuits 85

BLACK BEANS
Black Bean Cumin Sauce 232
Black Bean Salsa Salad 237
Black Bean Soup 57
BLUEBERRIES
Beaver Creek Blueberry Binge 262
Mountain Blueberry Pancakes 251
Bran Muffins 214
BREAD (See Biscuits, Muffins & Rolls also)
Almost Brioche Bread 79
Bread on a Stick 259
Bumper Crop Zucchini Bread 94
Classic Poppy Seed Bread 92
Dilly Casserole Bread 95
Edith's Cracked Wheat Bread 80
Fascinating Fast Bread 81
French Toast Santa Fe 101
Fresh Tomato and Green Onion Garlic Bread 98
Garlic Cheese Loaf 98
Grape Nut Bread 97
Health Bread 211
Hobo Bread 92
Irish Soda Bread 94
Jalapeño Corn Bread 238
Light Rye Bread with Anise Seed and Black Pepper 78
New Mexican Chile Bread 98
North African Coriander Bread 97
Orange Cranberry Bread 91
Palisade Peach Bread 93
Peach Preserve French Toast 106
Pecan and Red Onion Bread 97
Silverton Indian Fry Bread 238
BREAKFAST AND BRUNCH
Asparagus and Broccoli Quiche 108
Asparagus Gruyère Quiche 100
Baked Eggs and Bacon Florentine 217
Brunch Eggs with Spanish Sauce 103
Eggs in a Tortilla 251
Fiesta Brunch 100
French Toast Santa Fe 101
Garden Benedict 106
Gold Rush Casserole 101
Mountain Blueberry Pancakes 251
Omelet Olé 104
Peach Preserve French Toast 106
Salmon Strata 107
Scrambled Eggs Confetti 102
Scrambled Eggs with Asparagus 104
Sweet Pepper and Basil Frittata 105
BRIE
Linguine with Basil 196
Sugar and Nut Glazed Brie 18
Warmed Cranberry Brie 19
BROCCOLI
Asparagus and Broccoli Quiche 108

Broccoli and Cream Cheese 185
Broccoli, Peppers and Feta 184
Broccoli Salad 67
Low-Fat Broccoli, Bacon and Cheddar Toss 214
Tofu, Herbs and Vegetables 182
Whole Wheat Pasta with Vegetables 196
Brownies, Fantastic Frosted Fattening, 303
Burritos, Pork and Chile 226
Butter Cream Frosting 322
Butter Sauce for dipping 113

C

CABBAGE
Colcannon 180
Cranberry Red Cabbage 179
Oriental Cabbage Salad 66
Silver Dollar Slaw 254
CAKE
Absolutely All Chocolate Roll – Yule Log 306
Apple Cake with Hot Caramel Rum Sauce 298
Beaver Creek Blueberry Binge 262
Bessie's Chocolate Cake 293
Chocolate Angel Food Cake 220
Chocolate Sheet Cake 294
Enstrom's Oatmeal Chocolate Toffee Cake 294
Fantastic Frosted Fattening Brownies 303
Lemon Loaf Pound Cake 302
Pineapple Meringue Cake 300
Plum Cake 299
Pumpkin Apple Bundt Cake 219
Raisin Spice Cake 299
Raspberry Upside Down Cake 297
Talbott's Packing Shed Cake 293
Three Citrus Cake 296
Three–Layer Carrot Cake 301
Tweed Cake 292
CAKE FROSTING
Binge Icing 262
Butter Cream Frosting 322
Chocolate Mousse Frosting 322
Orange Cream Frosting 297
CANDY
Cherry Blossoms 275
Chocolate Covered Coconut Drops 278
Crackle Caramel Corn 279
Crunchy Microwave Chocolate Fudge 280
Double-Dipped Peanut Butter Balls 277
Mom's Favorite Fudge 278
Cantaloupe Splash Soup 42
CARAMEL
Crackle Caramel Corn 279
Hot Caramel Rum Sauce 298
Irresistible Almond Caramel Pie 289

CARROTS
Aspen Carrots 185
Braised Carrots with Mushrooms and Artichokes 186
Glazed Carrots 186
High Country Carrot Muffins 88
Ruby Carrots 187
Three–Layer Carrot Cake 301
Vegetable Melange 183
CHEESE
Asparagus Gruyère Quiche 100
Avalanche Manicotti 203
Baked French Bread Dip 34
Broccoli and Cream Cheese 185
Broccoli, Peppers and Feta 184
Cheese and Artichoke Appetizer 34
Cheese and Cream Sauce 188
Chile Relleno Torta 234
Cortez Chile con Queso 254
Crabby Cheese Crescents 25
Double-Decker High Altitude Cheese Biscuits 85
Garlic Cheese Loaf 98
Gold Rush Casserole 101
Hot Cheese Balls 23
Hot Gouda Cheese 21
Low-Fat Broccoli, Bacon and Cheddar Toss 214
Orzo with Mozzarella and Kalamata Olives 204
Ouray Swiss Cheese Soup 50
Sugar and Nut Glazed Brie 18
Three Cheese Ziti with Italian Sausage 198
Versatile Cheese Spread 35
Warmed Cranberry Brie 19
Western–Style Grits 103
CHEESECAKE
Cookies and Cream Cheesecake 315
Lemon Glazed Cheesecake 309
Smooth as Satin Cheesecake 314
Chef's Salt 128
CHERRIES
Cherry Blossoms 275
Lady Bug Cookies 276
CHICKEN
Barbecued Chicken and Ribs 258
Chicken & Wine 150
Chicken Almond Spread 21
Chicken and Artichokes Italian 152
Chicken and Sausage Jambalaya 159
Chicken and Shrimp Fettuccine 192
Chicken and Wild Rice Casserole 160
Chicken Breast with Warm Salsa 240
Chicken Enchiladas 229
Chicken Fajitas 260
Chicken on a Stick 260
Cobb Salad 63

Curried Chicken Artichoke Salad 65
Curried Chicken Salad 253
Japanese Chicken Salad 66
Korean Chicken 151
Marinated Chicken Enchiladas with Green
    Chile and Melon Salsa 228
Mexican Chicken Roll-ups 241
Mexican Corn Soup 224
Mushroom and Artichoke Chicken 216
Oriental Chicken Wontons 20
Parmesan Chicken 215
Perfect Grilled Chicken 151
Pufferbelly Pot Pie 158
Ridgeway Chicken Breasts 157
Rumaki Pâté 23
Shanghai Chicken Salad 209
Spanish Paella 154
Spanish Soft Tacos 231
Stacked Enchiladas 227
Sweetwater's Chicken Monte Cristo 155
Sweetwater's Tarragon Chicken Salad 75
Szechwan Confetti Salad 64
Weekend Chicken 156
White Chicken Chili 225
CHILI
Colorado Venison Chili 172
Crested Butte Chili Cheese Supreme 243
Volcano Green Chili 225
White Chicken Chili 225
CHOCOLATE
Absolutely All Chocolate Roll – Yule Log
    306
Bessie's Chocolate Cake 293
Black-Bottom Banana Bread 90
Chips and Nuts Muffins 87
Chocolate Angel Food Cake 220
Chocolate Angel Pie 288
Chocolate Chip Meringue Bars 266
Chocolate Covered Coconut Drops 278
Chocolate Mousse 307
Chocolate Mousse Frosting 322
Chocolate Sheet Cake 294
Cookies and Cream Cheesecake 315
Crunchy Microwave Chocolate Fudge 280
Dark Chocolate Fudge Sauce 332
Diana Torte 316
Double-Dipped Peanut Butter Balls 277
Enstrom's Oatmeal Chocolate Toffee Cake
    294
Fantastic Frosted Fattening Brownies 303
Fudge Cup 305
Fudge Pie 288
Milk Chocolate Pound Cake 295
Mocha Chip Cookies 273
Mocha Velvet Torte 308
Mom's Favorite Fudge 278
Triple Threat Chocolate Cookies 271

Turtle Cookies 266
Tweed Cake 292
Vienna Chocolate Bars 265
CHOWDER
Corn Chowder with Shrimp and Peppers 53
Wild Rice Clam Chowder 54
Cinnamon Rolls 86
Clam Chowder, Wild Rice, 54
Cobb Salad 63
Cobbler, Wild Berry 285
Coconut Drops, Chocolate Covered, 278
COFFEE CAKE
Colorado Coffee Cake 96
Toffee Coffee Cake 95
Colcannon 180
COOKIES
A Whopper of A Cookie 272
Apricot Bow Ties 269
Chocolate Chip Meringue Bars 266
Crisp Oat Cookies 272
Enstrom's Toffee Chip Cookies 273
Grandma Proctor's Filled Cookies 264
Grandma's Old Fashioned Amish Sugar
    Cookies 269
Lady Bug Cookies 276
Mincemeat Filled Cookies 277
Mocha Chip Cookies 273
Molasses Sugar Cookies 270
Old Fashioned Sugar Cookies 268
Orange Short Cookies 271
Peanut Butter Busters 275
Pecan Pie Squares 265
Sassafras Oatmeal Date Bars 267
Triple Threat Chocolate Cookies 271
Turtle Cookies 266
Vienna Chocolate Bars 265
Wild West Oatmeal Cookies 274
CORN
Corn Chowder with Shrimp and Peppers 53
Coyote Green Corn Tamales 233
Garlic Tamales with Black Bean Cumin
    Sauce 232
Jalapeño Corn Bread 238
Mexican Corn Soup 224
Olathe Sweet Corn Salad 218
Spicy Corn Relish 255
Cornbread, Cornbelt Special 93
Cornish Hens Flamed in Cognac 153
CRAB
Crab Claws with Mustard Sauce 115
Crab Fettucini 256
Crab Puffs with Sweet and Sour Sauce 19
Crab Tetrazzini 200
Crabby Cheese Crescents 25
Sausalito Crab Dip 25
Seafood Lasagna 115
Sole del Mar 116

Stir–Fry Seafood Pasta 195
CRANBERRIES
Cranberry Juice Punch 36
Cranberry Mousse with Raspberry Sauce
321
Cranberry Red Cabbage 179
Cranberry-Orange Compote 178
Orange Cranberry Bread 91
Warmed Cranberry Brie 19
Crème Fraîche 331
Crêpes, Spinach 188
Crested Butte Bananas in Foil 261
Cucumber Dill Sauce 110

D

Date Bars, Sassafras Oatmeal, 267
DESSERTS (See Cakes, Candy, Cheesecake, Cookies, &
Pies also)
Almond Toffee Tart 291
Bananas Foster 321
Chocolate Mousse 307
Cranberry Mousse with Raspberry Sauce
321
Crème Fraîche 331
Crested Butte Bananas in Foil 261
Dark Chocolate Fudge Sauce 332
Fresh Peach Sauce 332
Fresh Pear Ice 312
Fudge Cup 305
Greek Custard Strudel (Galotabouriko) 317
Individual Orange Flans 244
Ladyfingers 318
Lariat Fruit Leather 249
Lemon Ice Cream 312
Lemon Napoleons with Raspberry Sauce
310
Mocha Velvet Torte 308
Pears Melba 320
Rice Pudding 320
Southern Bread Pudding 319
Spring Berry Trifle 313
Tiramisu (Pick Me Up) 318
Trail Bars 249
White Chocolate Mousse with Raspberry
Jewel Sauce 304
DOVE
Bud's Greek Basting Sauce 150
DUCK
Braised Duck Pullman Style 168
Crisp Duck with Palisade Peaches 167
M.E.'s Duck Chorizo 167
Oriental Barbecue Duck Salad 170
Sweet and Sour Duck 169

E

EGGS
Asparagus and Broccoli Quiche 108
Asparagus Gruyère Quiche 100
Brunch Eggs with Spanish Sauce 103
Eggs in a Tortilla 251
Fiesta Brunch 100
Garden Benedict 106
Gold Rush Casserole 101
Omelet Olé 104
Peach Preserve French Toast 106
Salmon Strata 107
Scrambled Eggs Confetti 102
Scrambled Eggs with Asparagus 104
Sweet Pepper and Basil Frittata 105
The "Best Ever" Deviled Eggs 35
Vegetable Quiche 102
ELK
Elk Teriyaki 170
Mountain Man Jerky 248
Mountain Man Jerky Milk Gravy 248
West Slope Elk Stroganoff 171
Western Colorado Elk Curry 172
ENCHILADAS
Chicken Enchiladas 229
Enchilada Mole Sauce 230
Marinated Chicken Enchiladas with Green
Chile and Melon Salsa 228
Stacked Enchiladas 227

F

FETTUCCINE
Chicken and Shrimp Fettuccine 192
Crab Fettucini 256
Vegetable Fettuccine Alfredo 202
FISH (SEE INDIVIDUAL LISTINGS ALSO)
Better Beer–Batter for Fish Fillets 111
Fish D'Lish 123
Redstone Fish Fillets 120
Southwest Sole 239
Trout Pâté 29
Flans, Individual Orange, 244
French Dressing 75
French Toast Santa Fe 101
FRUIT (SEE INDIVIDUAL LISTINGS ALSO)
Fresh Fruit in Gingered White Wine 256
Lariat Fruit Leather 249
Spring Berry Trifle 313
Wild Berry Cobbler 285
FUDGE
Crunchy Microwave Chocolate Fudge 280
Mom's Favorite Fudge 278

G

GAME (SEE INDIVIDUAL LISTINGS ALSO)
Jung's Best Bird Marinade 174
Gazpacho 45
Glaze, Lemon 309
GRAINS
Edith's Cracked Wheat Bread 80

Tabbouleh 74
GRANOLA
  Trail Bars 249
Grape Nut Bread 97
Gravy, Mountain Man Jerky Milk, 248
GREEN BEANS
  Green Beans Elegant 176
  Herbed Green Beans 176
  Roasted Green Beans, Onion and Garlic
    176
Green Chile Sauce 228
Grits, Western–Style, 103

H

HALIBUT
  Fish D'Lish 123
  Sassy Seafood Salad 112
HAM
  Baked Ham with Spicy Mustard Sauce 143
  Buffet Ham 144
  Paul's Ham Salad 253
  Sweetwater's Chicken Monte Cristo 155
Hollandaise Sauce 106

I

Ice, Fresh Pear, 312
Ice Cream, Lemon, 312
Irish Creme Liqueur 38
Irish Soda Bread 94

J

JALAPEÑO
  Jalapeño Corn Bread 238
  Jalapeño Marinade 239
  Jalapeño Pickles 330
  Jalapeño Relish 235
JAMS & JELLIES
  Chile Jelly 326
  Palisade Peach Jam 325
  Rose Tree Jam 324

L

Ladyfingers 318
LAMB
  Bud's Greek Basting Sauce 150
  Butterflied Leg of Lamb with Herb–Wine
    Marinade 147
  Lamb Burgers 146
  Lamb Curry 149
  Leg of Lamb Swedish Style 148
  Rack of Lamb Dijon 146
Lasagna, Green Grocer, 193
LEEKS
  Potato Leek Soup 52
LEMON
  Lemon–Almond Stuffing 118
  Lemon Cream (A dip for crudités) 35

Lemon Filling 296
Lemon Glaze 309
Lemon Glazed Cheesecake 309
Lemon Ice Cream 312
Lemon Loaf Pound Cake 302
Lemon Meringue Pie 290
Lemon Mousse 311
Lemon Napoleons with Raspberry Sauce
  310
Three Citrus Cake 296
LIGHT AND HEALTHY
  Baked Eggs and Bacon Florentine 217
  Black Canyon Bean Salad 207
  Bran Muffins 214
  Chocolate Angel Food Cake 220
  Creamy Caesar Salad 207
  Greek-Style Pockets 212
  Health Bread 211
  Low-Fat Broccoli, Bacon and Cheddar Toss
    214
  Low-Fat Crème Anglaise 219
  Molded Gazpacho Salad 208
  Mushroom and Artichoke Chicken 216
  Olathe Sweet Corn Salad 218
  Parmesan Chicken 215
  Pork Chops Normandy 213
  Pumpkin Apple Bundt Cake 219
  Shanghai Chicken Salad 209
  Sliced and Diced Vegetables 210
  Vegetable Rice Toss 218
LIME
  Lime Garlic Shrimp with Mango Mint Salsa
    26
  Three Citrus Cake 296
Linguine with Basil 196

M

MARINADES
  Herb–Wine Marinade 147
  Jalapeño Marinade 239
  Jung's Best Bird Marinade 174
  Tomato–Soy Marinade 131
MOUSSE
  Chocolate Mousse 307
  Cranberry Mousse with Raspberry Sauce
    321
  Lemon Mousse 311
  White Chocolate Mousse with Raspberry
    Jewel Sauce 304
MUFFINS
  Bran Muffins 214
  Chips and Nuts Muffins 87
  High Country Carrot Muffins 88
  Refrigerator Buttermilk-Bran Muffins 89
  Spiced Apple Muffins 87
MUSHROOMS
  Braised Carrots with Mushrooms and
    Artichokes 186

Cream of Mushroom Soup 51
Marinated Mushroom Salad 68
Mushroom and Artichoke Chicken 216
Mushroom Spread 22
Sautéed Mushrooms and Spinach with
  Shallots 189
Stuffed Mushrooms 18
Vegetable Fettuccine Alfredo 202
Whole Wheat Pasta with Vegetables 196
MUSTARD
  Mustard Horseradish Sauce 131
  Mustard Sauce 115
  Not Your Average Mustard 330

N

NUTS (SEE INDIVIDUAL LISTINGS ALSO)
  Chips and Nuts Muffins 87
  Iron Man Trail Mix 247
  Sugar and Nut Glazed Brie 18

O

Oat Cookies, Crisp, 272
OATMEAL
  Enstrom's Oatmeal Chocolate Toffee Cake
    294
  Sassafras Oatmeal Date Bars 267
  Wild West Oatmeal Cookies 274
Omelet Olé 104
ONIONS
  Colcannon 180
  Onion Pissaladière 32
  Onion Soup Fondue 47
  Orange-Avocado-Onion Salad 70
  Roasted Green Beans, Onion and Garlic
    176
  Sherried Onion Gratin 177
ORANGE
  Cranberry-Orange Compote 178
  Individual Orange Flans 244
  Light Orange Dill Sauce 124
  Mandarin Salad 69
  Orange-Avocado-Onion Salad 70
  Orange Cranberry Bread 91
  Orange Cream Frosting 297
  Orange Rolls 84
  Orange Sauce 84
  Orange Short Cookies 271
  Pheasant in Elegant Orange Sauce 162
  Three Citrus Cake 296
ORZO
  Orzo Milanese 138
  Orzo with Mozzarella and Kalamata Olives
    204
  Osso Buco with Orzo Milanese 138

P

Pancakes, Mountain Blueberry, 251

PASTA
  Avalanche Manicotti 203
  Chicken and Shrimp Fettuccine 192
  Crab Fettucini 256
  Crab Tetrazzini 200
  Green Grocer Lasagna 193
  Linguine with Basil 196
  Orzo Milanese 138
  Orzo with Mozzarella and Kalamata Olives
    204
  Pasta al Limon 194
  Red Mountain Shells 195
  Sauce Alla Puttanesca 197
  Seafood Lasagna 115
  Sesame Noodles 201
  Southwestern Pasta Salad 236
  Spinach Stuffed Shells 201
  Stir–Fry Seafood Pasta 195
  Three Cheese Ziti with Italian Sausage 198
  Vegetable Fettuccine Alfredo 202
  Whole Wheat Pasta with Vegetables 196
PASTRY
  Greek Custard Strudel (Galotabouriko) 317
  Ladyfingers 318
  Lemon Napoleons with Raspberry Sauce
    310
  Never Fail Pie Crust 282
  Perfect Pastry 282
PÂTÉ
  Rumaki Pâté 23
  Trout Pâté 29
PEACHES
  Crisp Duck with Palisade Peaches 167
  Elam BLT Peach Margarita 39
  Fresh Peach Sauce 332
  Great Grandma's Fresh Peach Pie 283
  Orchard Mesa Spiced Peaches 327
  Palisade Growers Peach Pie Filling 283
  Palisade Peach Bread 93
  Palisade Peach Jam 325
  Peach Preserve French Toast 106
  Peach Smash 39
  Peach Soup 42
PEANUT BUTTER
  Double-Dipped Peanut Butter Balls 277
  Peanut Butter Busters 275
  Trail Bars 249
PEARS
  Fresh Pear Ice 312
  Pears Melba 320
PEAS
  Frozen Pea Salad 72
  Spinach, Pea, and Red Pepper Timbales 190
PECAN
  Pecan and Red Onion Bread 97
  Pecan Pie Squares 265
PEPPERS
  Broccoli, Peppers and Feta 184

Cold Pimiento Soup 44
Corn Chowder with Shrimp and Peppers 53
Josefinas 27
Roasted Peppers and Artichokes 31
Spinach, Pea, and Red Pepper Timbales 190
Sweet Pepper and Basil Frittata 105
Pesto Sauce 30
PHEASANT
Chilled Pheasant Salad Vinaigrette 163
Pheasant in Elegant Orange Sauce 162
PICKLES
Bread and Butter Pickles 328
Grand Valley Green Tomato Pickles 329
Jalapeño Pickles 330
Orchard Mesa Spiced Peaches 327
Pickled Beets 328
Pico de Gallo 222
PIES
Apple Pie Filling 331
Apple Pie with Warm Cinnamon Cider Sauce 284
Chocolate Angel Pie 288
Fudge Pie 288
Great Grandma's Fresh Peach Pie 283
Irresistible Almond Caramel Pie 289
Lemon Meringue Pie 290
Never Fail Pie Crust 282
Palisade Growers Peach Pie Filling 283
Paper Bag Apple Pie 286
Perfect Pastry 282
Strawberry Super Pie 287
Wild Berry Cobbler 285
PINEAPPLE
Pineapple Meringue Cake 300
Rose Tree Jam 324
PIÑONS
Garlic Rice with Piñons 194
Wild Rice with Piñons and Brandied Raisins 197
PLUM
Plum Cake 299
Plum–Marinated Spareribs 142
PORK (SEE BACON, HAM & SAUSAGE ALSO)
Barbecued Chicken and Ribs 258
Marinated Grilled Pork Chops 144
Medallions of Pork Tenderloin with Tarragon 145
Plum–Marinated Spareribs 142
Pork and Chile Burritos 226
Pork Chops Normandy 213
Red Mountain Stuffed Pork Chops 257
South of the Border Stew 60
Spareribs Hawaiian 143
Very Easy Fried Rice 199
Volcano Green Chili 225
POTATOES
Colcannon 180

Creamy Potato Soup 52
Potato Bacon Casserole 180
Potato Leek Soup 52
Roasted Parmesan Potato Wedges 180
PUDDINGS
Rice Pudding 320
Southern Bread Pudding 319
PUMPKIN
Pumpkin Apple Bundt Cake 219
Pumpkin Punch Bowl with Hot Mulled Cider 37

Q
Quail with Wild Rice and Roasted Shallots 166
QUICHE
Asparagus and Broccoli Quiche 108
Asparagus Gruyère Quiche 100
Vegetable Quiche 102

R
RAISINS
Iron Man Trail Mix 247
Raisin Spice Cake 299
Wild Rice with Piñons and Brandied Raisins 197
RASPBERRIES
Raspberry Jewel Sauce 304
Raspberry Sauce 310, 321
Raspberry Upside Down Cake 297
Raspberry Vinaigrette 68
Rose Tree Jam 324
RELISHES
Jalapeño Relish 235
Spicy Corn Relish 255
RICE
Arroz Durango 235
Garlic Rice with Piñons 194
Rice Fandango 199
Rice Pudding 320
Seafood and Wild Rice Salad 73
Vegetable Rice Toss 218
Very Easy Fried Rice 199
ROLLS
Cinnamon Rolls 86
Grandma B's Dinner Rolls 82
Orange Rolls 84
Quick Butter Dips 83
Sweet Walnut Crescents 82

S
SALAD
Black Bean Salsa Salad 237
Black Canyon Bean Salad 207
Bread Salad with Tomatoes 71
Broccoli Salad 67
Chilled Pheasant Salad Vinaigrette 163
Cobb Salad 63

Creamy Caesar Salad 207
Curried Chicken Artichoke Salad 65
Curried Chicken Salad 253
Ditch Bank Asparagus Toss 67
Elaine's Greek Salad 72
Frozen Pea Salad 72
Hail Caesar Salad 62
Japanese Chicken Salad 66
Layered Mexican Salad 237
Low-Fat Broccoli, Bacon and Cheddar
  Toss 214
Mandarin Salad 69
Marinated Mushroom Salad 68
Mixed Greens with Raspberry
  Vinaigrette 68
Molded Gazpacho Salad 208
Olathe Sweet Corn Salad 218
Orange-Avocado-Onion Salad 70
Oriental Barbecue Duck Salad 170
Oriental Cabbage Salad 66
Paul's Ham Salad 253
Sassy Seafood Salad 112
Seafood and Wild Rice Salad 73
Shanghai Chicken Salad 209
Silver Dollar Slaw 254
Southwestern Pasta Salad 236
Spinach and Strawberry Salad 70
Steak Salad 71
Sweetwater's Tarragon Chicken Salad 75
Szechwan Confetti Salad 64
Tabbouleh 74
Tomatoes Stuffed with Artichoke Hearts
  65
Twice-Dressed Salad 73
Waldorf Salad 62
SALAD DRESSINGS
Avocado Dressing 73
Betty's Dressing 76
Dog Team Dressing 76
French Dressing 75
Raspberry Vinaigrette 68
Romano Cheese Dressing 75
Special French Dressing 63
Thousand Island Dressing 76
SALMON
Gingered Salmon 119
Grilled Salmon with Dill Sauce 110
Leaf–Wrapped Stuffed Salmon 118
Orange Horseradish Crusted Salmon Fillet
  with a Light Orange Dill Sauce 124
Salmon Bisque 46
Salmon Spinach Pasty 125
Salmon Strata 107
Smoked Salmon Cheesecake 114
SALSA
Creamy Salsa Dip 22
Mango Mint Salsa 26

Melon Salsa 229
Warm Salsa 240
Salsa de Leonardo 223
SAUCES
Barbecue Sauce 133
Béchamel Sauce 200
Black Bean Cumin Sauce 232
Bourbon Sauce 319
Bud's Greek Basting Sauce 150
Butter Sauce for dipping 113
Cheese and Cream Sauce 188
Crème Fraîche 331
Cucumber Dill Sauce 110
Dark Chocolate Fudge Sauce 332
Enchilada Mole Sauce 230
Fresh Peach Sauce 332
Great Barbecue Sauce 333
Green Chile Sauce 228
Hollandaise Sauce 106
Hot Caramel Rum Sauce 298
Hunters' Horseradish Sauce 136
Light Orange Dill Sauce 124
Low-Fat Crème Anglaise 219
Melon Salsa 229
Mountain Man Mustard Sauce 133
Mustard Horseradish Sauce 131
Mustard Sauce 115
Not Your Average Mustard 330
Orange Sauce 84
Pesto Sauce 30
Pico de Gallo 222
Raspberry Jewel Sauce 304
Raspberry Sauce 310, 321
Salsa de Leonardo 223
Sassy Sauce 112
Sauce Alla Puttanesca 197
Sauce Béarnaise 333
Spanish Sauce 103
Spicy Mustard Sauce 143
Sweet and Sour Sauce 19
Warm Cinnamon Cider Sauce 285
Warm Salsa 240
Your Favorite Tomato Sauce 334
SAUSAGE
Boliche Asado de Colorado 137
Chicken and Sausage Jambalaya 159
Fiesta Brunch 100
M.E.'s Duck Chorizo 167
Red Mountain Shells 195
Sausage and Mushroom Strudel 140
Sausage Strudel 28
Spanish Paella 154
Spinach Stuffed Shells 201
Three Cheese Ziti with Italian Sausage 198
SCALLOPS
Seafood la Joya 117
Sole del Mar 116

SEAFOOD *(See Crab, Fish, Scallops & Shrimp also)*
Seafood and Wild Rice Salad 73
Seafood la Joya 117
Seafood Lasagna 115
Seafood Stars 24
SESAME
Sesame Noodles 201
Sesame Shrimp Toast 24
SHRIMP
Chicken and Shrimp Fettuccine 192
Corn Chowder with Shrimp and Peppers 53
Grilled Marinated Shrimp 113
Lime Garlic Shrimp with Mango Mint Salsa 26
Sassy Seafood Salad 112
Seafood la Joya 117
Seafood Lasagna 115
Sesame Shrimp Toast 24
Shrimp and Artichoke Casserole 121
Shrimp Mold 26
Shrimp New Orleans 25, 126
Shrimp on the Bar–B 116
Sole del Mar 116
Stir–Fry Seafood Pasta 195
Szechwan Shrimp 122
Telluride Shrimp Jambalaya 113
Very Easy Fried Rice 199
Smoked Salmon Cheesecake 114
SOLE
Sole del Mar 116
Southwest Sole 239
SOUP
Beatrice Farnham Otto's Tomato Bisque 48
Black Bean Soup 57
Cantaloupe Splash Soup 42
Chilled Summer Squash Soup with Curry 43
Cold Pimiento Soup 44
Cream of Mushroom Soup 51
Creamy Potato Soup 52
Four Corners Tortilla Soup 224
Gazpacho 45
Gourmet Spinach Soup 50
Mexican Corn Soup 224
Onion Soup Fondue 47
Ouray Swiss Cheese Soup 50
Peach Soup 42
Potato Leek Soup 52
Salmon Bisque 46
Today's Recipe: Tomato Soup 49
Veggie Southwest Soup 56
Wild Rice Soup 55
SOUTHWESTERN FARE
Arroz Durango 235
Beaver Creek Trout in Jalapeño Marinade 239
Black Bean Salsa Salad 237

Chicken Breast with Warm Salsa 240
Chicken Enchiladas 229
Chicken Fajitas 260
Chile Relleno Torta 234
Coyote Green Corn Tamales 233
Crested Butte Chili Cheese Supreme 243
Enchilada Mole Sauce 230
Four Corners Tortilla Soup 224
Garlic Tamales with Black Bean Cumin Sauce 232
Holy Guacamole 223
Individual Orange Flans 244
Jalapeño Corn Bread 238
Jalapeño Relish 235
Layered Mexican Salad 237
Marinated Chicken Enchiladas with Green Chile and Melon Salsa 228
Mexican Chicken Roll-ups 241
Mexican Corn Soup 224
Pico de Gallo 222
Pork and Chile Burritos 226
Salsa Beef 242
Salsa de Leonardo 223
Silverton Indian Fry Bread 238
South of the Border Stew 60
Southwest Sole 239
Southwestern Pasta Salad 236
Spanish Soft Tacos 231
Stacked Enchiladas 227
Tamale Pie 234
Volcano Green Chili 225
Western Wontons 222
White Chicken Chili 225
Spanakopita 33
Spareribs Hawaiian 143
SPINACH
Baked Eggs and Bacon Florentine 217
Gourmet Spinach Soup 50
Omelet Olé 104
Salmon Spinach Pasty 125
Sautéed Mushrooms and Spinach with Shallots 189
Scalloped Spinach 187
Spanakopita 33
Spinach and Strawberry Salad 70
Spinach Artichoke Casserole 189
Spinach Crêpes 188
Spinach, Pea, and Red Pepper Timbales 190
Spinach Stuffed Shells 201
SQUASH
Baked Acorn Squash with Cranberry-Orange Compote 178
Chilled Summer Squash Soup with Curry 43
Grilled Garlic Squash 179
Thanksgiving Squash 179
Vegetable Fettuccine Alfredo 202

Vegetarian Winter Squash Stew 58
Steak Ore House 129
Steak Rolls with Mushrooms 134
Steak Salad 71
STEW
  South of the Border Stew 60
  Veal and Barley Stew 59
  Vegetarian Winter Squash Stew 58
STRAWBERRIES
  Spinach and Strawberry Salad 70
  Strawberry Super Pie 287
Stuffing, Lemon–Almond, 118
Sweet Pepper and Basil Frittata 105

T

Tabbouleh 74
Tacos, Spanish Soft, 231
TAMALES
  Coyote Green Corn Tamales 233
  Garlic Tamales with Black Bean Cumin
    Sauce 232
  Tamale Pie 234
Tart, Almond Toffee, 291
Thousand Island Dressing 76
Tiramisu (Pick Me Up) 318
TOFFEE
  Almond Toffee Tart 291
  Enstrom's Oatmeal Chocolate Toffee Cake
    294
  Enstrom's Toffee Chip Cookies 273
  Toffee Coffee Cake 95
Tofu, Herbs and Vegetables 182
TOMATO
  Avalanche Manicotti 203
  Beatrice Farnham Otto's Tomato Bisque 48
  Bread Salad with Tomatoes 71
  Fresh Tomato and Green Onion Garlic
    Bread 98
  Gazpacho 45
  Grand Valley Green Tomato Pickles 329
  Sauce Alla Puttanesca 197
  Today's Recipe: Tomato Soup 49
  Tomatoes Stuffed with Artichoke Hearts 65
  Tomato–Soy Marinade 131
  Your Favorite Tomato Sauce 334
TORTES
  Diana Torte 316
  Mocha Velvet Torte 308
Trail Bars 249
Trifle, Spring Berry, 313
TROUT
  Beaver Creek Trout in Jalapeño Marinade
    239
  Mountain Trout Prepared in Foil 259
  Roaring Fork Oven Crisp Trout 122
  Sautéed Trout 126
  Trout Pâté 29

TURKEY
  Greek-Style Pockets 212
  Italian Meatloaf 132

V

VEAL
  Apple–Stuffed Veal Rolls 139
  Osso Buco with Orzo Milanese 138
  Veal and Barley Stew 59
VEGETABLES (See individual listings also)
  Farmers' Market Vegetable Roast 181
  Sliced and Diced Vegetables 210
  Tofu, Herbs and Vegetables 182
  Vegetable Fettuccine Alfredo 202
  Vegetable Melange 183
  Vegetable Quiche 102
  Vegetable Rice Toss 218
  Vegetarian Winter Squash Stew 58
  Veggie Southwest Soup 56
  Whole Wheat Pasta with Vegetables 196
VENISON
  Colorado Venison Chili 172
  Grilled Venison with Apricot and Green
    Peppercorn 173
  Mountain Man Jerky 248
  Mountain Man Jerky Milk Gravy 248
  Tamale Pie 234
  Venison with Stone Fruits and Berry Sauce
    174

W

Waldorf Salad 62
White Chocolate Mousse with Raspberry Jewel
    Sauce 304
Whole Wheat Pasta with Vegetables 196
Wild Berry Cobbler 285
WILD RICE
  Chicken and Wild Rice Casserole 160
  Quail with Wild Rice and Roasted Shallots
    166
  Wild Rice Clam Chowder 54
  Wild Rice Soup 55
  Wild Rice with Piñons and Brandied Raisins
    197

Y

Yams and Apples 178

Z

ZUCCHINI
  Bumper Crop Zucchini Bread 94
  Farmers' Market Vegetable Roast 181
  Vegetable Fettuccine Alfredo 202
  Vegetable Melange 183

Order Form

RECIPES FROM CAMPFIRE TO CANDLELIGHT

Name _____

Address _____

City _____

State _____

Zip _____

Phone _____

Send Check or money order payable to:

West of the Rockies
P.O. Box 3221 • Grand Junction, Colorado 81502
phone/fax 303-243-7790
Please do not send cash. Sorry, no C.O.D.'s

ISBN # 0-9641314-0-4

Item	Quantity	Unit	Total Price
West of the Rockies Cookbook		17.95	
Watercolor Cover Art Print, signed		15.00	
		Subtotal	$ _____
Applicable Colorado Sales Tax (Residents only):			$ _____
Shipping/Handling (3.00 each book)			$ _____
Total enclosed			$ _____

All profits from the sale of this cookbook will be reinvested in the community through projects supported by the Junior Service League.

Order Form

RECIPES FROM CAMPFIRE TO CANDLELIGHT

Name _____

Address _____

City _____

State _____

Zip _____

Phone _____

Send Check or money order payable to:

West of the Rockies
P.O. Box 3221 • Grand Junction, Colorado 81502
phone/fax 303-243-7790
Please do not send cash. Sorry, no C.O.D.'s

ISBN # 0-9641314-0-4

Item	Quantity	Unit	Total Price
West of the Rockies Cookbook		17.95	
Watercolor Cover Art Print, signed		15.00	
		Subtotal	$ _____
Applicable Colorado Sales Tax (Residents only):			$ _____
Shipping/Handling (3.00 each book)			$ _____
Total enclosed			$ _____

All profits from the sale of this cookbook will be reinvested in the community through projects supported by the Junior Service League.